CAPTAIN AMERICA

NO ESCAPE

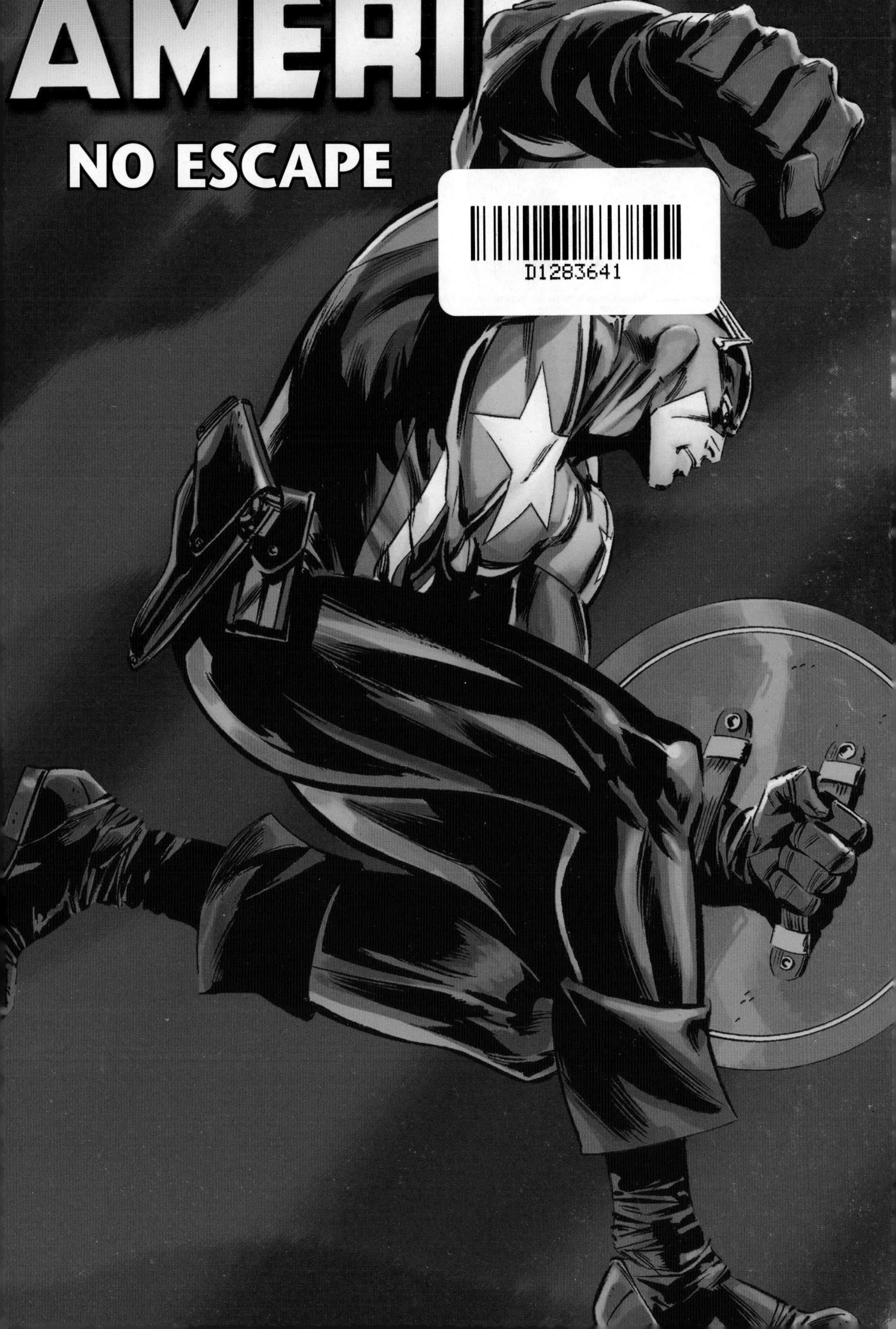

CAPTAIN AMERICA

NO ESCAPE

WRITER: Ed Brubaker
PENCILS: Butch Guice
with Mitch Breitweiser (Issue #607)
INKS: Butch Guice
with Mitch Breitweiser, Mark Pennington,
Rick Magyar & Andrew Hennessy
COLOR ART: Dean White
with Elizabeth Dismang, Paul Mounts & Frank Martin
LETTERER: VC's Joe Caramagna
COVER ART: Marko Djurdjevic
ASSOCIATE EDITOR: Lauren Sankovitch
EDITOR: Tom Brevoort

Captain America created by Joe Simon & Jack Kirby

Collection Editor: Jennifer Grünwald
Editorial Assistants: James Emmett & Joe Hochstein
Assistant Editors: Alex Starbuck & Nelson Ribeiro
Editor, Special Projects: Mark D. Beazley
Senior Editor, Special Projects: Jeff Youngquist
Senior Vice President of Sales: David Gabriel

Editor in Chief: Joe Quesada • Publisher: Dan Buckley • Executive Producer: Alan Fine

CAPTAIN AMERICA: NO ESCAPE. Contains material originally published in magazine form as CAPTAIN AMERICA #606-610. First printing 2011. Hardcover ISBN# 978-0-7851-4512-7. Softcover ISBN# 978-0-7851-4513-4. Published by MARVEL WORLDWIDE, INC., a subsidiary of MARVEL ENTERTAINMENT, LLC. OFFICE OF PUBLICATION: 417 5th Avenue, New York, NY 10016. Copyright © 2010 and 2011 Marvel Characters, Inc. All rights reserved. Hardcover, $19.99 per copy in the U.S. and $22.50 in Canada (GST #R127032852). Softcover: $15.99 per copy in the U.S. and $17.99 in Canada (GST #R127032852). Canadian Agreement #40668537. All characters featured in this issue and the distinctive names and likenesses thereof, and all related indicia are trademarks of Marvel Characters, Inc. No similarity between any of the names, characters, persons, and/or institutions in this magazine with those of any living or dead person or institution is intended, and any such similarity which may exist is purely coincidental. **Printed in the U.S.A.** ALAN FINE, EVP - Office of the President, Marvel Worldwide, Inc. and EVP & CMO Marvel Characters B.V.; DAN BUCKLEY, Chief Executive Officer and Publisher - Print, Animation & Digital Media; JIM SOKOLOWSKI, Chief Operating Officer; DAVID BOGART, SVP of Business Affairs & Talent Management; MICHAEL PASCIULLO, VP Merchandising & Communications; JIM O'KEEFE, VP of Operations & Logistics; DAN CARR, Executive Director of Publishing Technology; JUSTIN F. GABRIE, Director of Publishing & Editorial Operations; SUSAN CRESPI, Editorial Operations Manager; ALEX MORALES, Publishing Operations Manager; STAN LEE, Chairman Emeritus. For information regarding advertising in Marvel Comics or on Marvel.com, please contact Ron Stern, VP of Business Development, at rstern@marvel.com. For Marvel subscription inquiries, please call 800-217-9158. Manufactured between 10/25/10 and 11/24/10 (hardcover), and 10/25/10 and 5/25/11 (softcover), by R.R. DONNELLEY, INC., SALEM, VA, USA.

10 9 8 7 6 5 4 3 2 1

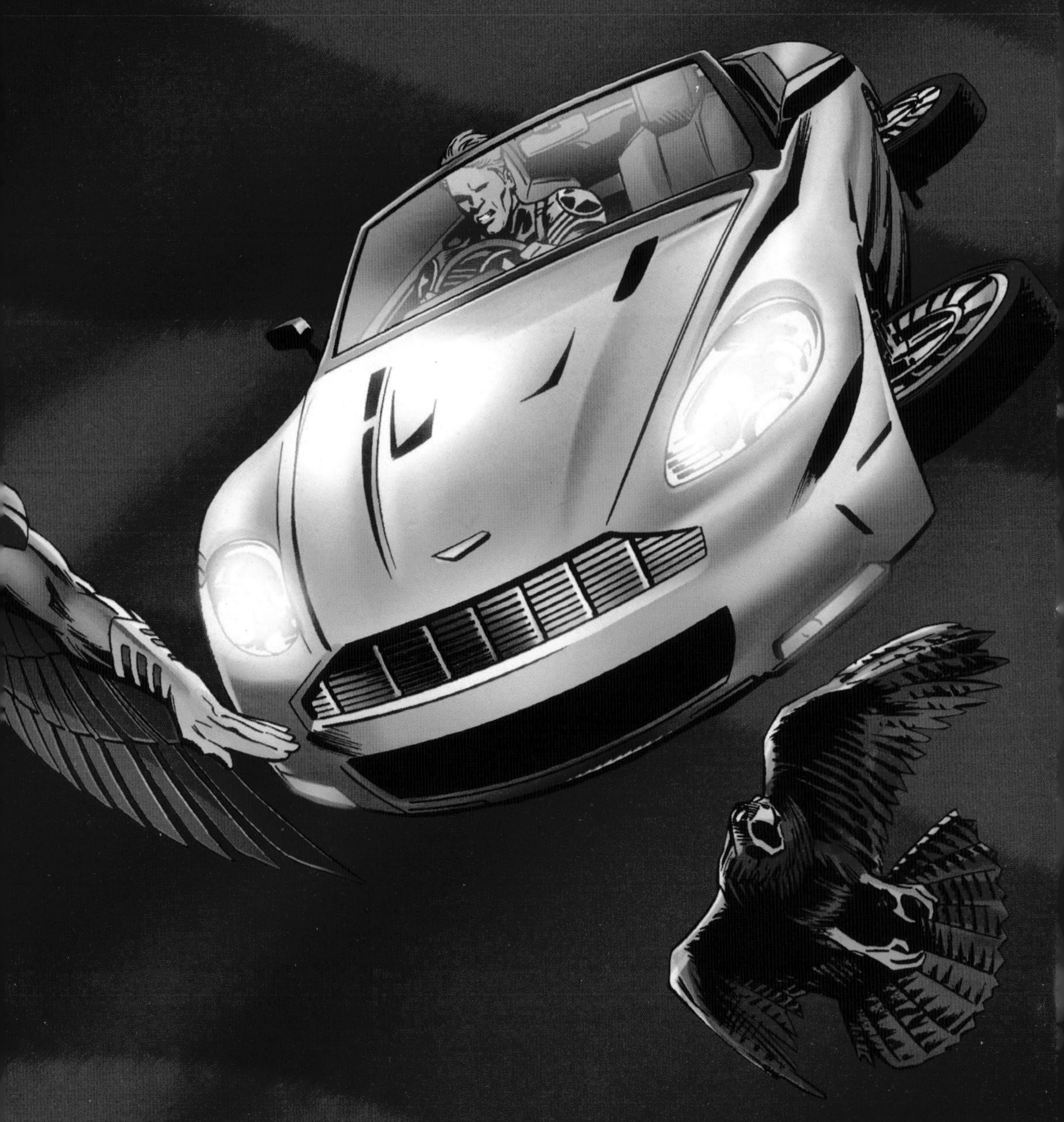

PREVISOULY:

After the apparent murder of Steve Rogers, the man who was Captain America, Cap's former partner during World War II, James "Bucky" Barnes, has taken on Steve's mantle and his mission. Even now that Steve Rogers has returned from the grave, Bucky continues to wield the shield as Captain America.

But not everybody is happy that Bucky, thought killed in the closing days of the war, is still alive.

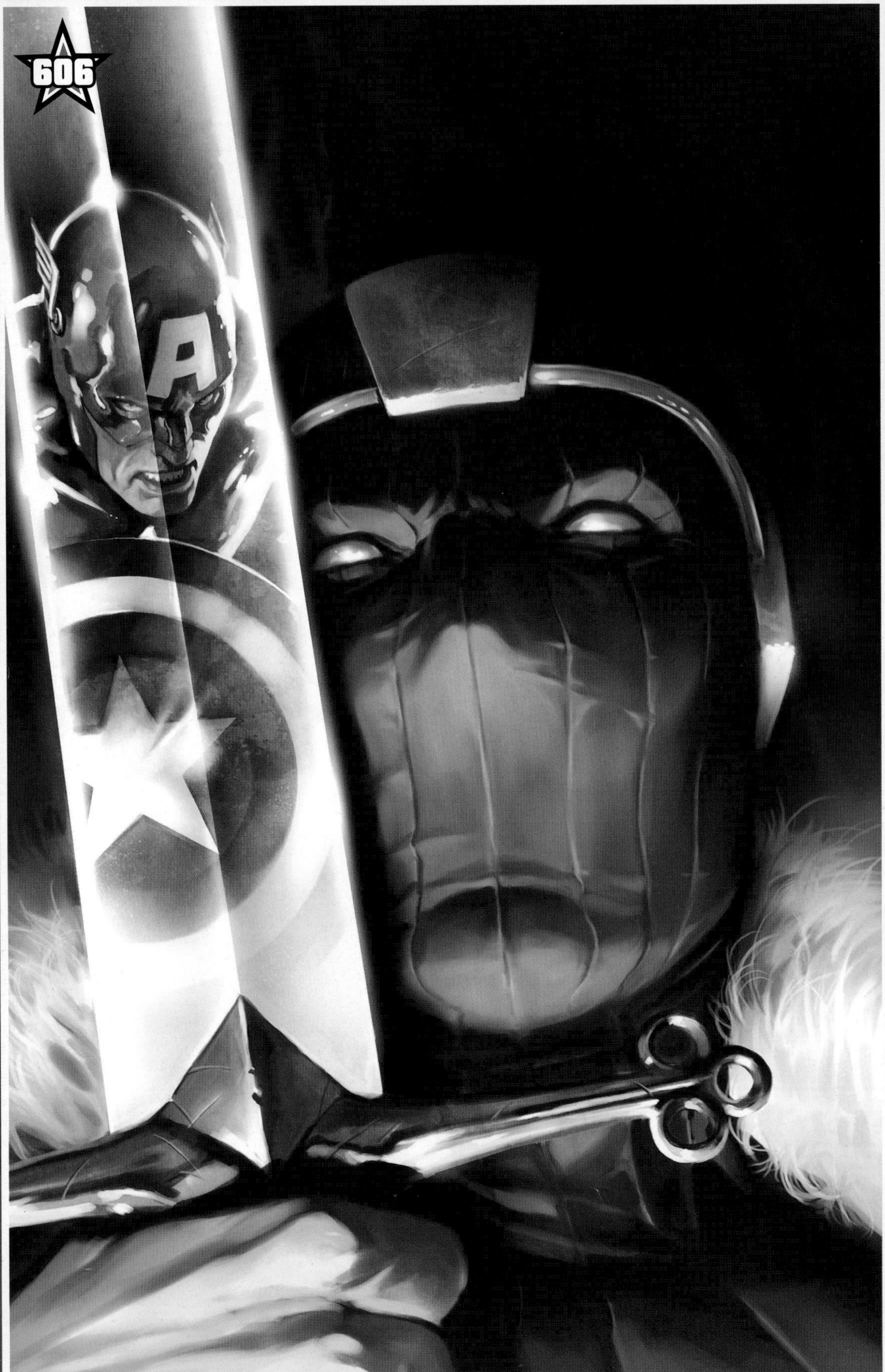
606

NO ESCAPE PART 1

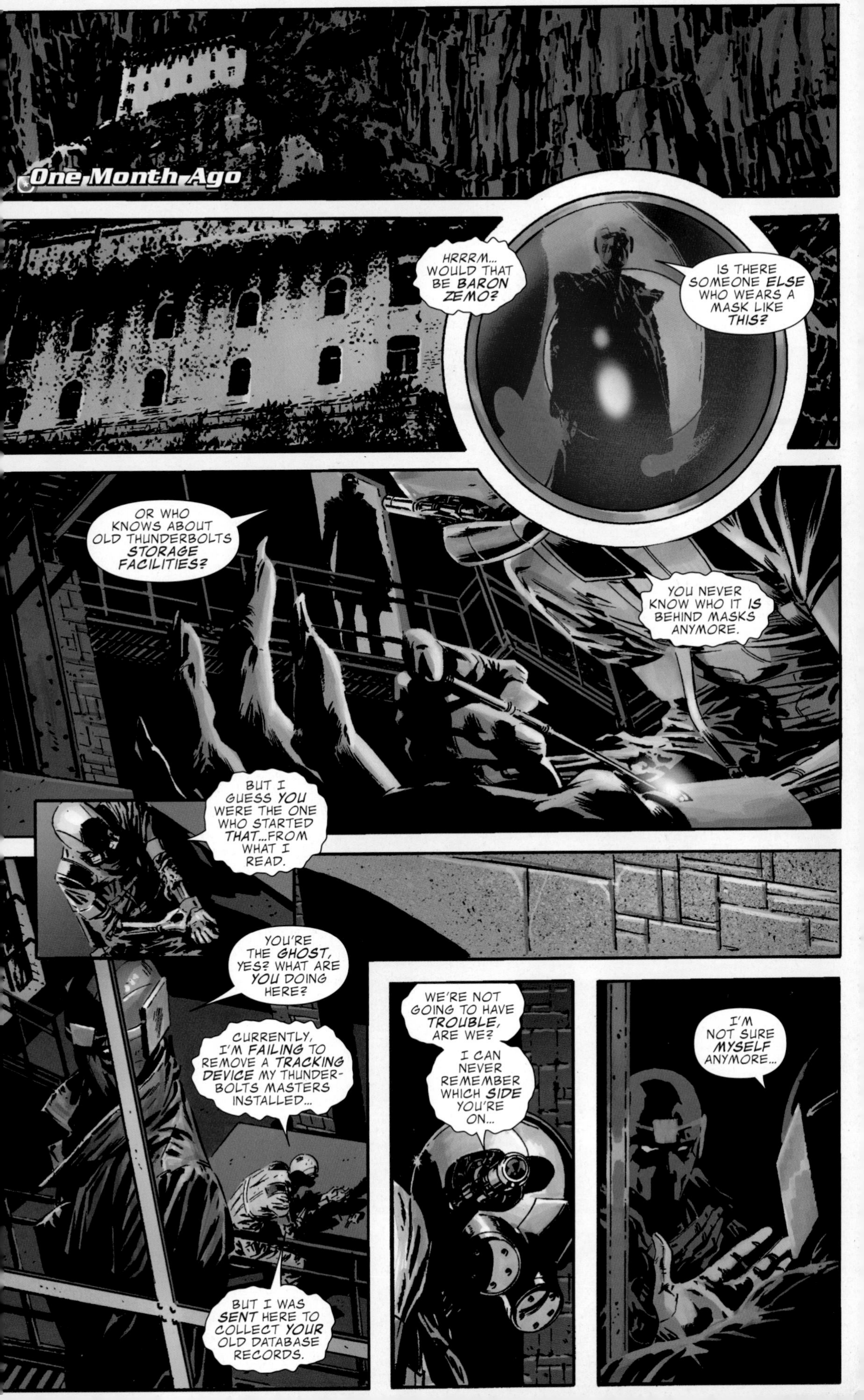
One Month Ago
HRRRM... WOULD THAT BE BARON ZEMO?
IS THERE SOMEONE ELSE WHO WEARS A MASK LIKE THIS?
OR WHO KNOWS ABOUT OLD THUNDERBOLTS STORAGE FACILITIES?
YOU NEVER KNOW WHO IT IS BEHIND MASKS ANYMORE.
BUT I GUESS YOU WERE THE ONE WHO STARTED THAT...FROM WHAT I READ.
YOU'RE THE GHOST, YES? WHAT ARE YOU DOING HERE?
CURRENTLY, I'M FAILING TO REMOVE A TRACKING DEVICE MY THUNDER-BOLTS MASTERS INSTALLED...
BUT I WAS SENT HERE TO COLLECT YOUR OLD DATABASE RECORDS.
WE'RE NOT GOING TO HAVE TROUBLE, ARE WE?
I CAN NEVER REMEMBER WHICH SIDE YOU'RE ON...
I'M NOT SURE MYSELF ANYMORE...

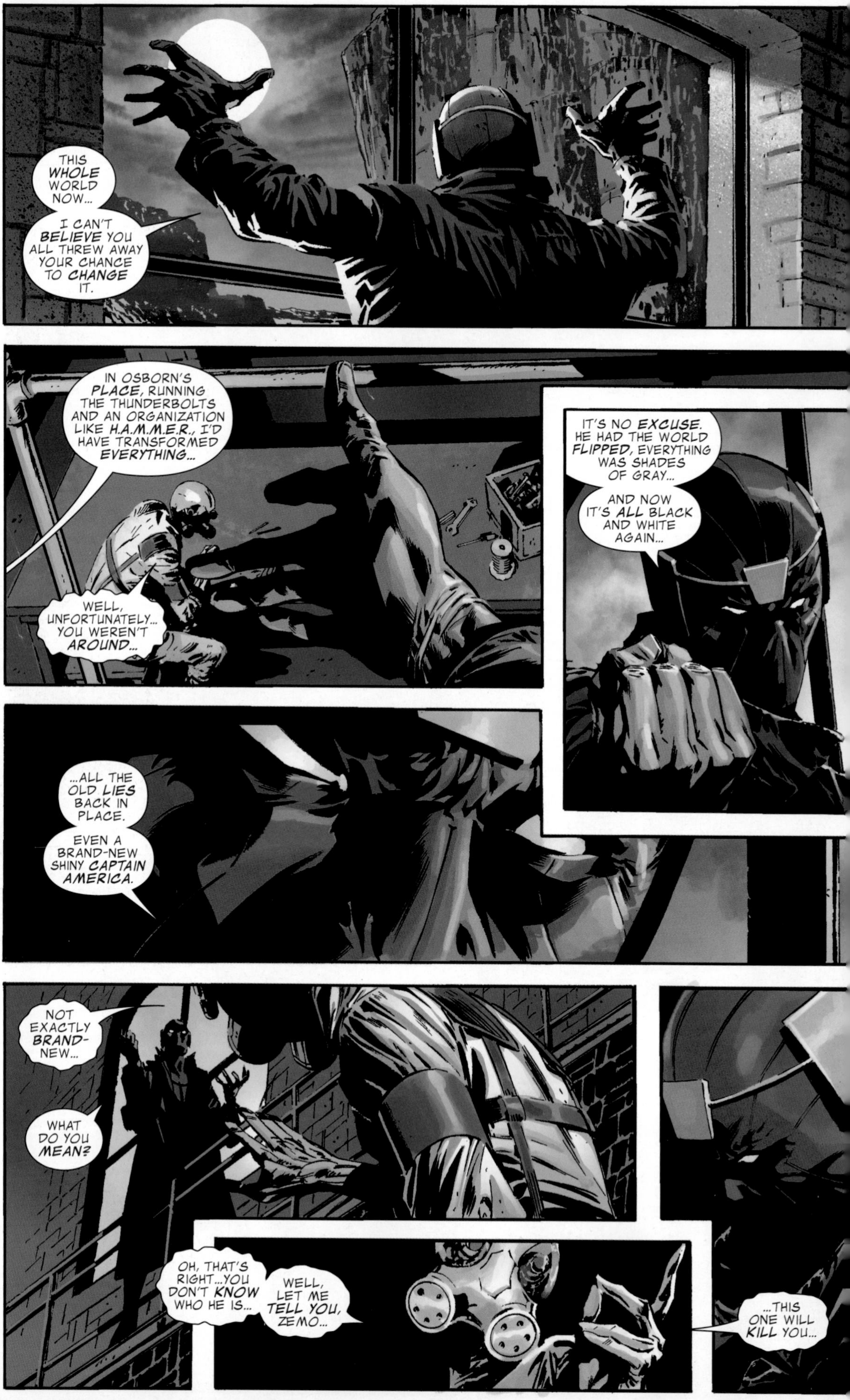
THIS WHOLE WORLD NOW...
I CAN'T BELIEVE YOU ALL THREW AWAY YOUR CHANCE TO CHANGE IT.
IN OSBORN'S PLACE, RUNNING THE THUNDERBOLTS AND AN ORGANIZATION LIKE H.A.M.M.E.R., I'D HAVE TRANSFORMED EVERYTHING...
WELL, UNFORTUNATELY... YOU WEREN'T AROUND...
IT'S NO EXCUSE. HE HAD THE WORLD FLIPPED, EVERYTHING WAS SHADES OF GRAY...
AND NOW IT'S ALL BLACK AND WHITE AGAIN...
...ALL THE OLD LIES BACK IN PLACE.
EVEN A BRAND-NEW SHINY CAPTAIN AMERICA.
NOT EXACTLY BRAND-NEW...
WHAT DO YOU MEAN?
OH, THAT'S RIGHT...YOU DON'T KNOW WHO HE IS...
WELL, LET ME TELL YOU, ZEMO...
...THIS ONE WILL KILL YOU...

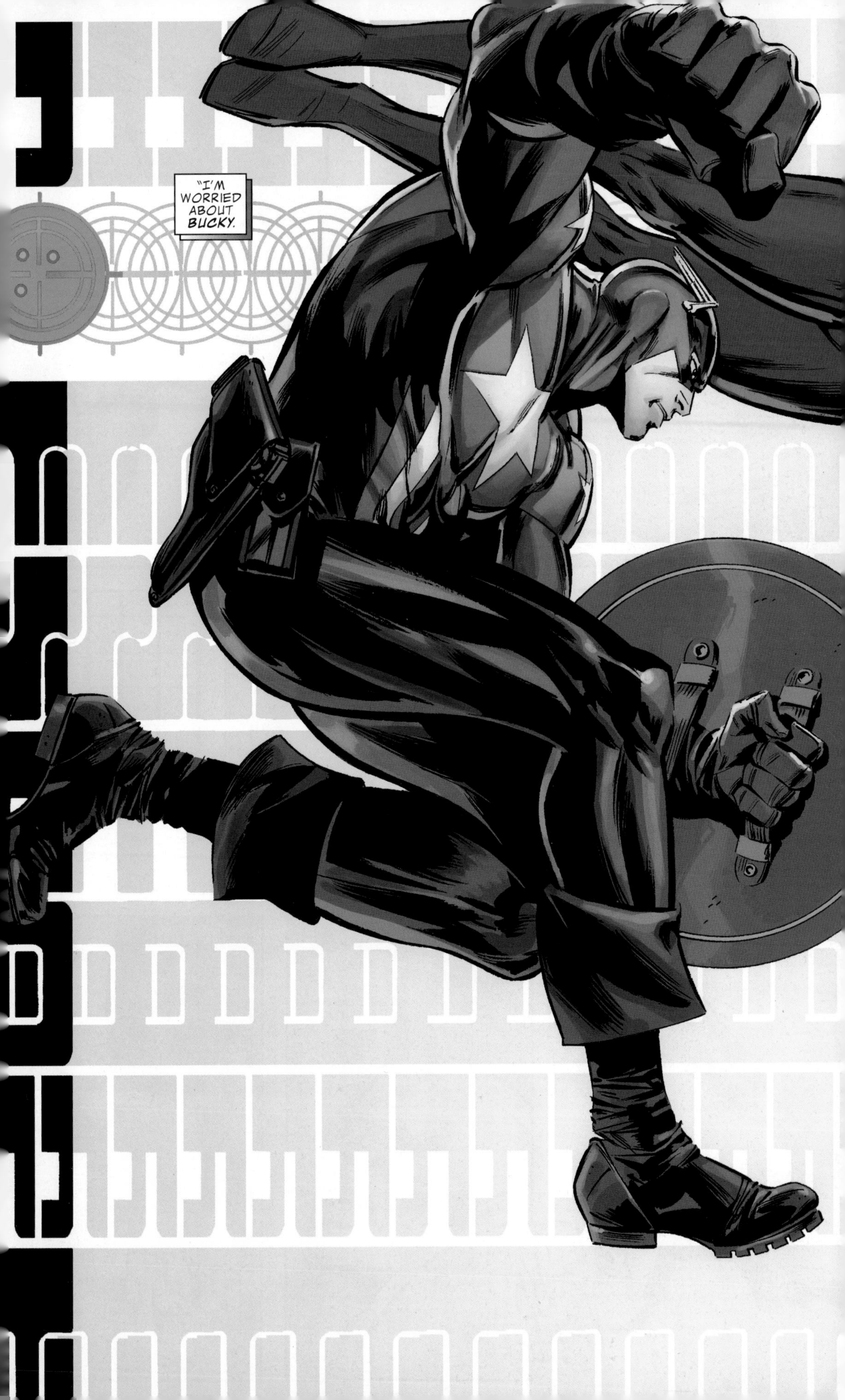
"I'M WORRIED ABOUT BUCKY.

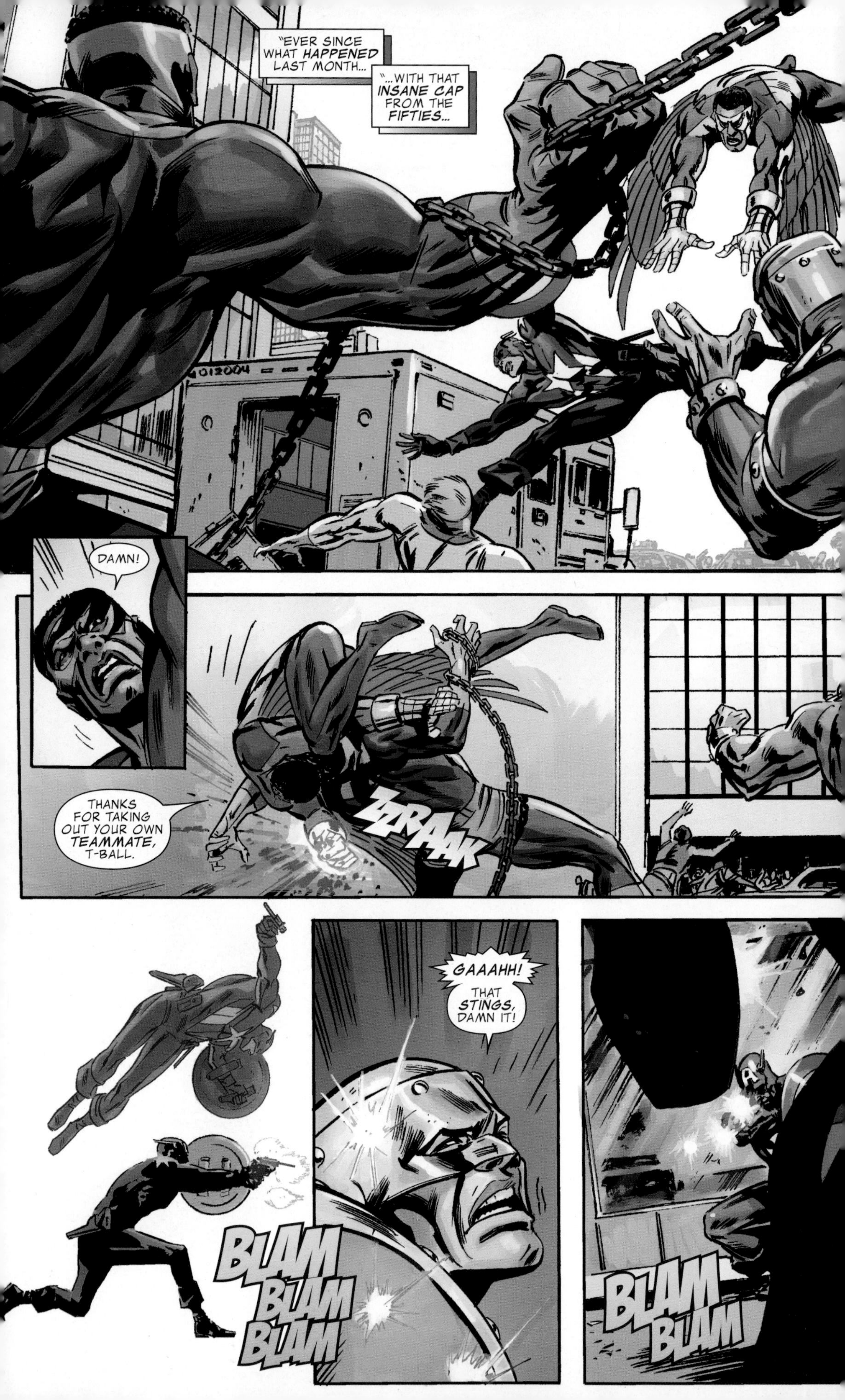
"EVER SINCE WHAT HAPPENED LAST MONTH...
"...WITH THAT INSANE CAP FROM THE FIFTIES...
DAMN!
THANKS FOR TAKING OUT YOUR OWN TEAMMATE, T-BALL.
ZZRAAK
BLAM BLAM BLAM
GAAAHH!
THAT STINGS, DAMN IT!
BLAM BLAM

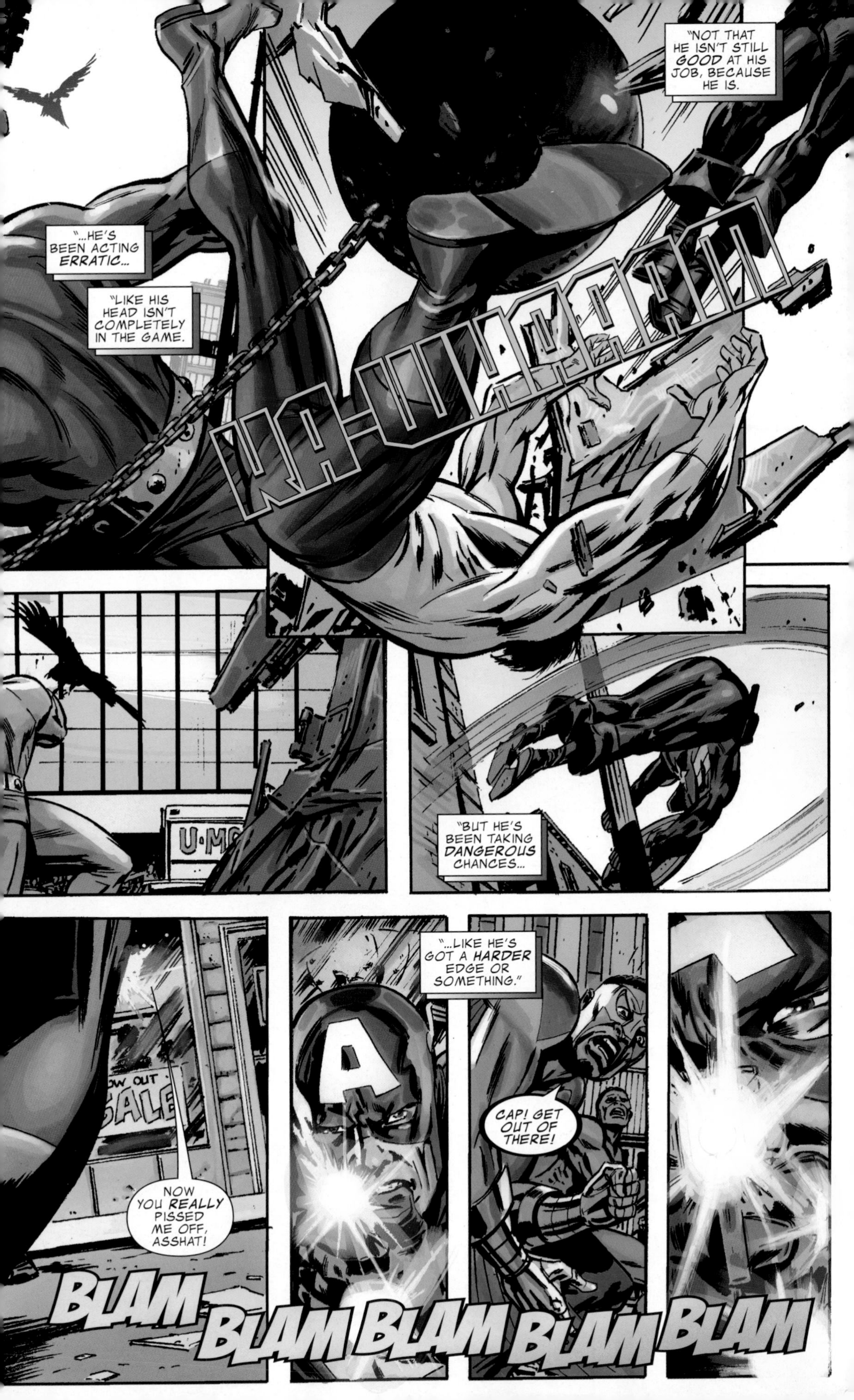
"NOT THAT HE ISN'T STILL GOOD AT HIS JOB, BECAUSE HE IS.
"...HE'S BEEN ACTING ERRATIC...
"LIKE HIS HEAD ISN'T COMPLETELY IN THE GAME.
"BUT HE'S BEEN TAKING DANGEROUS CHANCES...
"...LIKE HE'S GOT A HARDER EDGE OR SOMETHING."
NOW YOU REALLY PISSED ME OFF, ASSHAT!
CAP! GET OUT OF THERE!
BLAM
BLAM BLAM BLAM BLAM

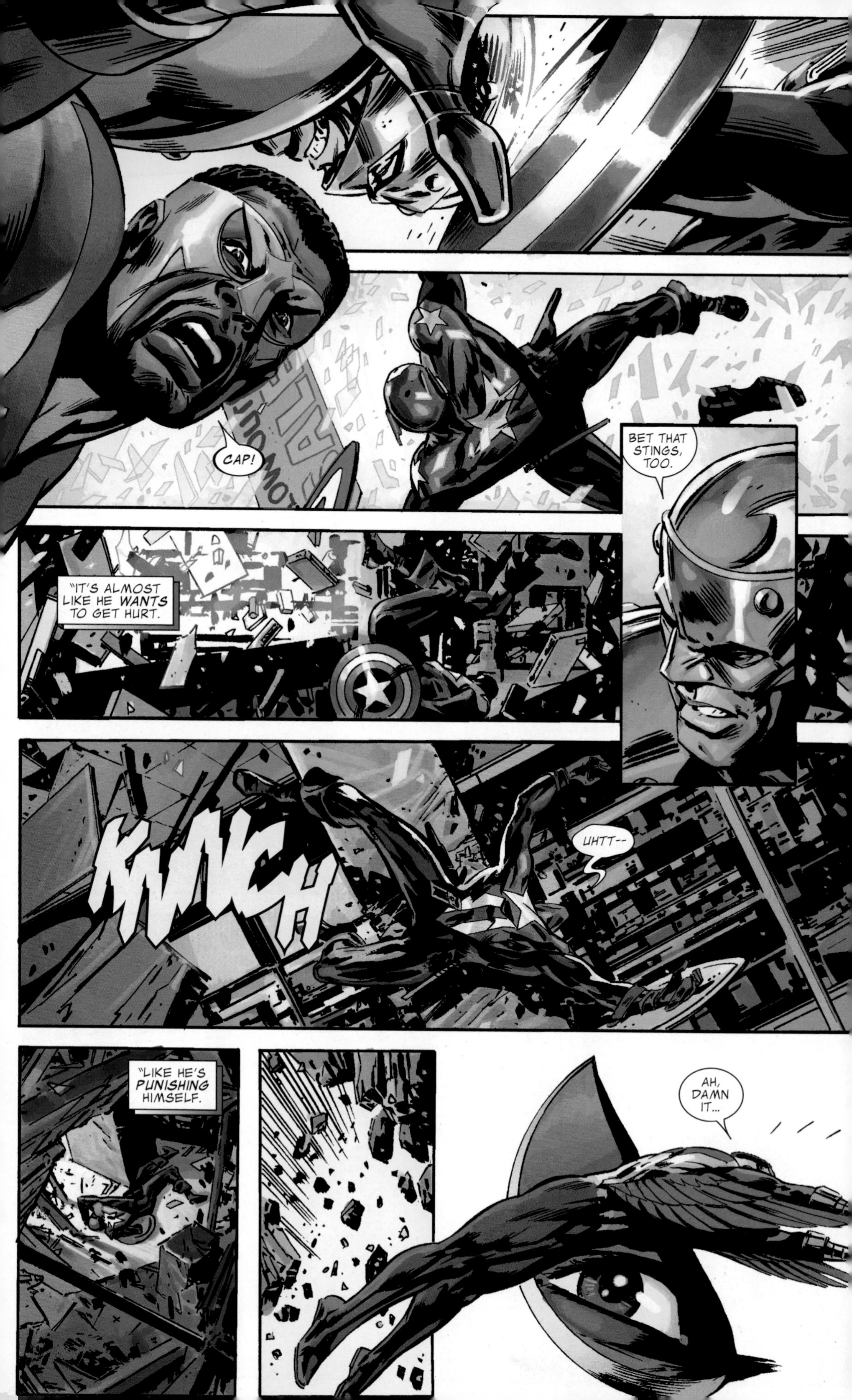
CAP!
BET THAT STINGS, TOO.
"IT'S ALMOST LIKE HE WANTS TO GET HURT.
UHTT--
"LIKE HE'S PUNISHING HIMSELF.
AH, DAMN IT...

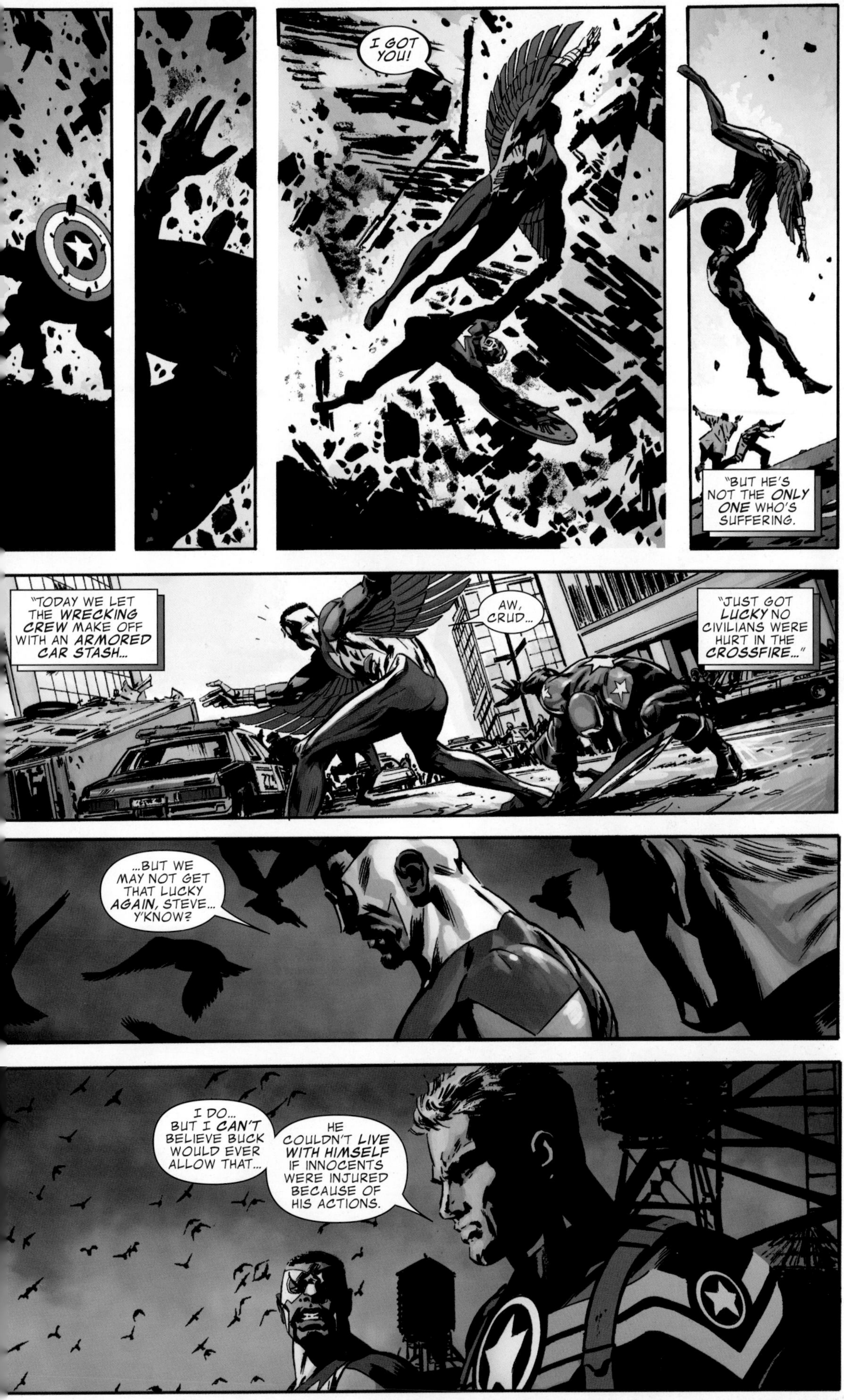
I GOT YOU!
"BUT HE'S NOT THE ONLY ONE WHO'S SUFFERING.
"TODAY WE LET THE WRECKING CREW MAKE OFF WITH AN ARMORED CAR STASH...
AW, CRUD...
"JUST GOT LUCKY NO CIVILIANS WERE HURT IN THE CROSSFIRE..."
...BUT WE MAY NOT GET THAT LUCKY AGAIN, STEVE... Y'KNOW?
I DO... BUT I CAN'T BELIEVE BUCK WOULD EVER ALLOW THAT...
HE COULDN'T LIVE WITH HIMSELF IF INNOCENTS WERE INJURED BECAUSE OF HIS ACTIONS.

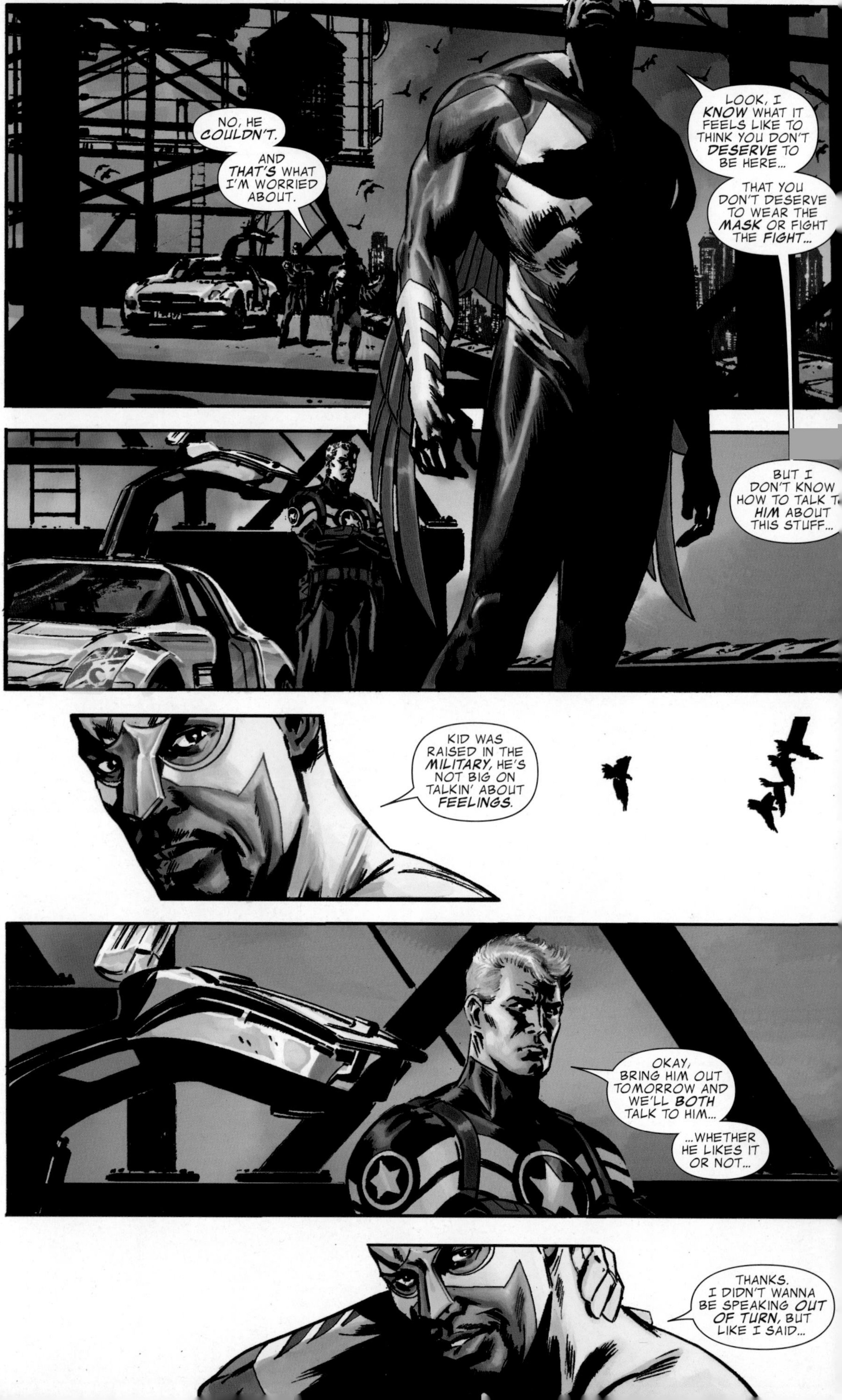
NO, HE COULDN'T.
AND THAT'S WHAT I'M WORRIED ABOUT.
LOOK, I KNOW WHAT IT FEELS LIKE TO THINK YOU DON'T DESERVE TO BE HERE...
THAT YOU DON'T DESERVE TO WEAR THE MASK OR FIGHT THE FIGHT...
BUT I DON'T KNOW HOW TO TALK T HIM ABOUT THIS STUFF...
KID WAS RAISED IN THE MILITARY, HE'S NOT BIG ON TALKIN' ABOUT FEELINGS.
OKAY, BRING HIM OUT TOMORROW AND WE'LL BOTH TALK TO HIM...
...WHETHER HE LIKES IT OR NOT...
THANKS. I DIDN'T WANNA BE SPEAKING OUT OF TURN, BUT LIKE I SAID...

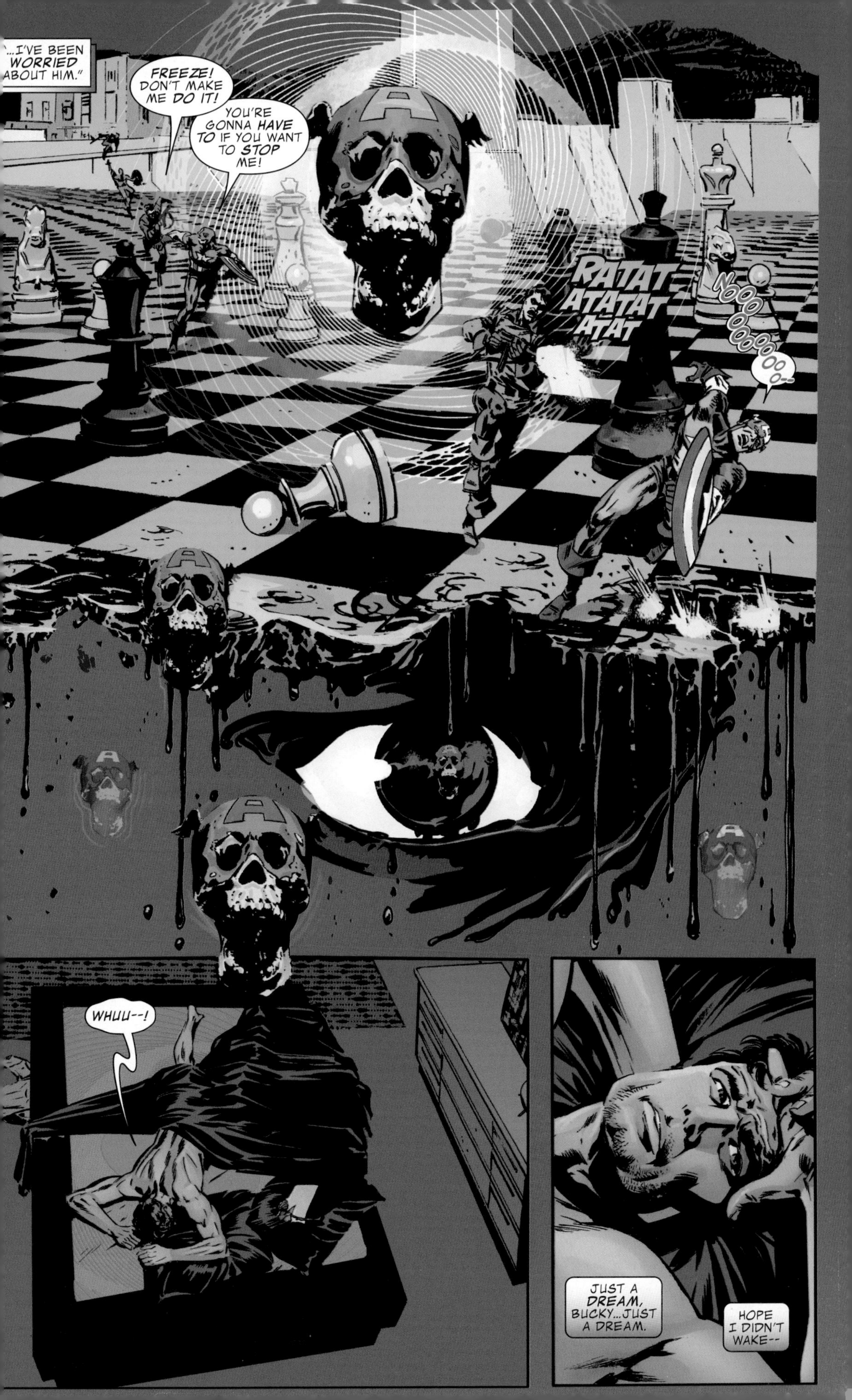
"...I'VE BEEN WORRIED ABOUT HIM."
FREEZE! DON'T MAKE ME DO IT!
YOU'RE GONNA HAVE TO IF YOU WANT TO STOP ME!
RATAT ATATAT ATAT
NOOOOOOOOO--
WHUU--!
JUST A DREAM, BUCKY...JUST A DREAM.
HOPE I DIDN'T WAKE--

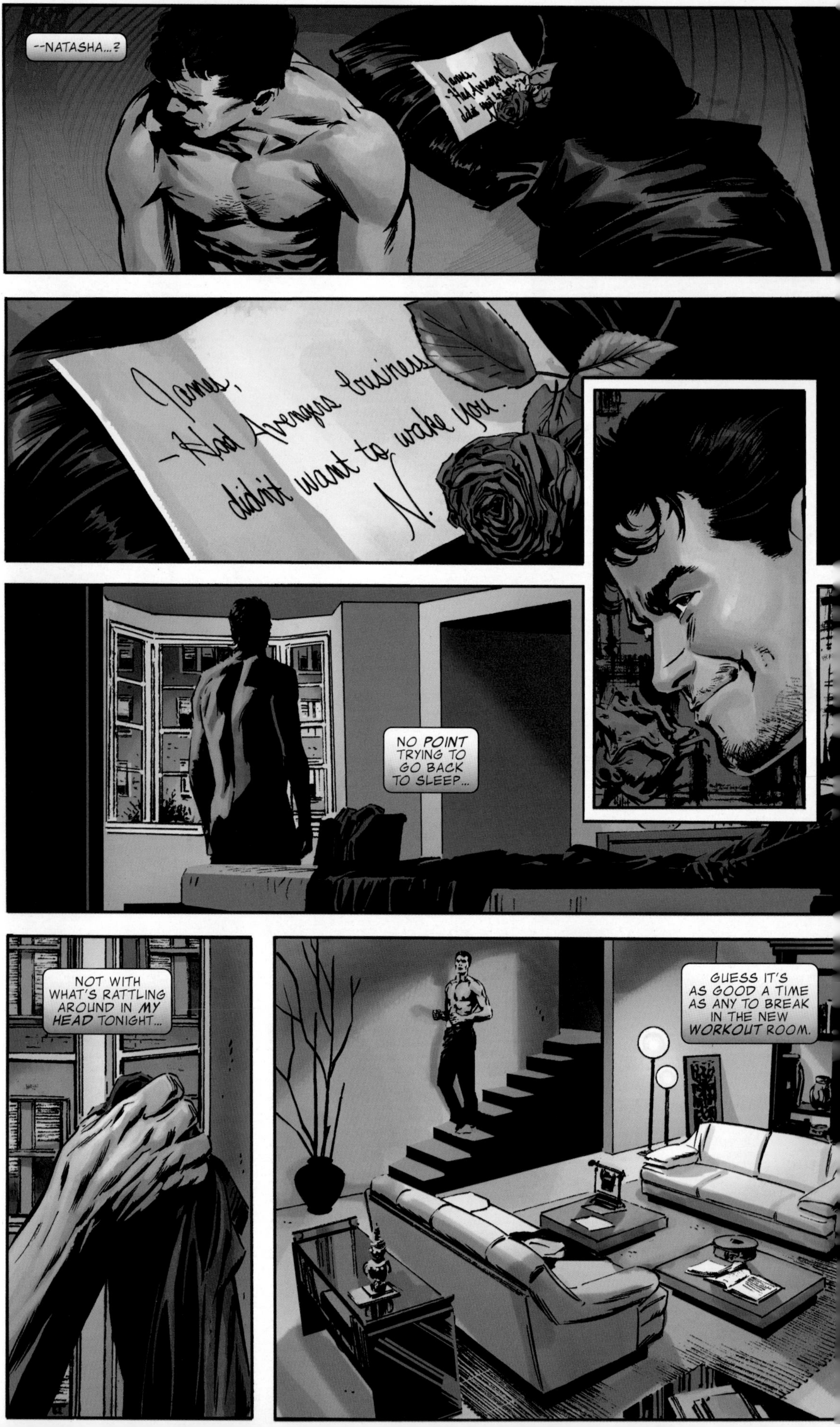
--NATASHA...?
James,
-Had Avengers business
didn't want to wake you.
N.
NO POINT TRYING TO GO BACK TO SLEEP...
NOT WITH WHAT'S RATTLING AROUND IN MY HEAD TONIGHT...
GUESS IT'S AS GOOD A TIME AS ANY TO BREAK IN THE NEW WORKOUT ROOM.

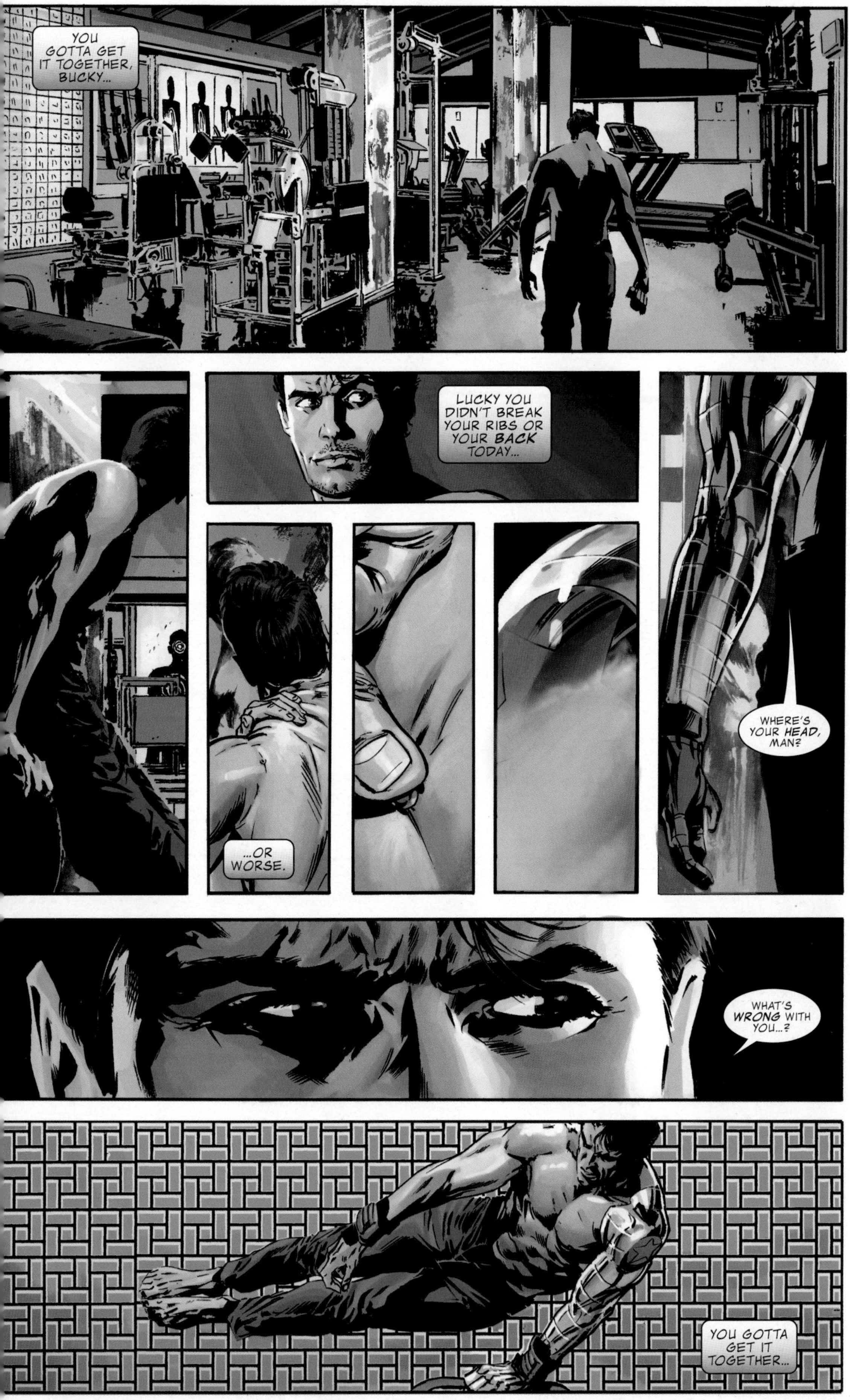
YOU GOTTA GET IT TOGETHER, BUCKY...
LUCKY YOU DIDN'T BREAK YOUR RIBS OR YOUR BACK TODAY...
...OR WORSE.
WHERE'S YOUR HEAD, MAN?
WHAT'S WRONG WITH YOU...?
YOU GOTTA GET IT TOGETHER...

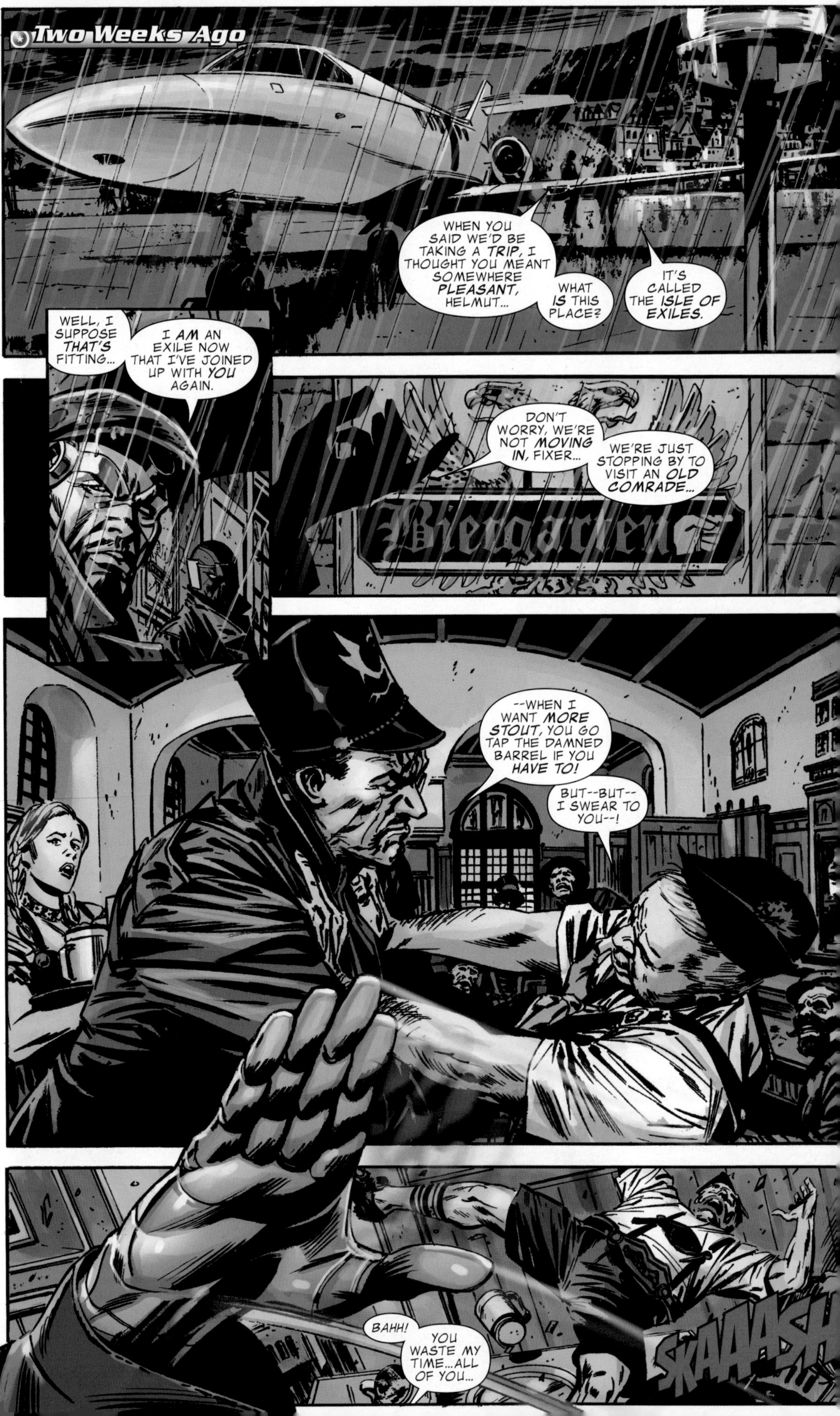
Two Weeks Ago
WHEN YOU SAID WE'D BE TAKING A TRIP, I THOUGHT YOU MEANT SOMEWHERE PLEASANT, HELMUT...
WHAT IS THIS PLACE?
IT'S CALLED THE ISLE OF EXILES.
WELL, I SUPPOSE THAT'S FITTING...
I AM AN EXILE NOW THAT I'VE JOINED UP WITH YOU AGAIN.
DON'T WORRY, WE'RE NOT MOVING IN, FIXER...
WE'RE JUST STOPPING BY TO VISIT AN OLD COMRADE...
--WHEN I WANT MORE STOUT, YOU GO TAP THE DAMNED BARREL IF YOU HAVE TO!
BUT--BUT--I SWEAR TO YOU--!
BAHH!
YOU WASTE MY TIME...ALL OF YOU...
SKAAASH

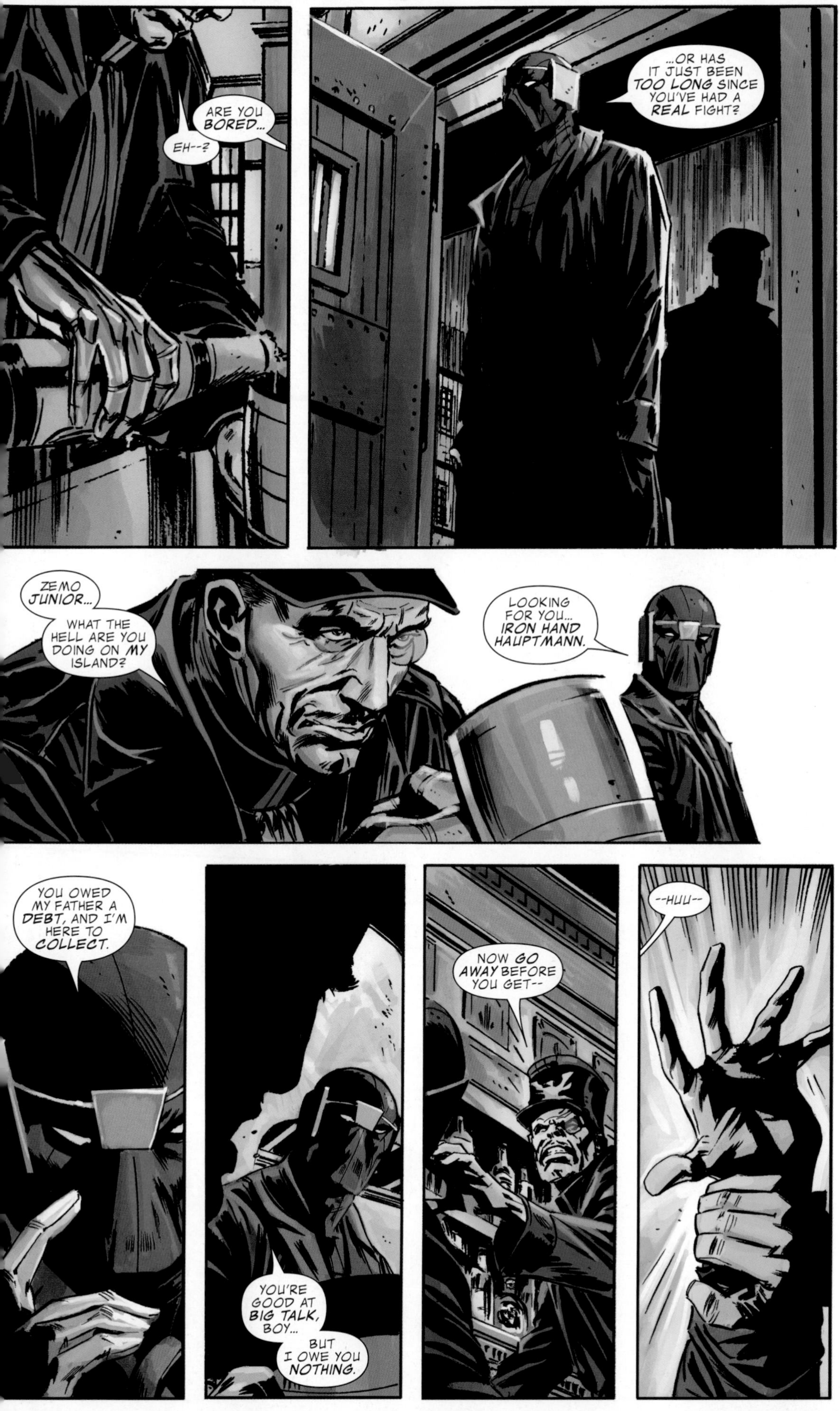
ARE YOU BORED...
EH--?
...OR HAS IT JUST BEEN TOO LONG SINCE YOU'VE HAD A REAL FIGHT?
ZEMO JUNIOR...
WHAT THE HELL ARE YOU DOING ON MY ISLAND?
LOOKING FOR YOU... IRON HAND HAUPTMANN.
YOU OWED MY FATHER A DEBT, AND I'M HERE TO COLLECT.
YOU'RE GOOD AT BIG TALK, BOY...
BUT I OWE YOU NOTHING.
NOW GO AWAY BEFORE YOU GET--
--HUU--

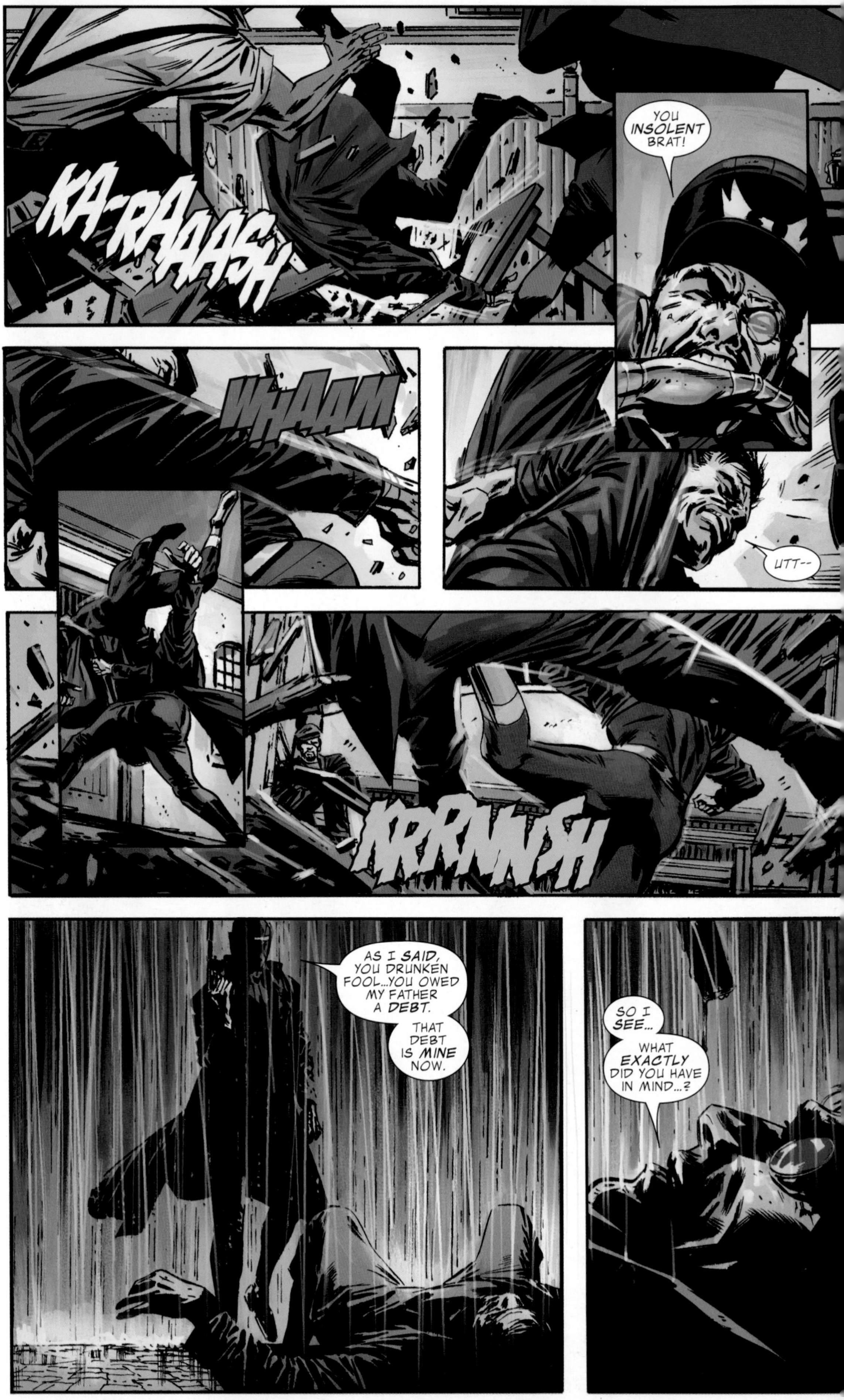
KA-RAAASH
YOU INSOLENT BRAT!
WHAAM
UTT--
KRRNNSH
AS I SAID, YOU DRUNKEN FOOL...YOU OWED MY FATHER A DEBT.
THAT DEBT IS MINE NOW.
SO I SEE...
WHAT EXACTLY DID YOU HAVE IN MIND...?

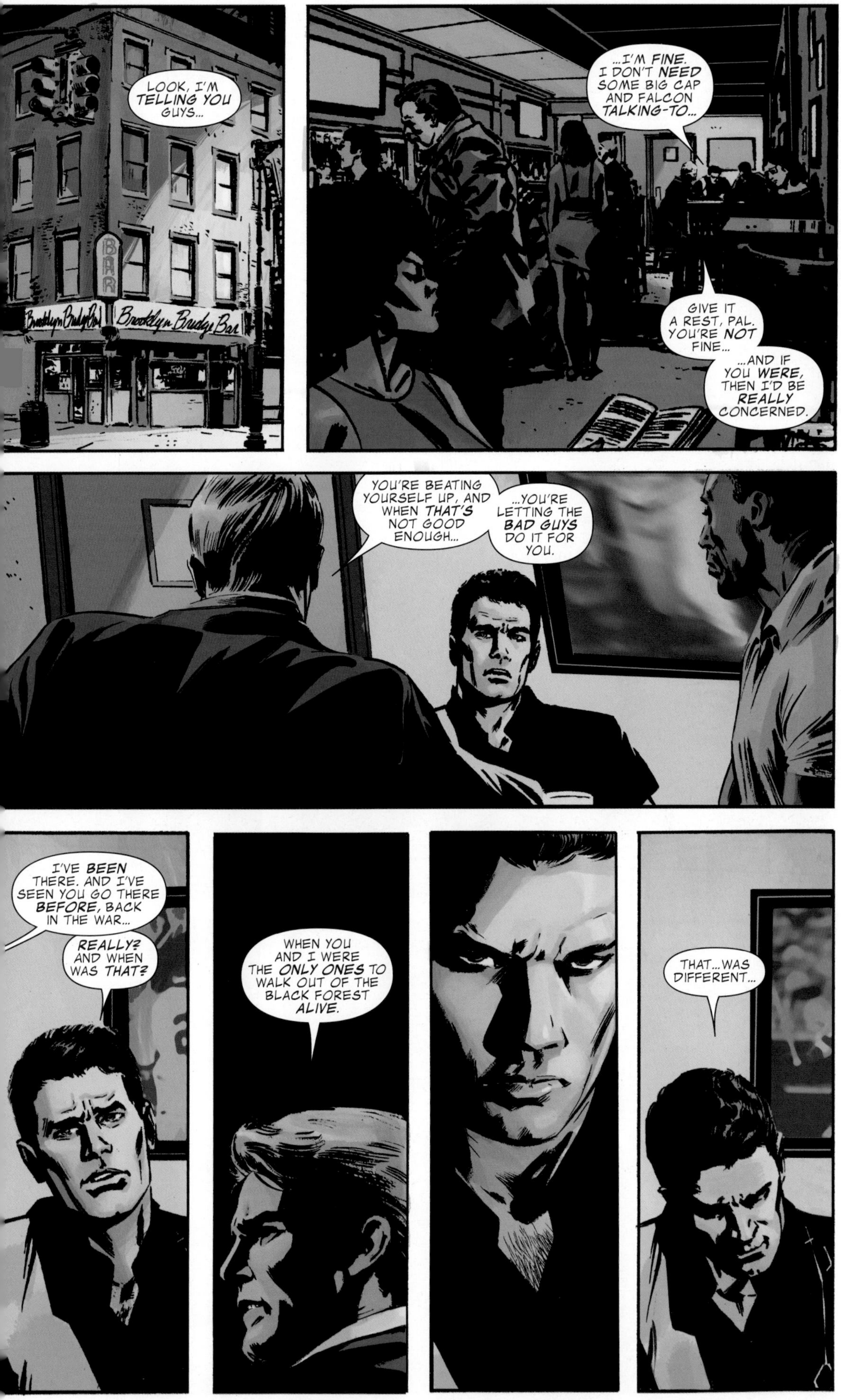

LOOK, I'M TELLING YOU GUYS...
BAR
Brooklyn Bridge Bar
Brooklyn Bridge Bar
...I'M FINE. I DON'T NEED SOME BIG CAP AND FALCON TALKING-TO...
GIVE IT A REST, PAL. YOU'RE NOT FINE...
...AND IF YOU WERE, THEN I'D BE REALLY CONCERNED.
YOU'RE BEATING YOURSELF UP, AND WHEN THAT'S NOT GOOD ENOUGH...
...YOU'RE LETTING THE BAD GUYS DO IT FOR YOU.
I'VE BEEN THERE. AND I'VE SEEN YOU GO THERE BEFORE, BACK IN THE WAR...
REALLY? AND WHEN WAS THAT?
WHEN YOU AND I WERE THE ONLY ONES TO WALK OUT OF THE BLACK FOREST ALIVE.
THAT...WAS DIFFERENT...

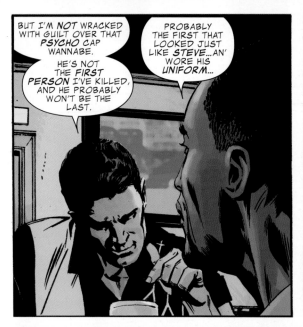

BUT I'M *NOT* WRACKED WITH GUILT OVER THAT *PSYCHO* CAP WANNABE.

HE'S NOT THE *FIRST PERSON* I'VE KILLED, AND HE PROBABLY WON'T BE THE LAST.

PROBABLY THE FIRST THAT LOOKED JUST LIKE *STEVE*...AN' WORE HIS *UNIFORM*...

I GOTTA GET ANOTHER BEER...

WHAT D'YOU THINK, MAN?

HE'S *HEARING* US, EVEN IF HE WON'T ADMIT IT.

NEVER COULD ADMIT ANY *WEAKNESS*, COULD YOU, *BUCKY?*

HERE YOU GO. SORRY FOR THE *WAIT*... IT'S MY *FIRST NIGHT*.

MUST BE SOMETHING YOU LEARNED, GROWING UP IN THE MILITARY.

DENY PAIN, DENY FEAR... DENY IT *ALL.*

Tipping isn't A CITY In China!

DON'T SWEAT IT... KEEP THE CHANGE.

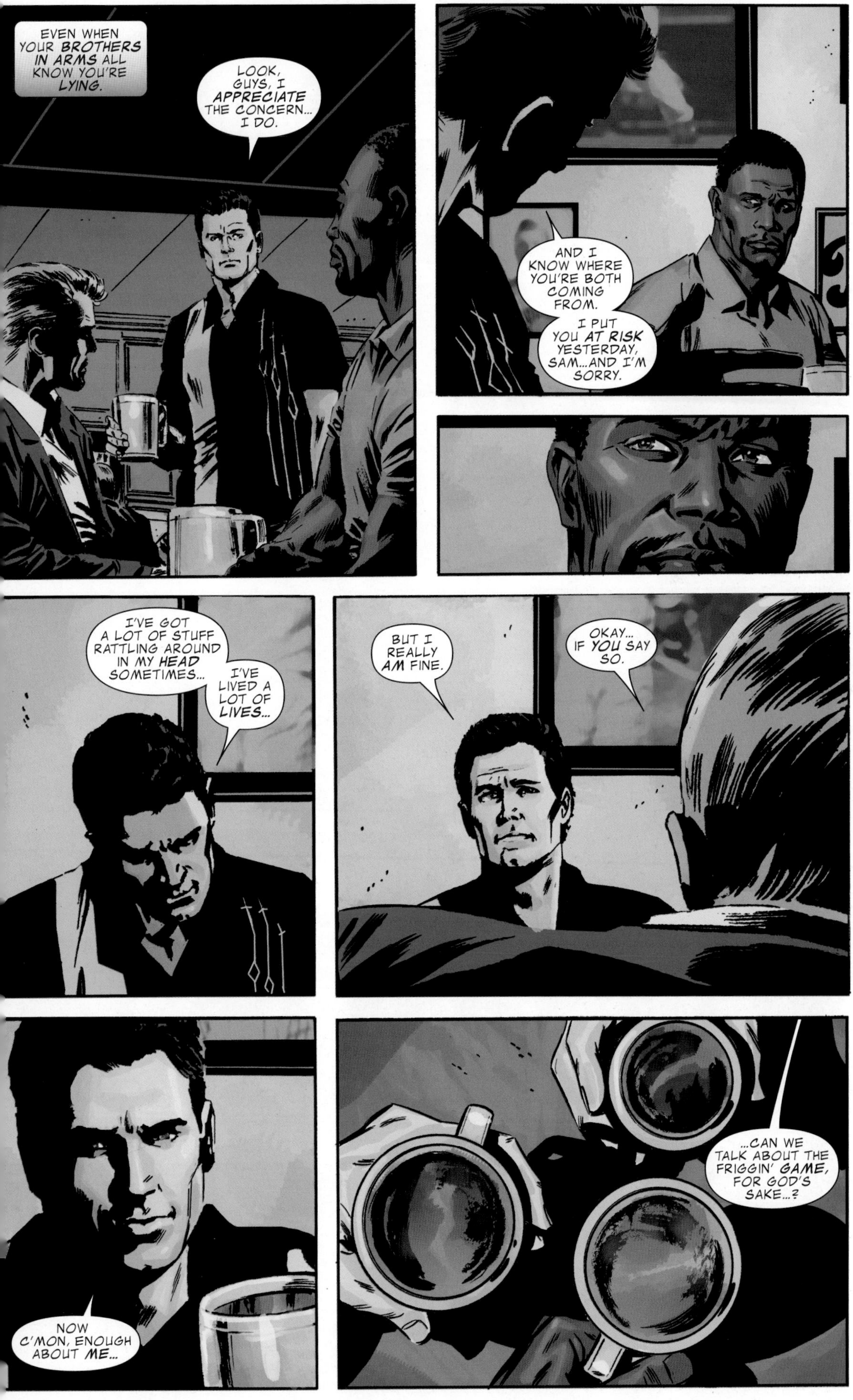

EVEN WHEN YOUR BROTHERS IN ARMS ALL KNOW YOU'RE LYING.
LOOK, GUYS, I APPRECIATE THE CONCERN... I DO.
AND I KNOW WHERE YOU'RE BOTH COMING FROM.
I PUT YOU AT RISK YESTERDAY, SAM...AND I'M SORRY.
I'VE GOT A LOT OF STUFF RATTLING AROUND IN MY HEAD SOMETIMES...
I'VE LIVED A LOT OF LIVES...
BUT I REALLY AM FINE.
OKAY... IF YOU SAY SO.
NOW C'MON, ENOUGH ABOUT ME...
...CAN WE TALK ABOUT THE FRIGGIN' GAME, FOR GOD'S SAKE...?

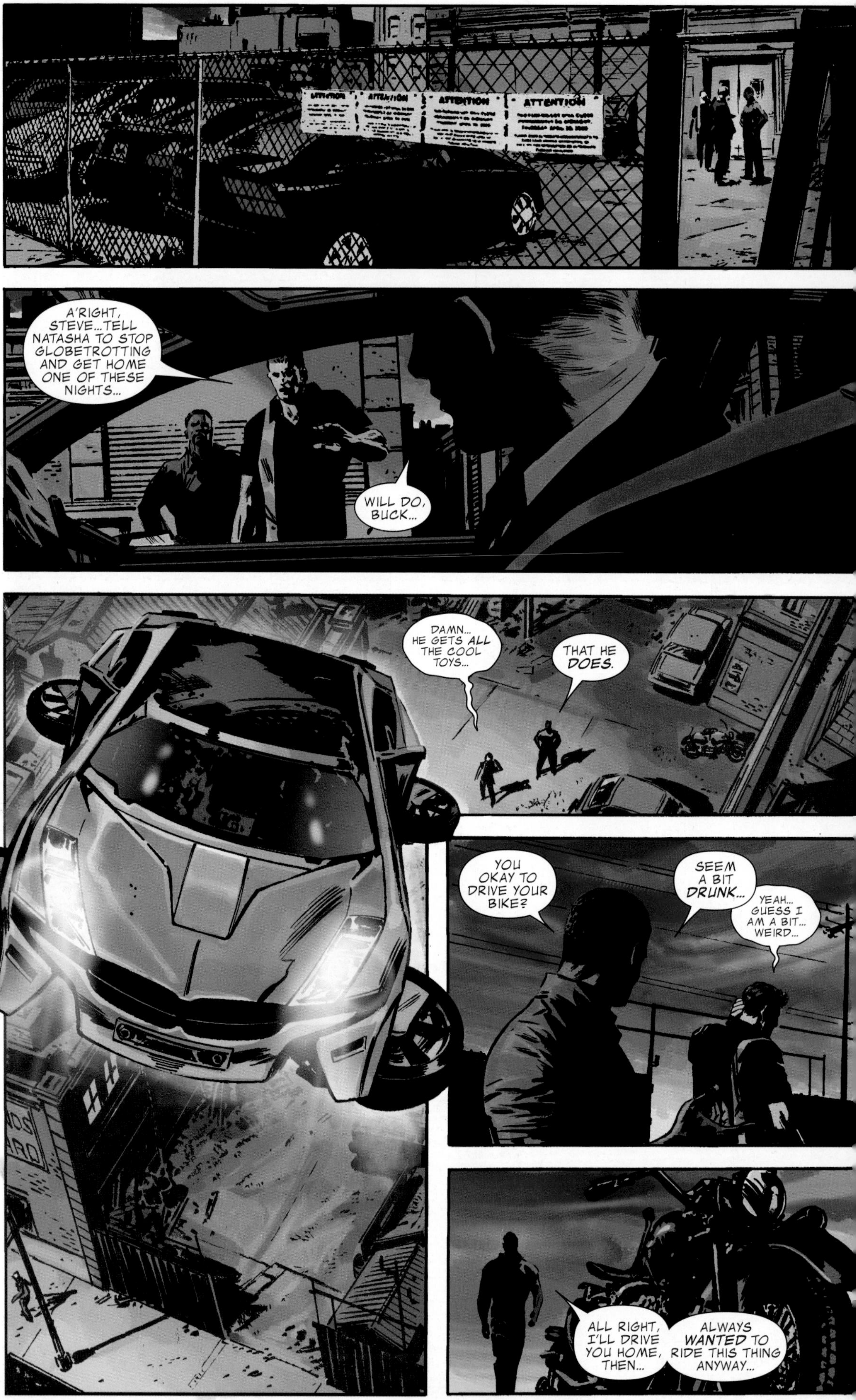
ATTENTION
ATTENTION
ATTENTION
ATTENTION
A'RIGHT, STEVE...TELL NATASHA TO STOP GLOBETROTTING AND GET HOME ONE OF THESE NIGHTS...
WILL DO, BUCK...
DAMN... HE GETS *ALL* THE COOL TOYS...
THAT HE *DOES*.
YOU OKAY TO DRIVE YOUR BIKE?
SEEM A BIT *DRUNK*...
YEAH... GUESS I AM A BIT... WEIRD...
ALL RIGHT, I'LL DRIVE YOU HOME, THEN...
ALWAYS *WANTED* TO RIDE THIS THING ANYWAY...

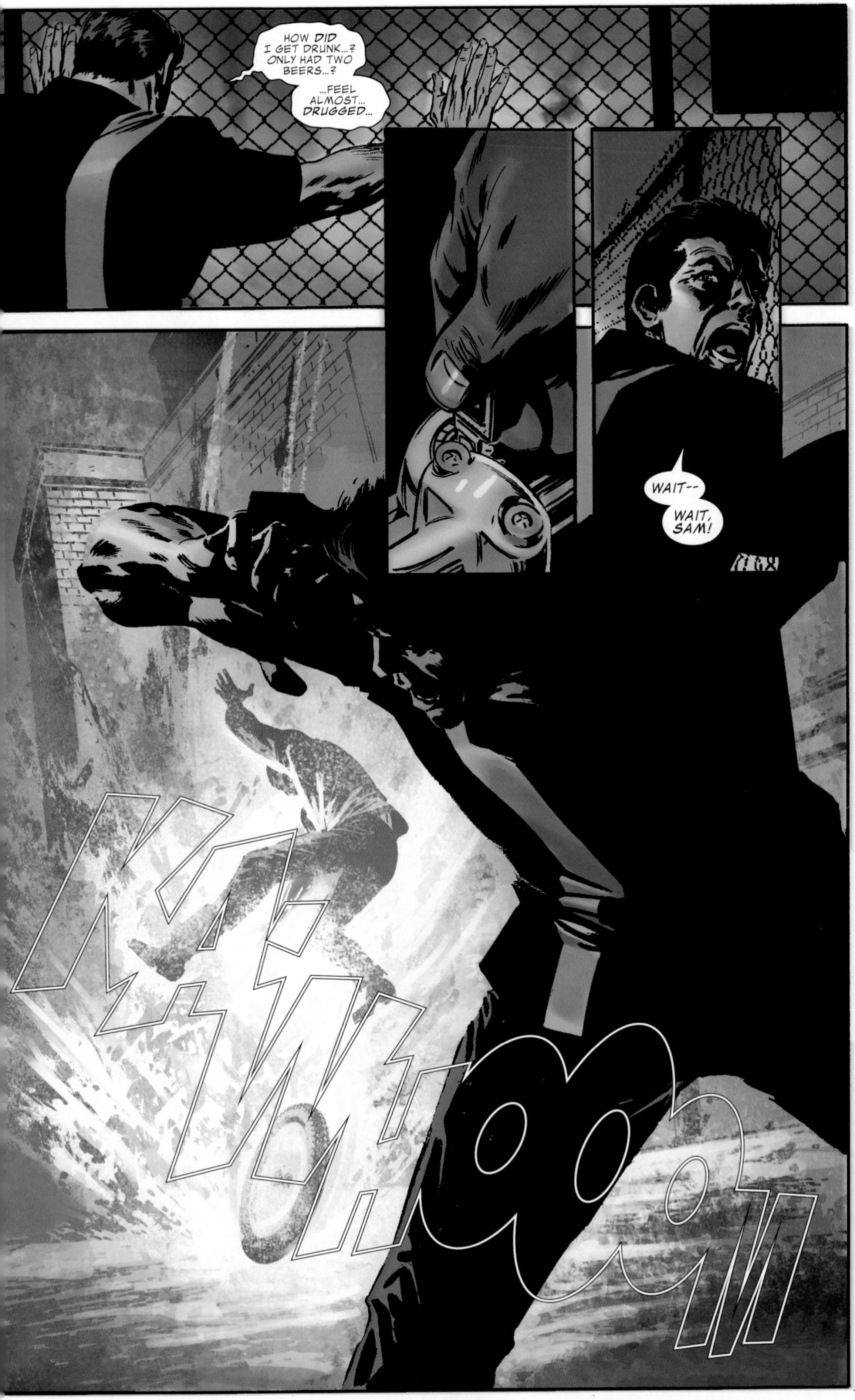

HOW DID I GET DRUNK...? ONLY HAD TWO BEERS...?
...FEEL ALMOST... DRUGGED...
WAIT--
WAIT, SAM!
KAWHOOM

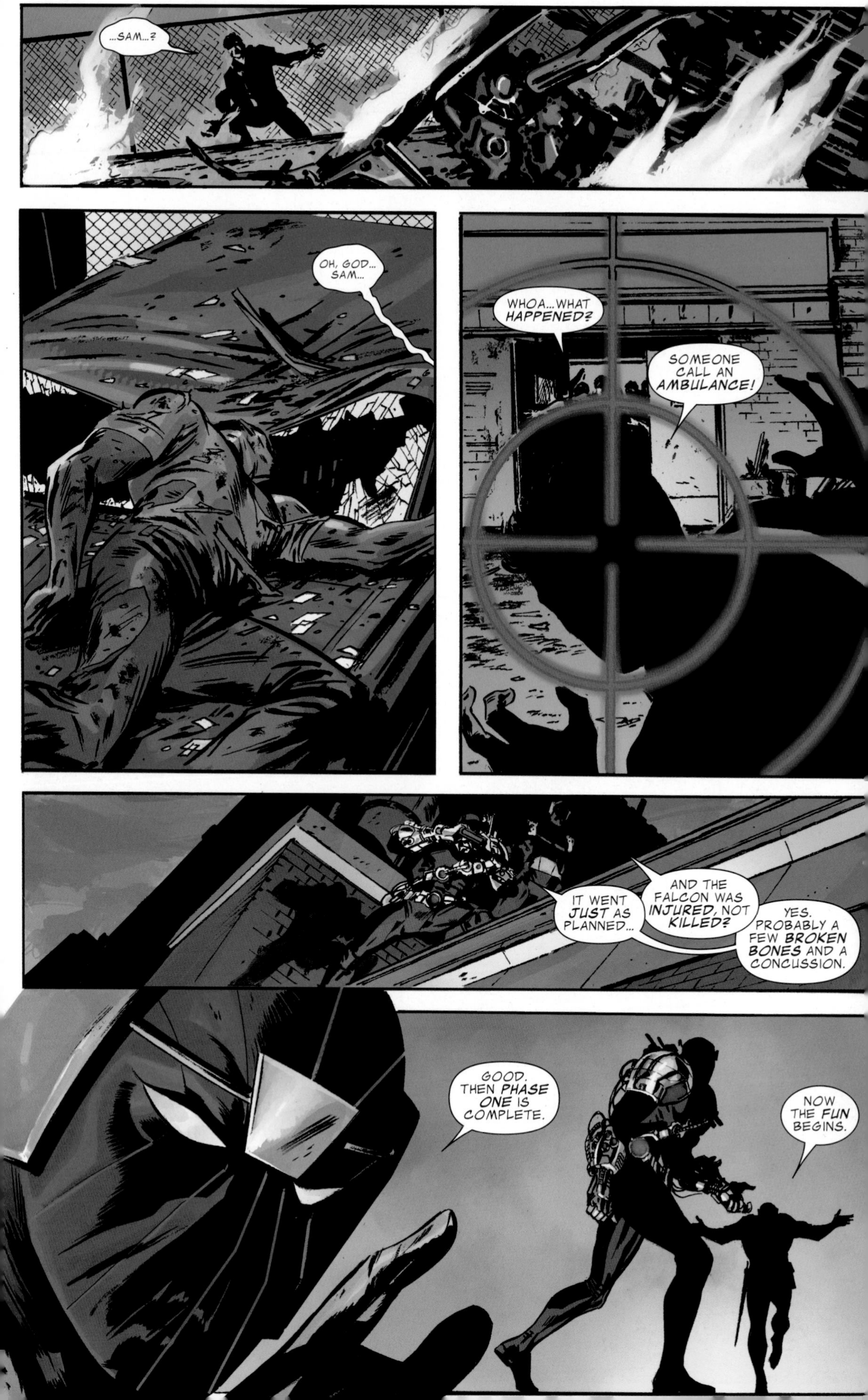
...SAM...?
OH, GOD... SAM...
WHOA...WHAT HAPPENED?
SOMEONE CALL AN AMBULANCE!
AND THE FALCON WAS INJURED, NOT KILLED?
IT WENT JUST AS PLANNED...
YES. PROBABLY A FEW BROKEN BONES AND A CONCUSSION.
GOOD. THEN PHASE ONE IS COMPLETE.
NOW THE FUN BEGINS.

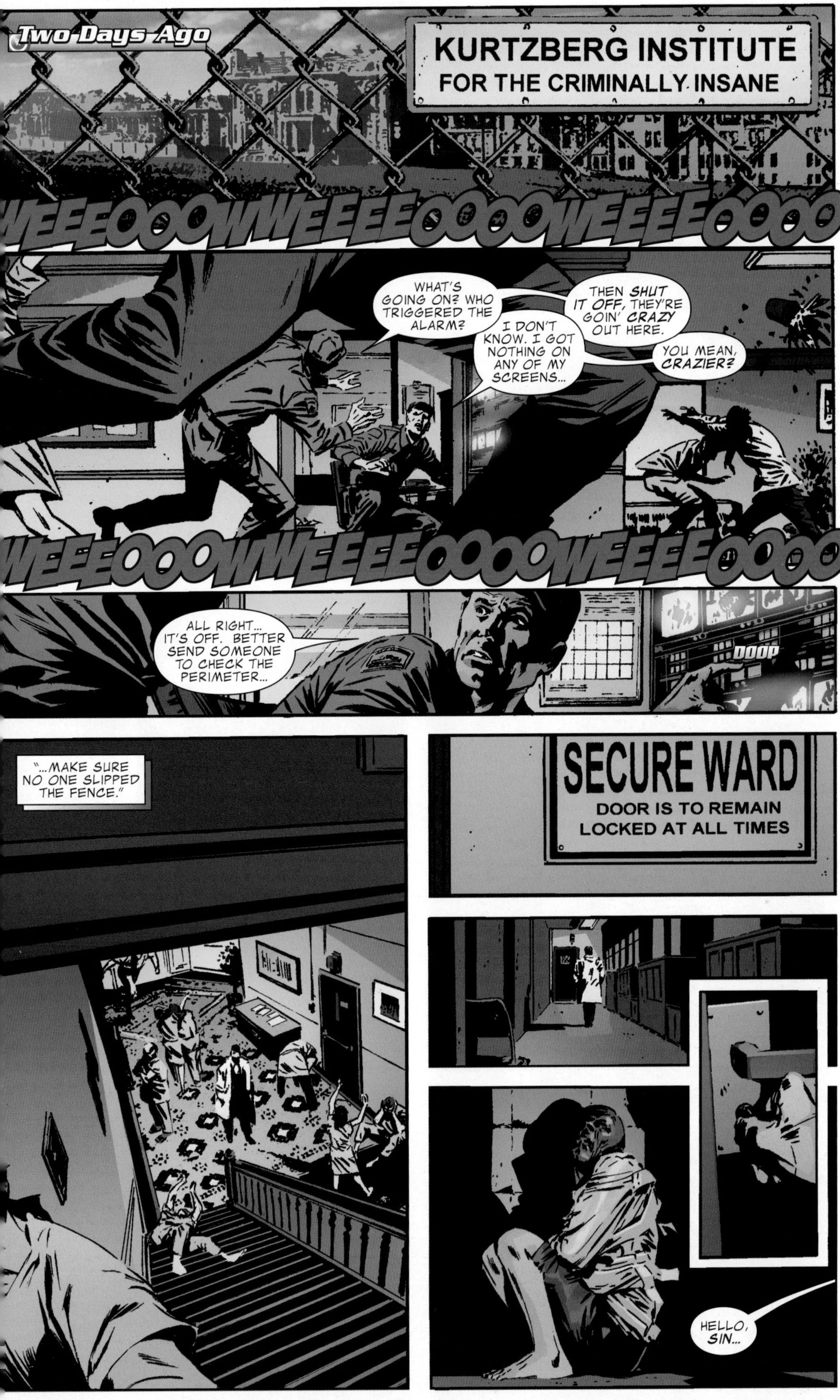
Two Days Ago
KURTZBERG INSTITUTE
FOR THE CRIMINALLY INSANE
WEEEOOOWWEEEEOOOOWEEEEOOOO
WHAT'S GOING ON? WHO TRIGGERED THE ALARM?
I DON'T KNOW. I GOT NOTHING ON ANY OF MY SCREENS...
THEN SHUT IT OFF, THEY'RE GOIN' CRAZY OUT HERE.
YOU MEAN, CRAZIER?
WEEEOOOWWEEEEOOOOWEEEEOOOO
ALL RIGHT... IT'S OFF. BETTER SEND SOMEONE TO CHECK THE PERIMETER...
DOOP
"...MAKE SURE NO ONE SLIPPED THE FENCE."
SECURE WARD
DOOR IS TO REMAIN
LOCKED AT ALL TIMES
HELLO, SIN...

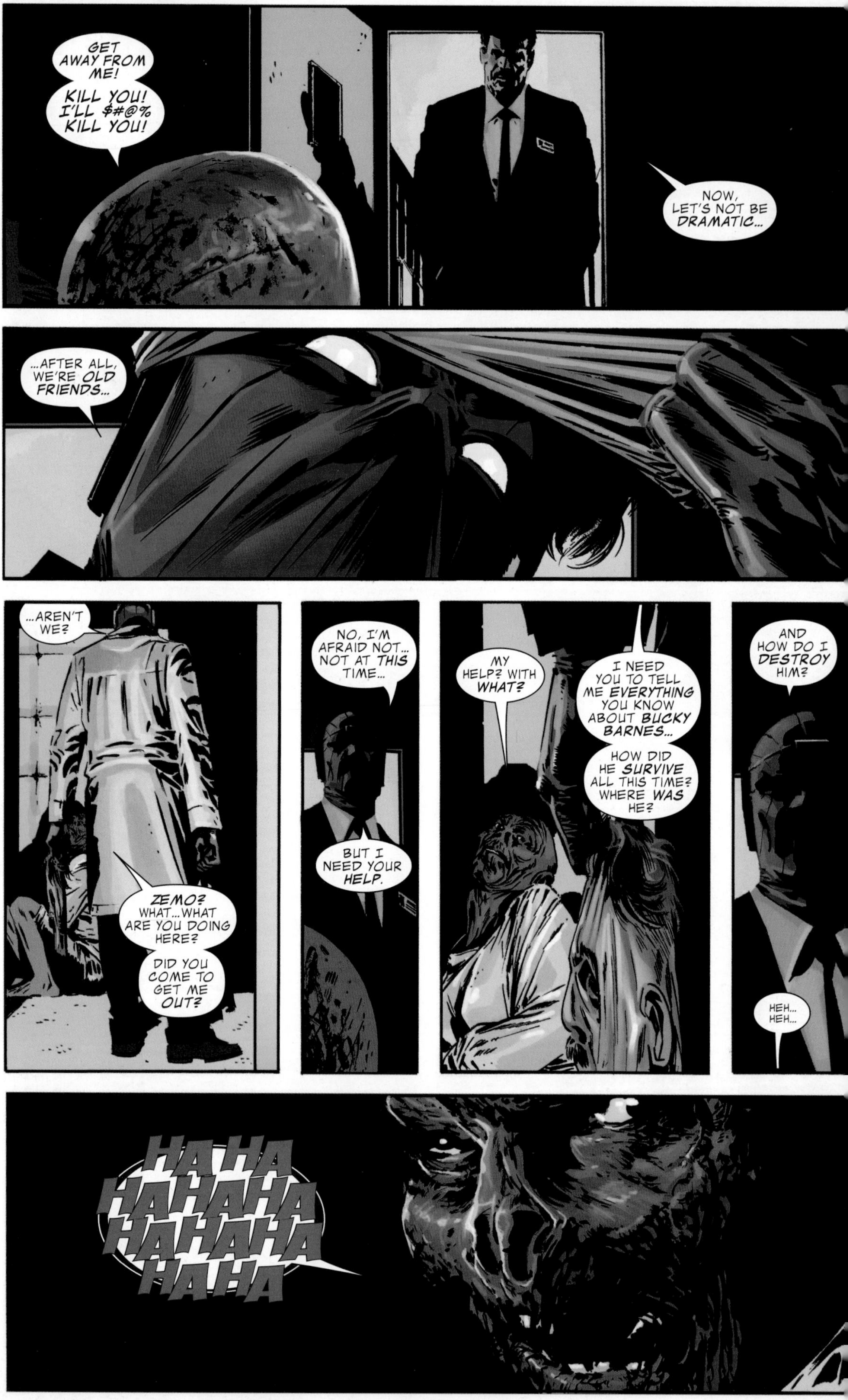
GET AWAY FROM ME!
KILL YOU! I'LL $#@% KILL YOU!
NOW, LET'S NOT BE DRAMATIC...
...AFTER ALL, WE'RE OLD FRIENDS...
...AREN'T WE?
ZEMO? WHAT...WHAT ARE YOU DOING HERE?
DID YOU COME TO GET ME OUT?
NO, I'M AFRAID NOT... NOT AT THIS TIME...
BUT I NEED YOUR HELP.
MY HELP? WITH WHAT?
I NEED YOU TO TELL ME EVERYTHING YOU KNOW ABOUT BUCKY BARNES...
HOW DID HE SURVIVE ALL THIS TIME? WHERE WAS HE?
AND HOW DO I DESTROY HIM?
HEH... HEH...
HAHA HAHAHA HAHAHA HAHA

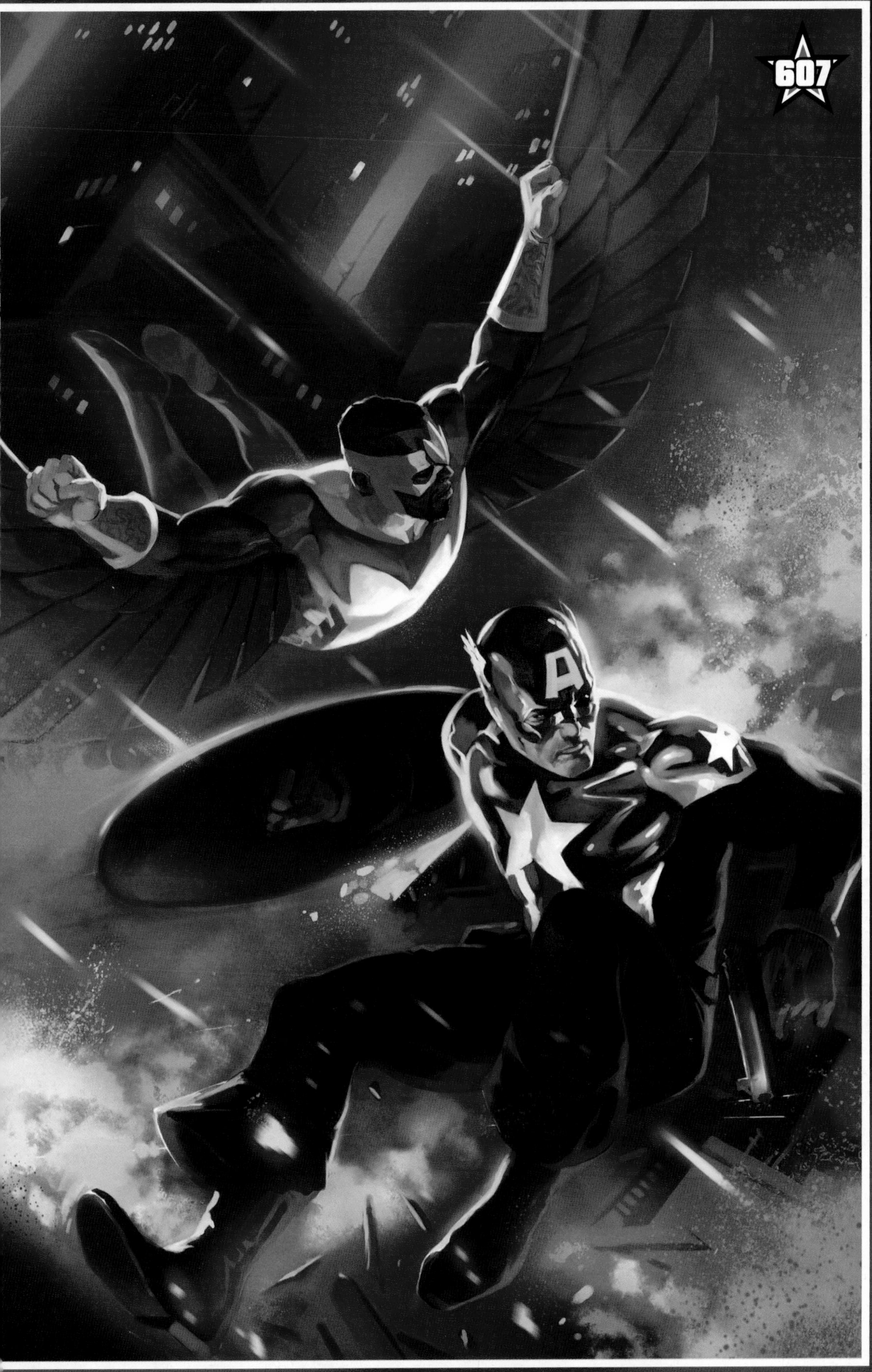
607

NO ESCAPE PART 2

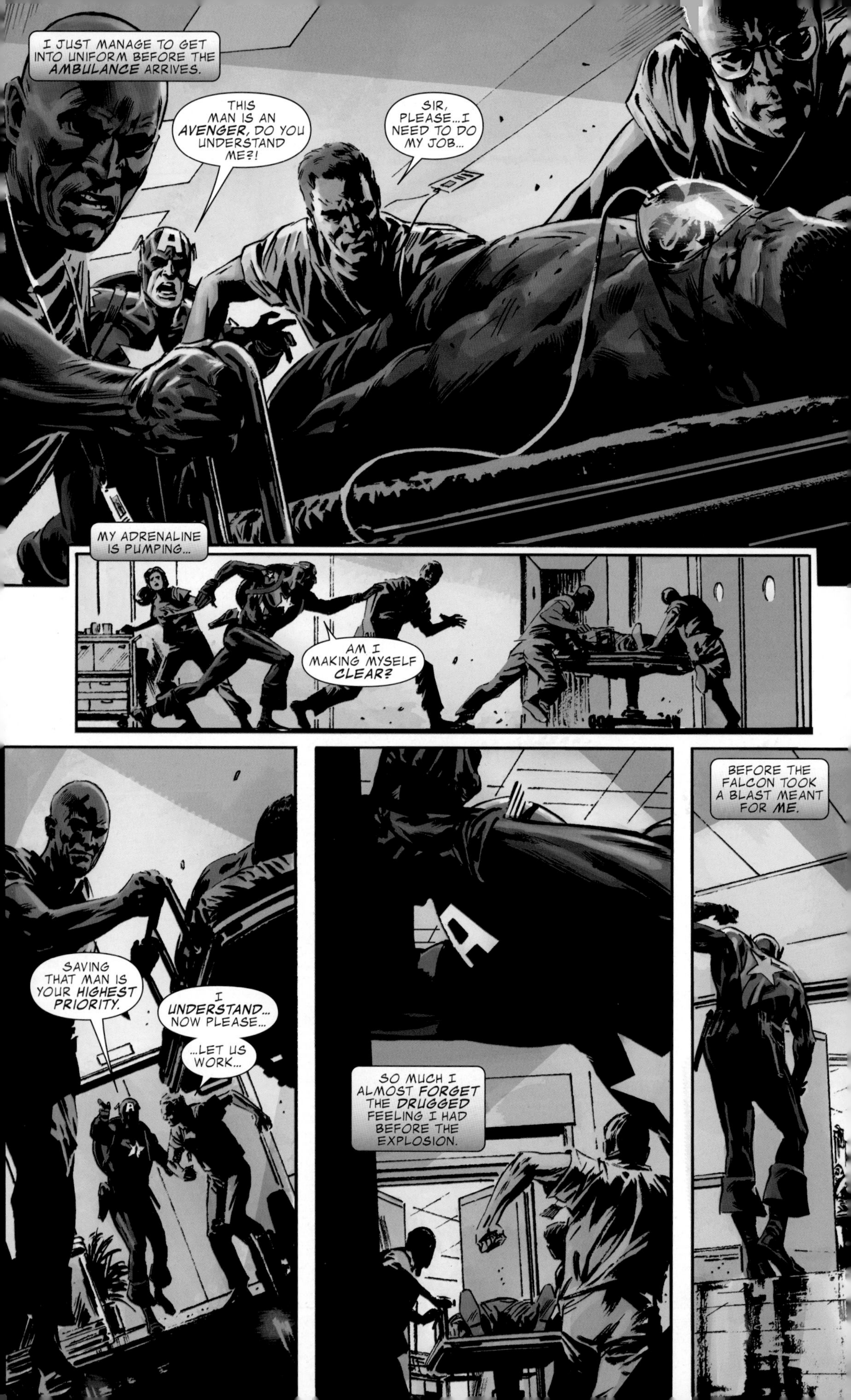
I JUST MANAGE TO GET INTO UNIFORM BEFORE THE AMBULANCE ARRIVES.
THIS MAN IS AN AVENGER, DO YOU UNDERSTAND ME?!
SIR, PLEASE...I NEED TO DO MY JOB...
MY ADRENALINE IS PUMPING...
AM I MAKING MYSELF CLEAR?
SAVING THAT MAN IS YOUR HIGHEST PRIORITY.
I UNDERSTAND... NOW PLEASE...
...LET US WORK...
SO MUCH I ALMOST FORGET THE DRUGGED FEELING I HAD BEFORE THE EXPLOSION.
BEFORE THE FALCON TOOK A BLAST MEANT FOR ME.

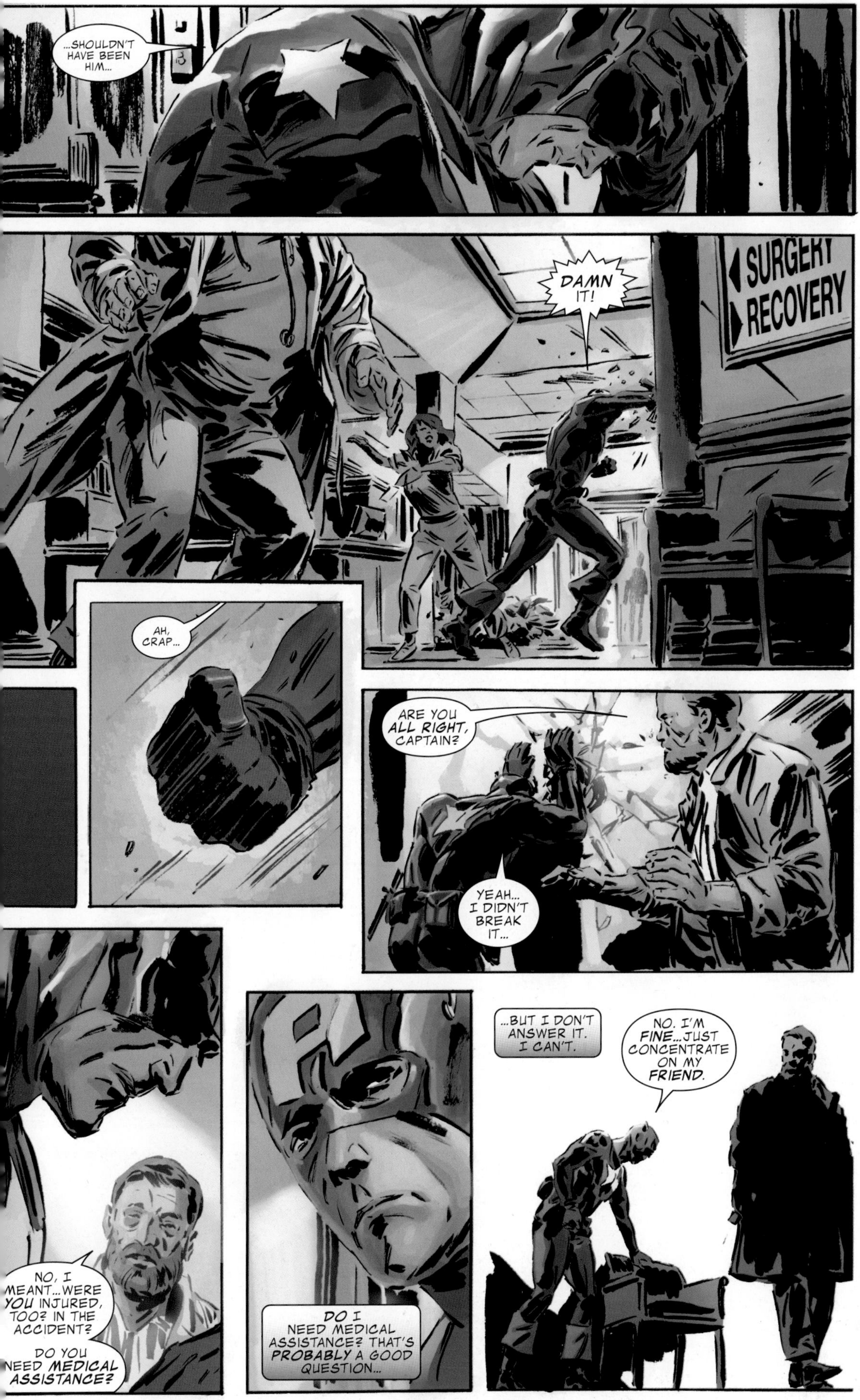
...SHOULDN'T HAVE BEEN HIM...
DAMN IT!
SURGERY
RECOVERY
AH, CRAP...
ARE YOU ALL RIGHT, CAPTAIN?
YEAH... I DIDN'T BREAK IT...
NO, I MEANT...WERE YOU INJURED, TOO? IN THE ACCIDENT?
DO YOU NEED MEDICAL ASSISTANCE?
DO I NEED MEDICAL ASSISTANCE? THAT'S PROBABLY A GOOD QUESTION...
...BUT I DON'T ANSWER IT. I CAN'T.
NO. I'M FINE...JUST CONCENTRATE ON MY FRIEND.

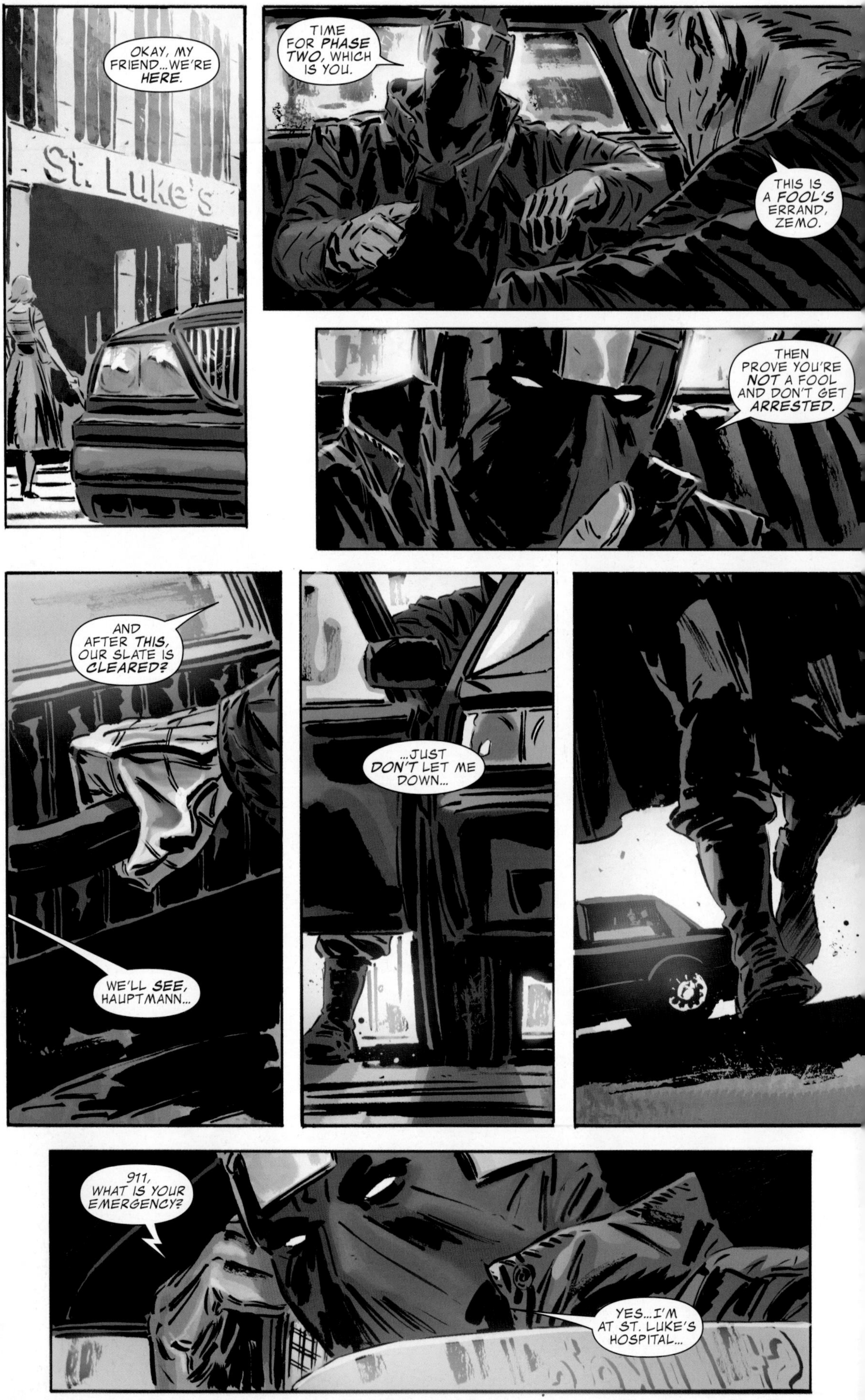
OKAY, MY FRIEND...WE'RE HERE.
St. Luke's
TIME FOR PHASE TWO, WHICH IS YOU.
THIS IS A FOOL'S ERRAND, ZEMO.
THEN PROVE YOU'RE NOT A FOOL AND DON'T GET ARRESTED.
AND AFTER THIS, OUR SLATE IS CLEARED?
WE'LL SEE, HAUPTMANN...
...JUST DON'T LET ME DOWN...
911, WHAT IS YOUR EMERGENCY?
YES...I'M AT ST. LUKE'S HOSPITAL...

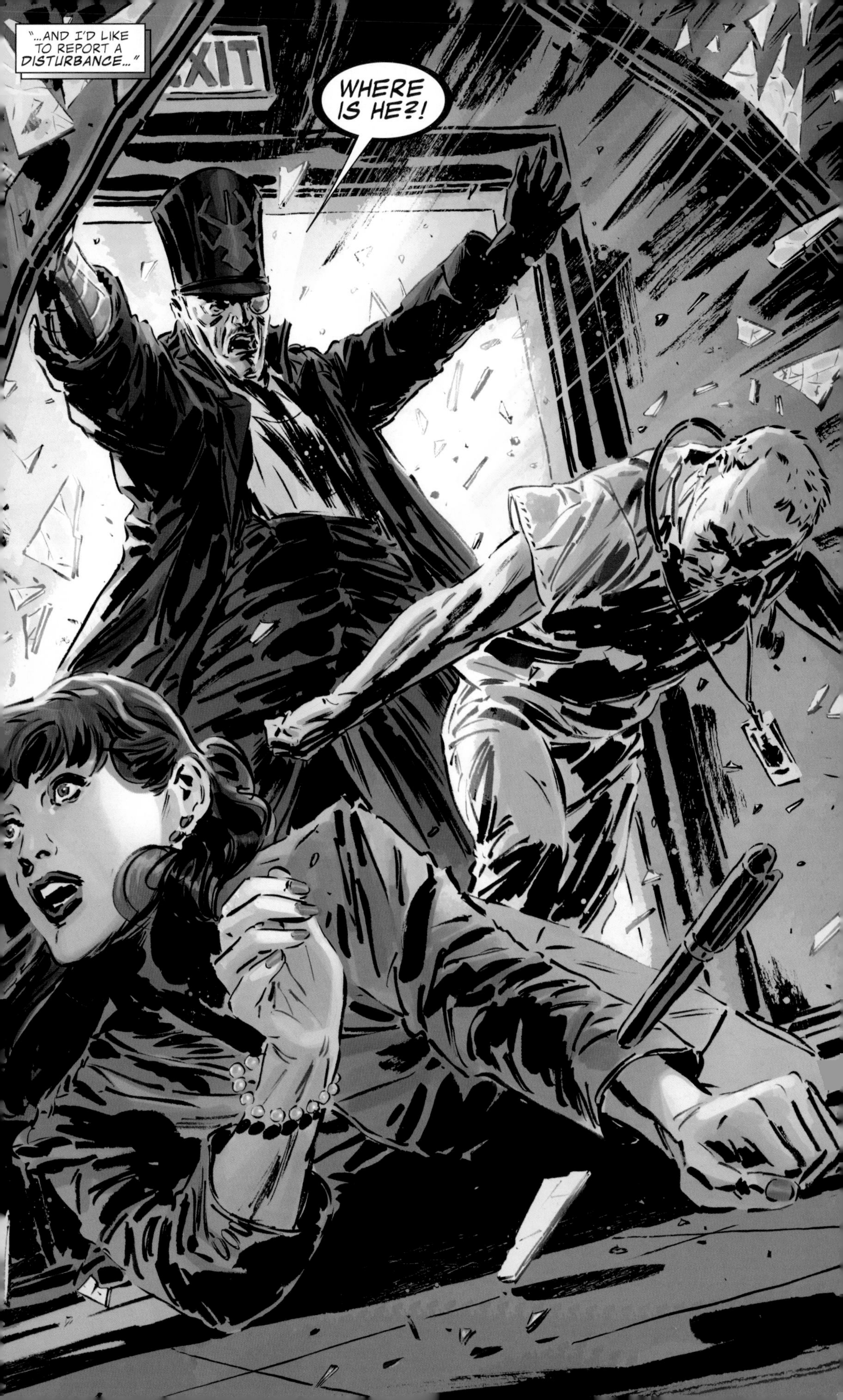
"...AND I'D LIKE TO REPORT A DISTURBANCE..."
WHERE IS HE?!
EXIT

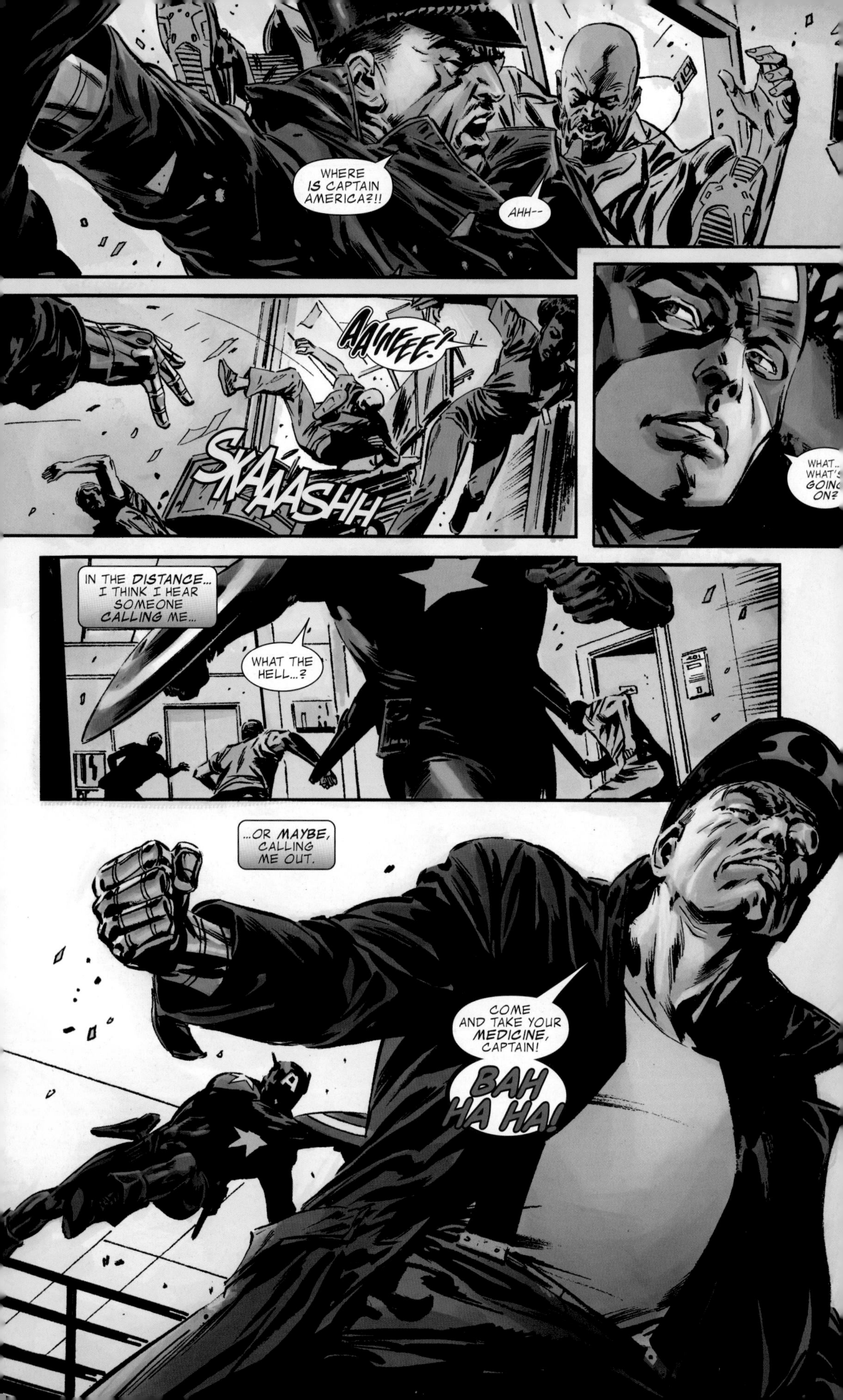
WHERE IS CAPTAIN AMERICA?!!
AHH--
AAWEEE!
SKAAASHH
WHAT... WHAT'S GOING ON?
IN THE DISTANCE... I THINK I HEAR SOMEONE CALLING ME...
WHAT THE HELL...?
...OR MAYBE, CALLING ME OUT.
COME AND TAKE YOUR MEDICINE, CAPTAIN!
BAH HA HA!

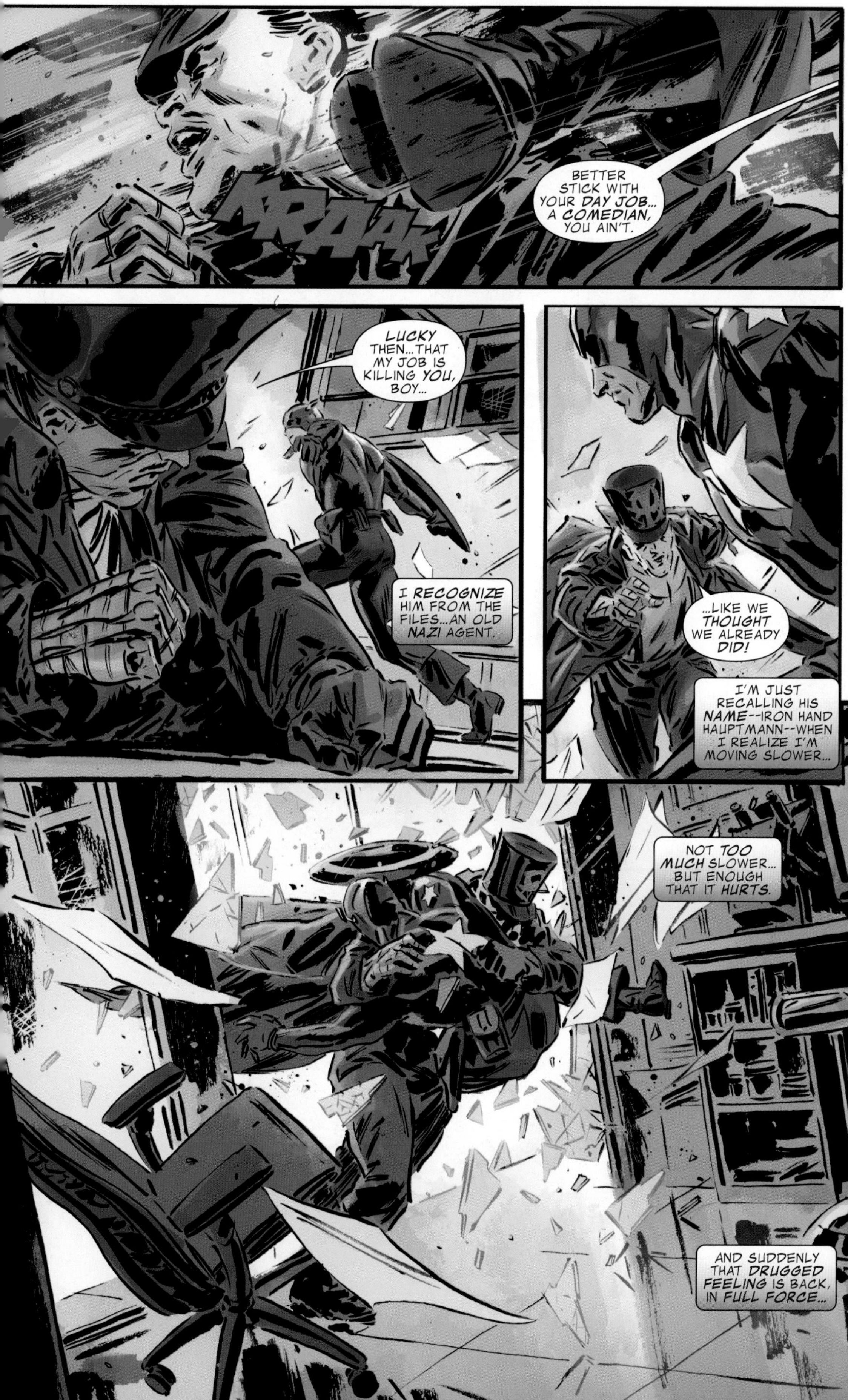

KRAAAK
BETTER STICK WITH YOUR DAY JOB... A COMEDIAN, YOU AIN'T.
LUCKY THEN...THAT MY JOB IS KILLING YOU, BOY...
I RECOGNIZE HIM FROM THE FILES...AN OLD NAZI AGENT.
...LIKE WE THOUGHT WE ALREADY DID!
I'M JUST RECALLING HIS NAME--IRON HAND HAUPTMANN--WHEN I REALIZE I'M MOVING SLOWER...
NOT TOO MUCH SLOWER... BUT ENOUGH THAT IT HURTS.
AND SUDDENLY THAT DRUGGED FEELING IS BACK, IN FULL FORCE...

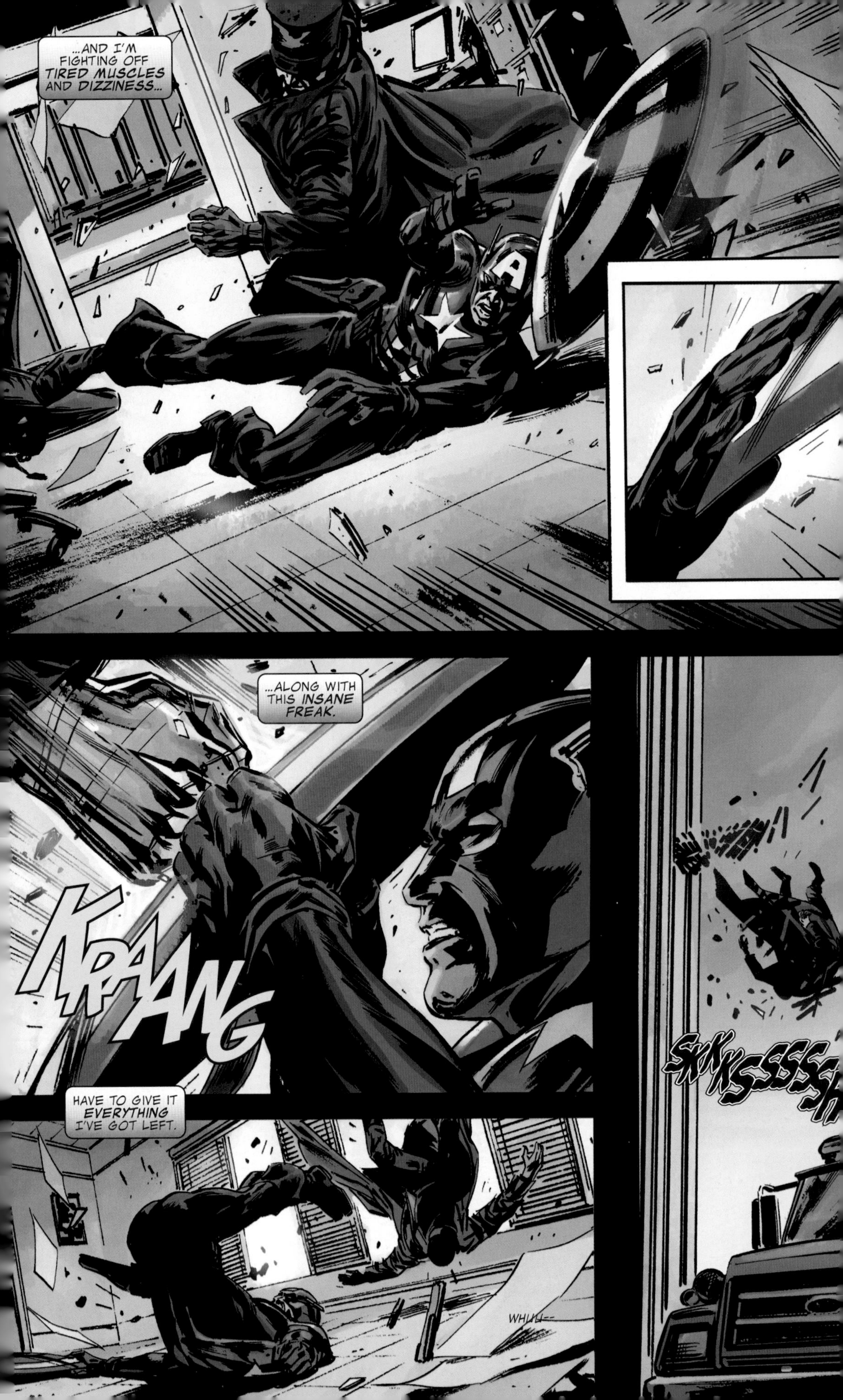
...AND I'M FIGHTING OFF TIRED MUSCLES AND DIZZINESS...
...ALONG WITH THIS INSANE FREAK.
KRAANG
HAVE TO GIVE IT EVERYTHING I'VE GOT LEFT.
WHUU--

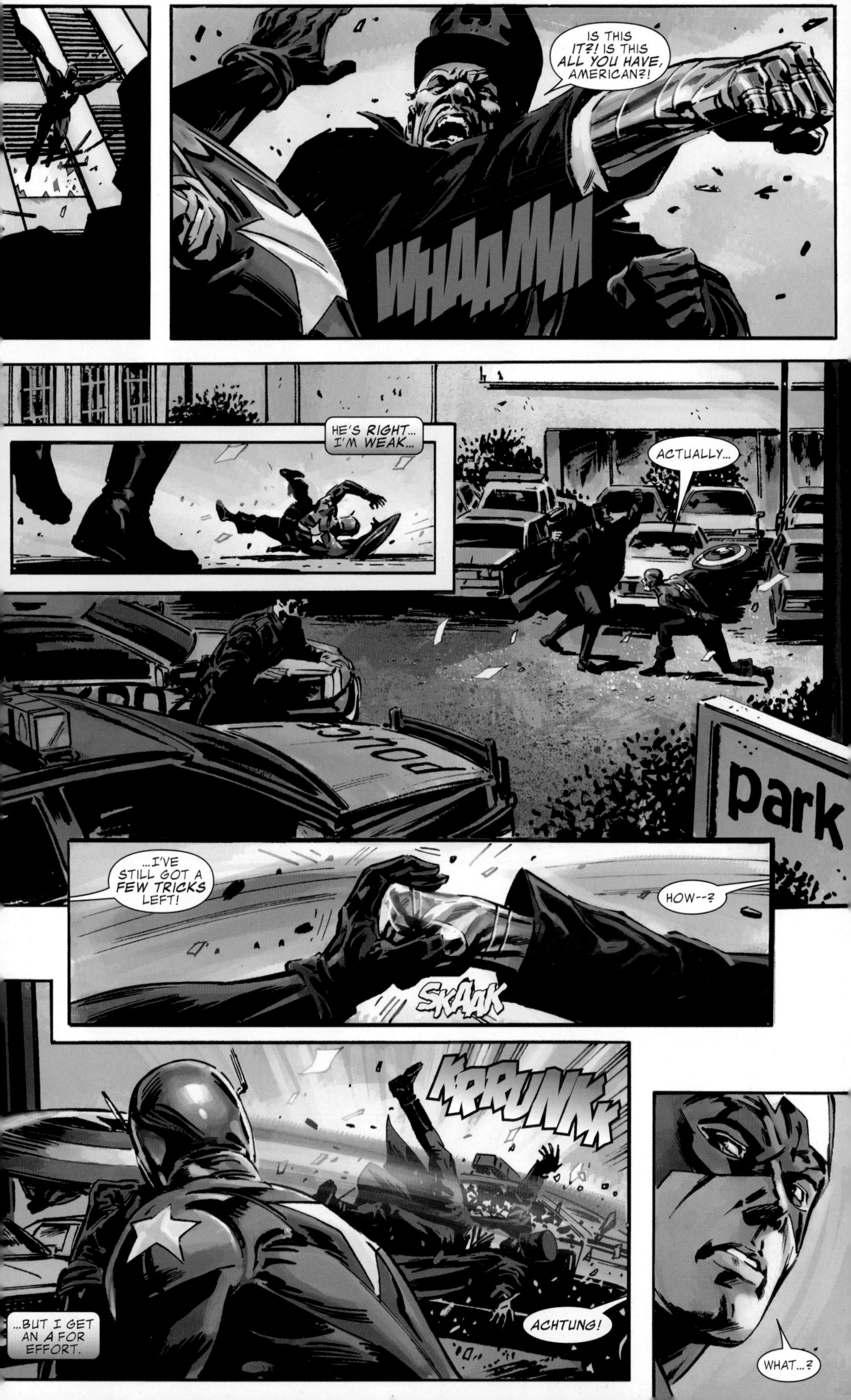
IS THIS IT?! IS THIS ALL YOU HAVE, AMERICAN?!
WHAAMM
HE'S RIGHT... I'M WEAK...
ACTUALLY...
park
...I'VE STILL GOT A FEW TRICKS LEFT!
HOW--?
SKAAK
KRRUNKK
...BUT I GET AN A FOR EFFORT.
ACHTUNG!
WHAT...?

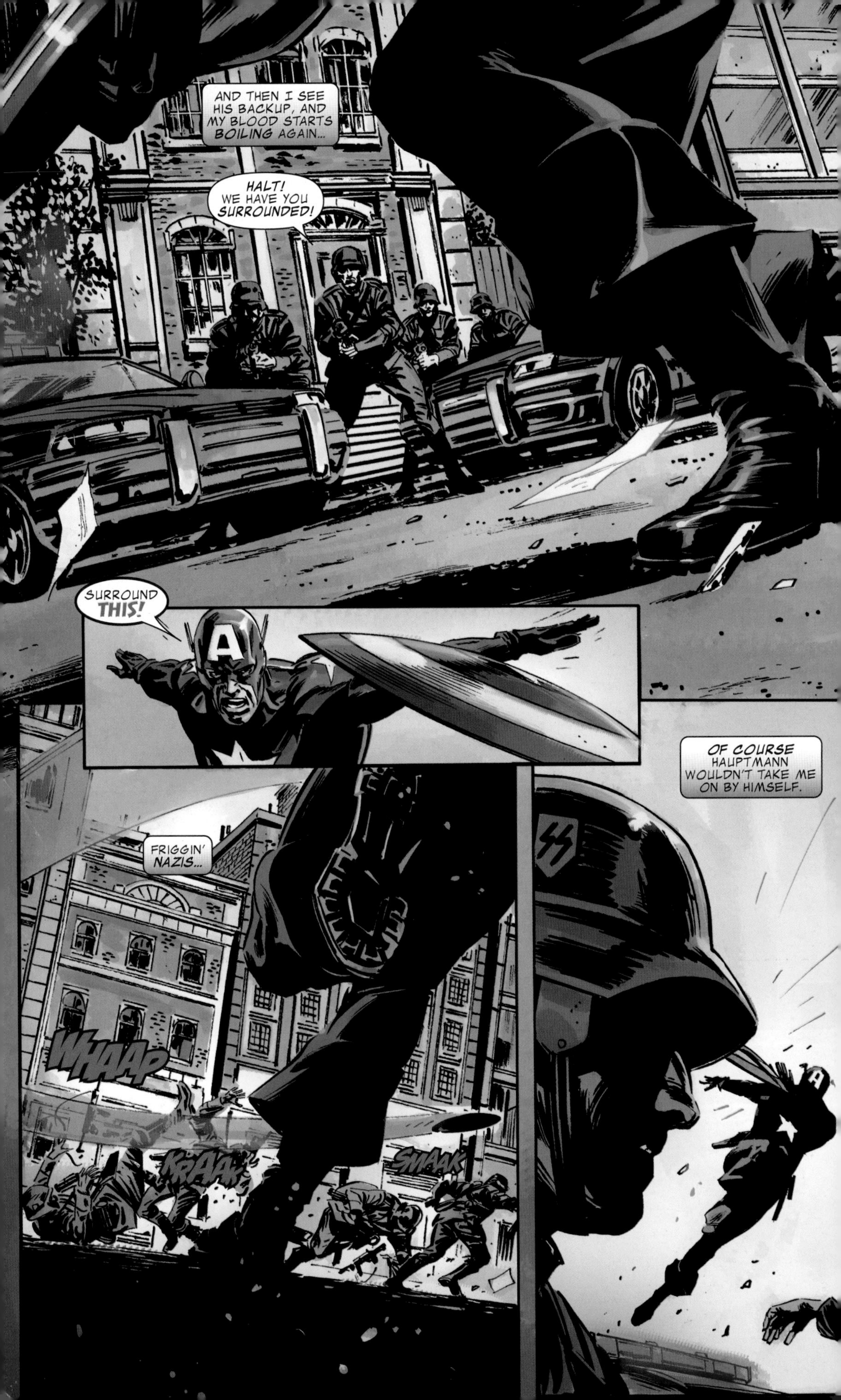

AND THEN I SEE HIS BACKUP, AND MY BLOOD STARTS BOILING AGAIN...
HALT! WE HAVE YOU SURROUNDED!
SURROUND THIS!
FRIGGIN' NAZIS...
WHAAP
KRAAK
SMAAK
OF COURSE HAUPTMANN WOULDN'T TAKE ME ON BY HIMSELF.

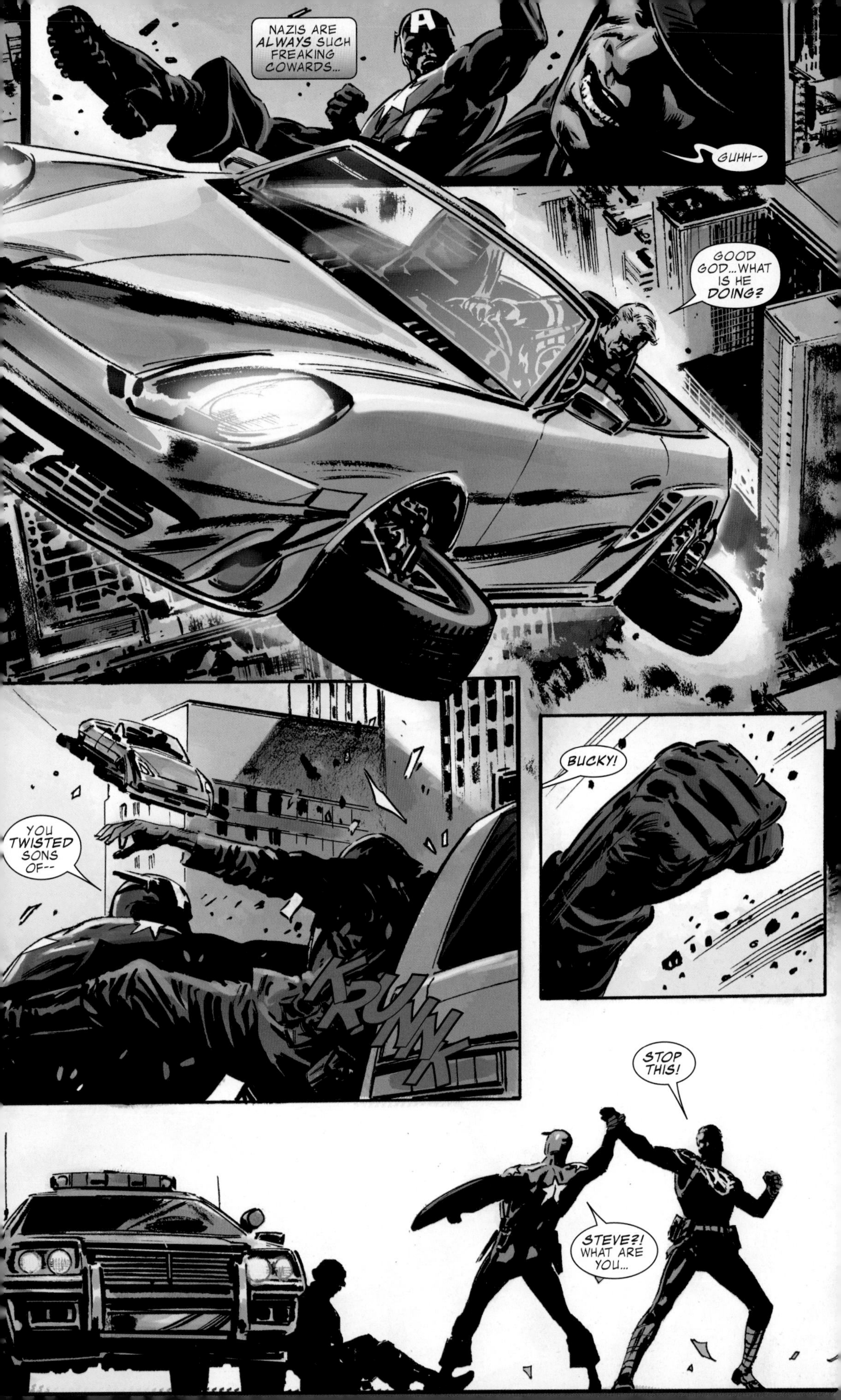
NAZIS ARE ALWAYS SUCH FREAKING COWARDS...
GUHH--
GOOD GOD...WHAT IS HE DOING?
YOU TWISTED SONS OF--
KRUNK
BUCKY!
STOP THIS!
STEVE?! WHAT ARE YOU...

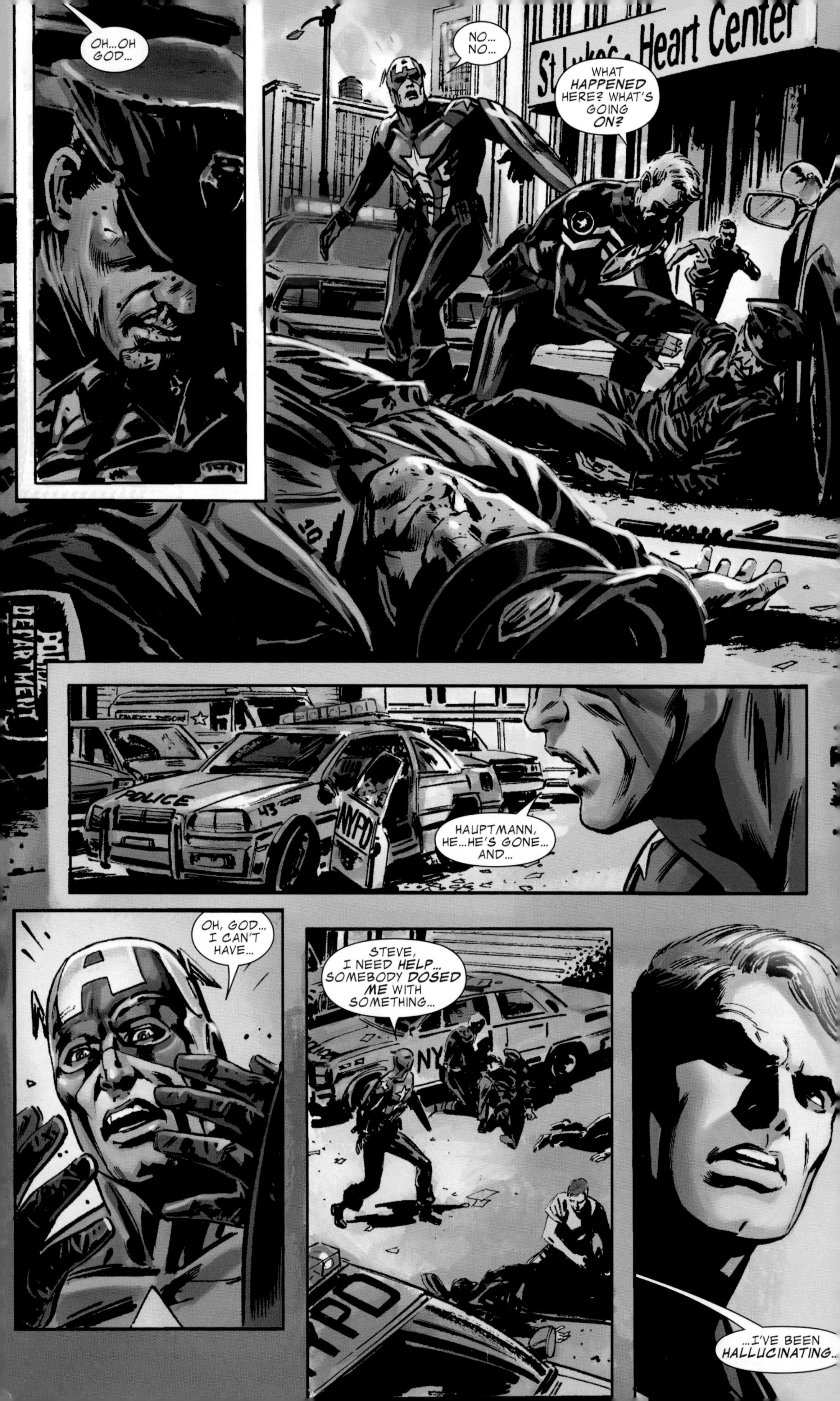

OH...OH GOD...
NO... NO...
St Luke's Heart Center
WHAT HAPPENED HERE? WHAT'S GOING ON?
POLICE DEPARTMENT
POLICE
NYPD
HAUPTMANN, HE...HE'S GONE... AND...
OH, GOD... I CAN'T HAVE...
STEVE, I NEED HELP... SOMEBODY DOSED ME WITH SOMETHING...
...I'VE BEEN HALLUCINATING...

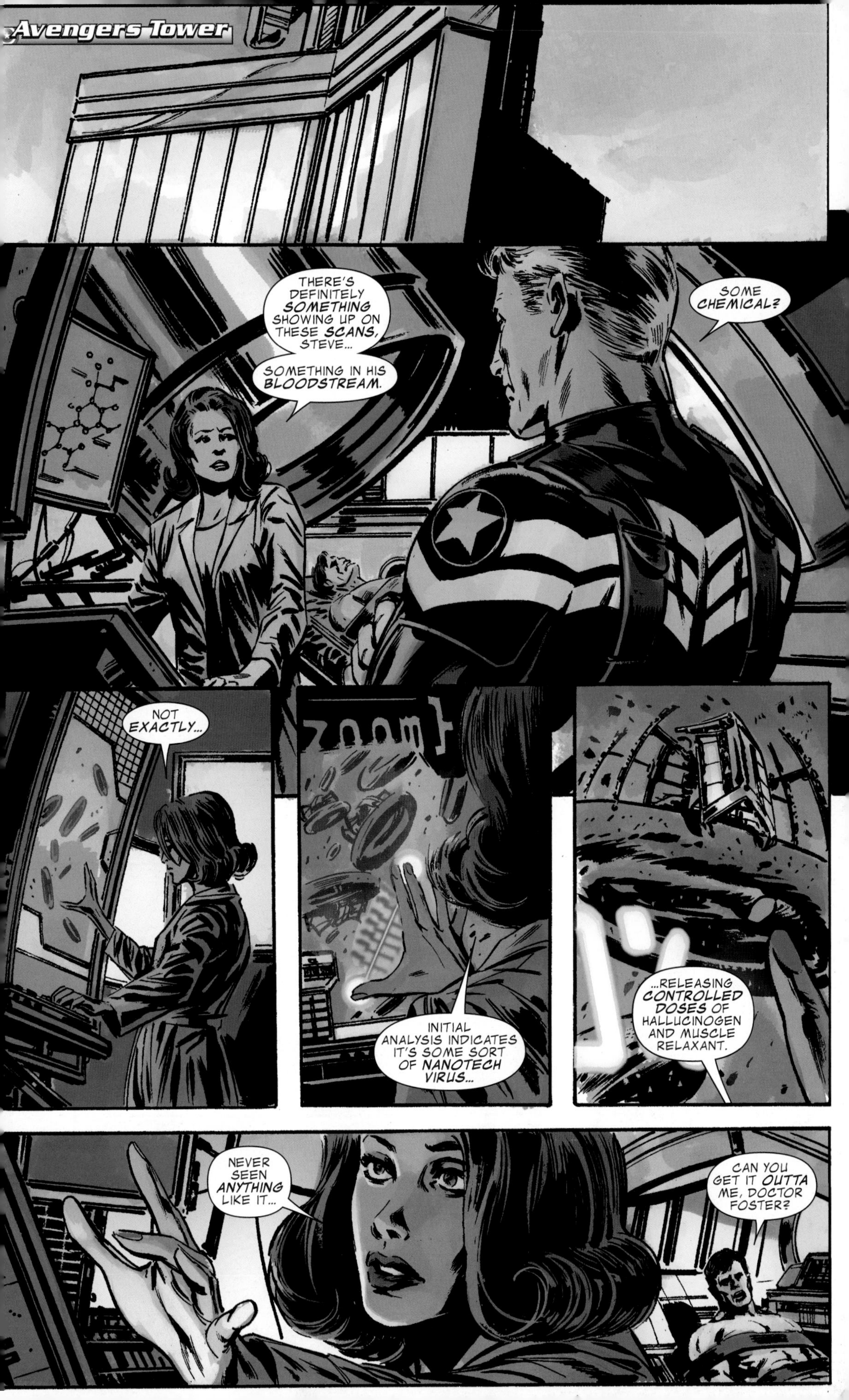
Avengers Tower
THERE'S DEFINITELY SOMETHING SHOWING UP ON THESE SCANS, STEVE...
SOMETHING IN HIS BLOODSTREAM.
SOME CHEMICAL?
NOT EXACTLY...
zoom
INITIAL ANALYSIS INDICATES IT'S SOME SORT OF NANOTECH VIRUS...
...RELEASING CONTROLLED DOSES OF HALLUCINOGEN AND MUSCLE RELAXANT.
NEVER SEEN ANYTHING LIKE IT...
CAN YOU GET IT OUTTA ME, DOCTOR FOSTER?

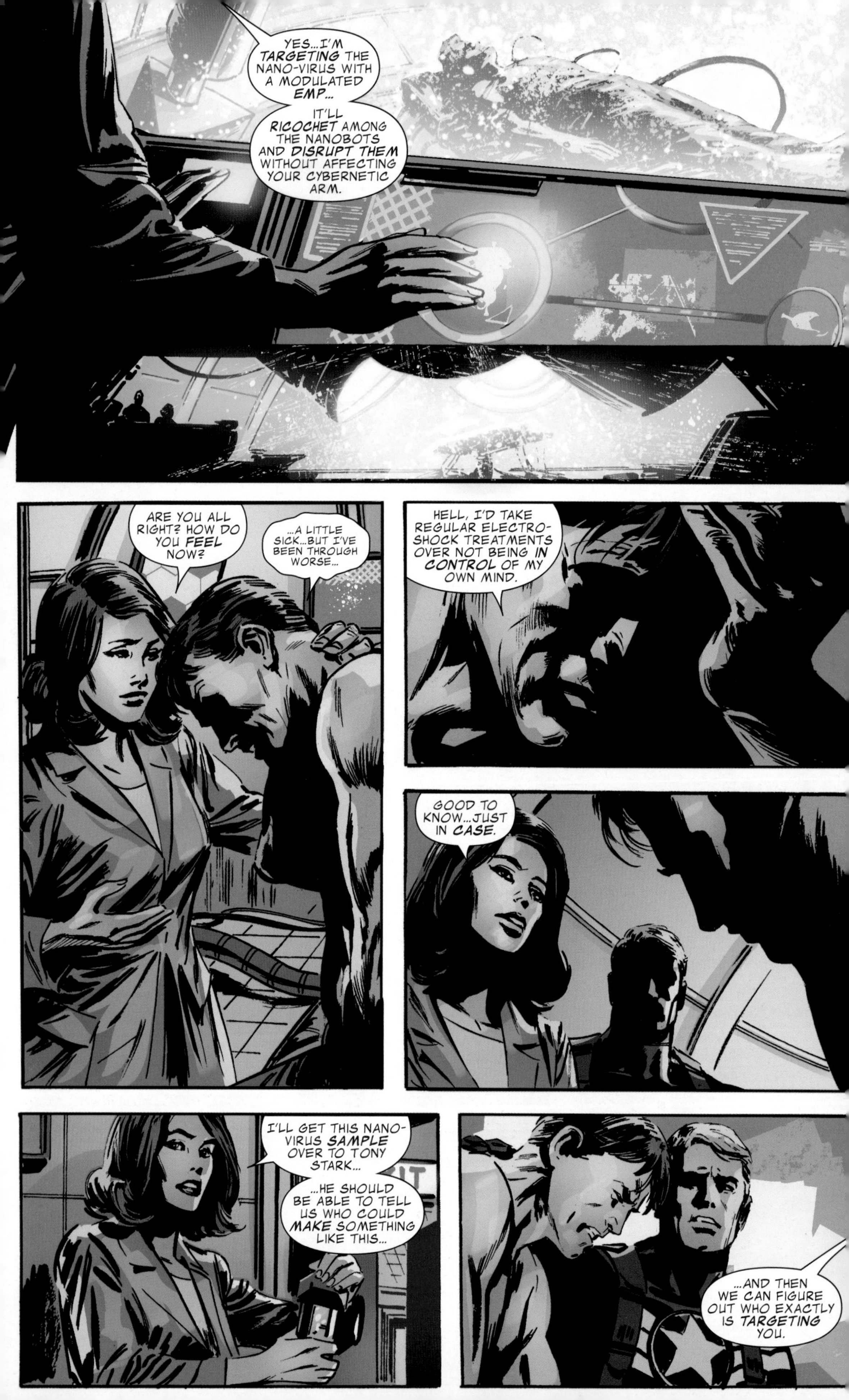
YES...I'M TARGETING THE NANO-VIRUS WITH A MODULATED EMP...
IT'LL RICOCHET AMONG THE NANOBOTS AND DISRUPT THEM WITHOUT AFFECTING YOUR CYBERNETIC ARM.
ARE YOU ALL RIGHT? HOW DO YOU FEEL NOW?
...A LITTLE SICK...BUT I'VE BEEN THROUGH WORSE...
HELL, I'D TAKE REGULAR ELECTRO-SHOCK TREATMENTS OVER NOT BEING IN CONTROL OF MY OWN MIND.
GOOD TO KNOW...JUST IN CASE.
I'LL GET THIS NANO-VIRUS SAMPLE OVER TO TONY STARK...
...HE SHOULD BE ABLE TO TELL US WHO COULD MAKE SOMETHING LIKE THIS...
...AND THEN WE CAN FIGURE OUT WHO EXACTLY IS TARGETING YOU.

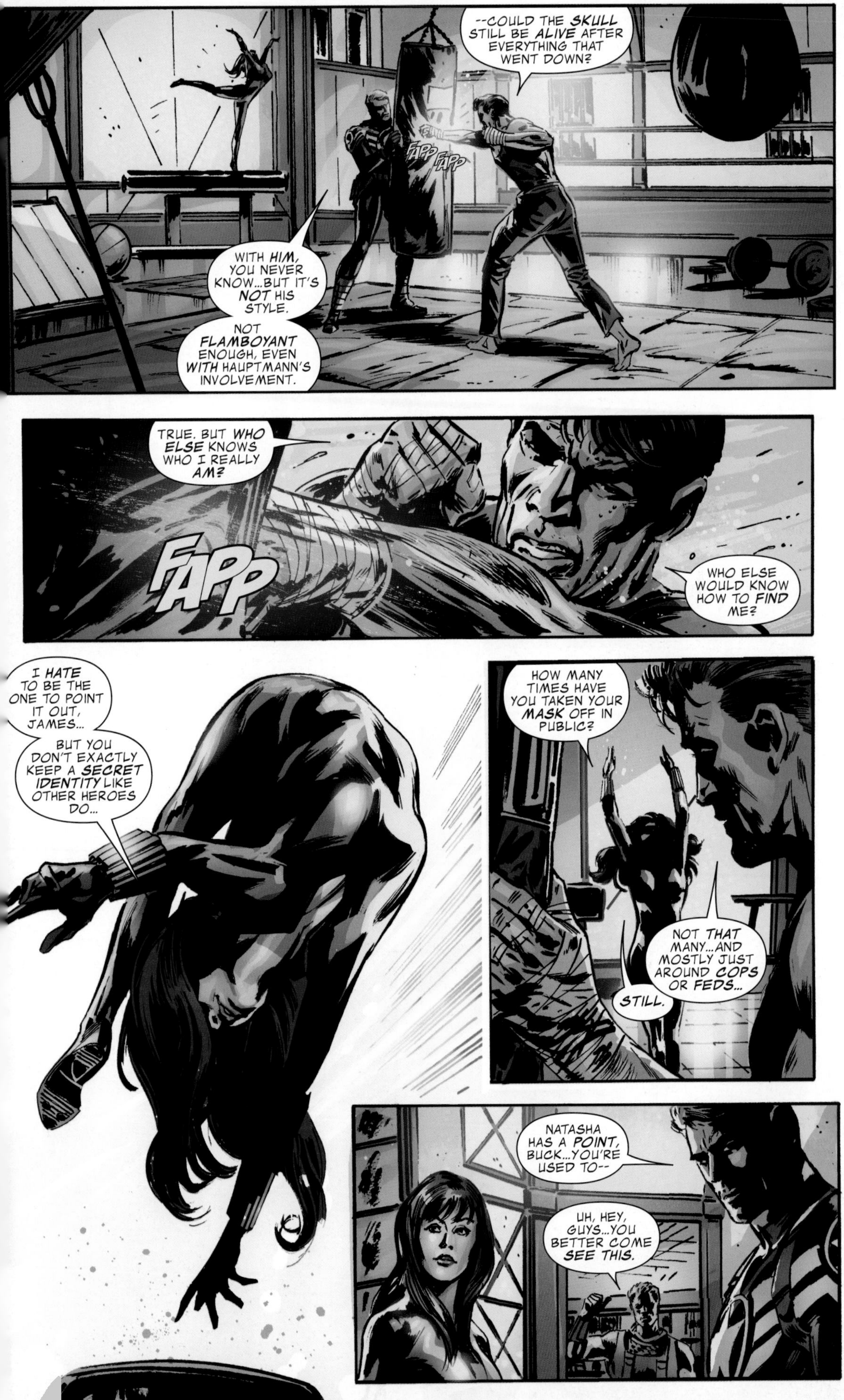
--COULD THE SKULL STILL BE ALIVE AFTER EVERYTHING THAT WENT DOWN?
FAPP FAPP
WITH HIM, YOU NEVER KNOW...BUT IT'S NOT HIS STYLE.
NOT FLAMBOYANT ENOUGH, EVEN WITH HAUPTMANN'S INVOLVEMENT.
TRUE. BUT WHO ELSE KNOWS WHO I REALLY AM?
FAPP
WHO ELSE WOULD KNOW HOW TO FIND ME?
I HATE TO BE THE ONE TO POINT IT OUT, JAMES...
BUT YOU DON'T EXACTLY KEEP A SECRET IDENTITY LIKE OTHER HEROES DO...
HOW MANY TIMES HAVE YOU TAKEN YOUR MASK OFF IN PUBLIC?
NOT THAT MANY...AND MOSTLY JUST AROUND COPS OR FEDS...
STILL.
NATASHA HAS A POINT, BUCK...YOU'RE USED TO--
UH, HEY, GUYS...YOU BETTER COME SEE THIS.

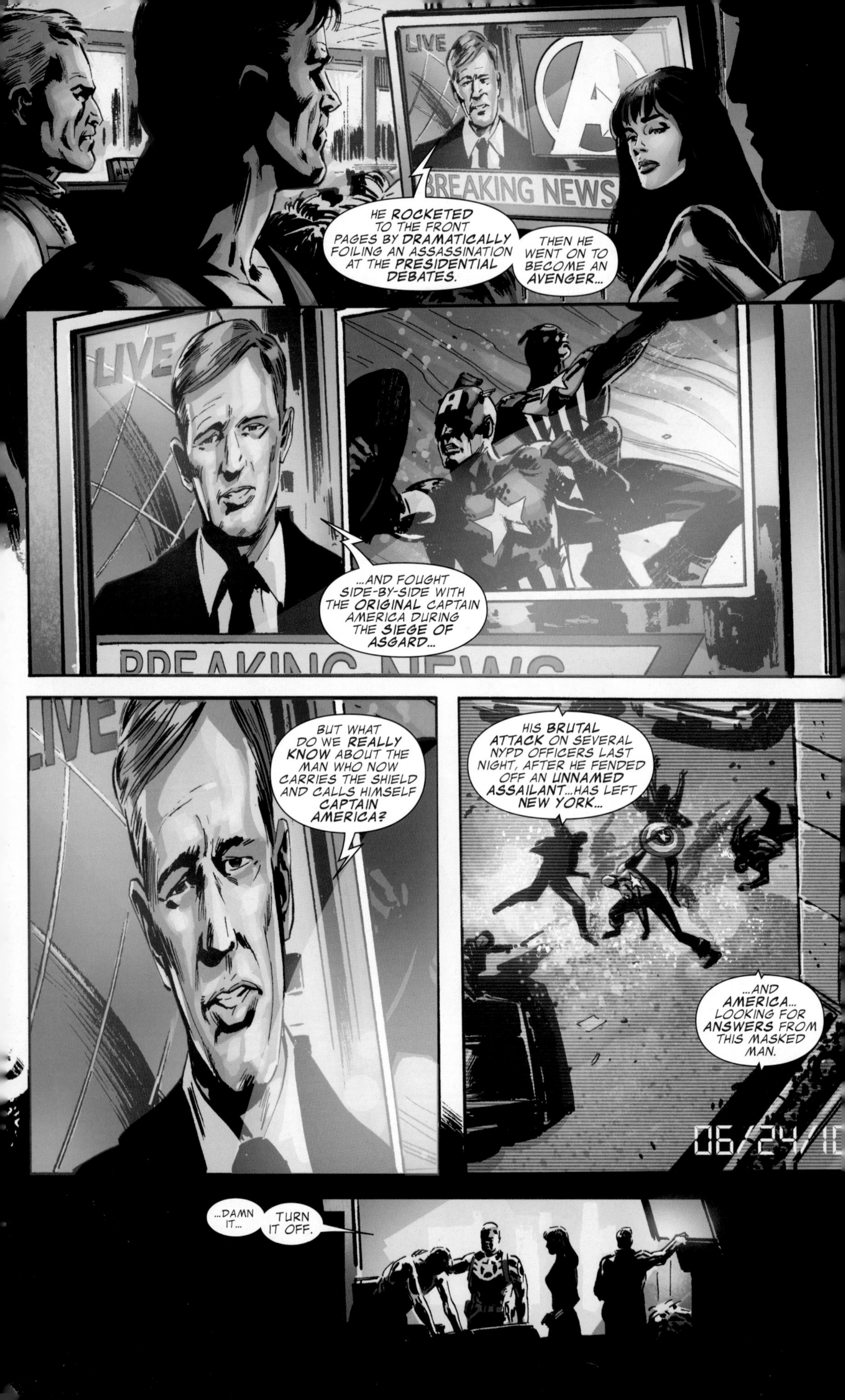

LIVE
BREAKING NEWS
HE ROCKETED TO THE FRONT PAGES BY DRAMATICALLY FOILING AN ASSASSINATION AT THE PRESIDENTIAL DEBATES.
THEN HE WENT ON TO BECOME AN AVENGER...
LIVE
...AND FOUGHT SIDE-BY-SIDE WITH THE ORIGINAL CAPTAIN AMERICA DURING THE SIEGE OF ASGARD...
BUT WHAT DO WE REALLY KNOW ABOUT THE MAN WHO NOW CARRIES THE SHIELD AND CALLS HIMSELF CAPTAIN AMERICA?
HIS BRUTAL ATTACK ON SEVERAL NYPD OFFICERS LAST NIGHT, AFTER HE FENDED OFF AN UNNAMED ASSAILANT...HAS LEFT NEW YORK...
...AND AMERICA... LOOKING FOR ANSWERS FROM THIS MASKED MAN.
...DAMN IT...
TURN IT OFF.

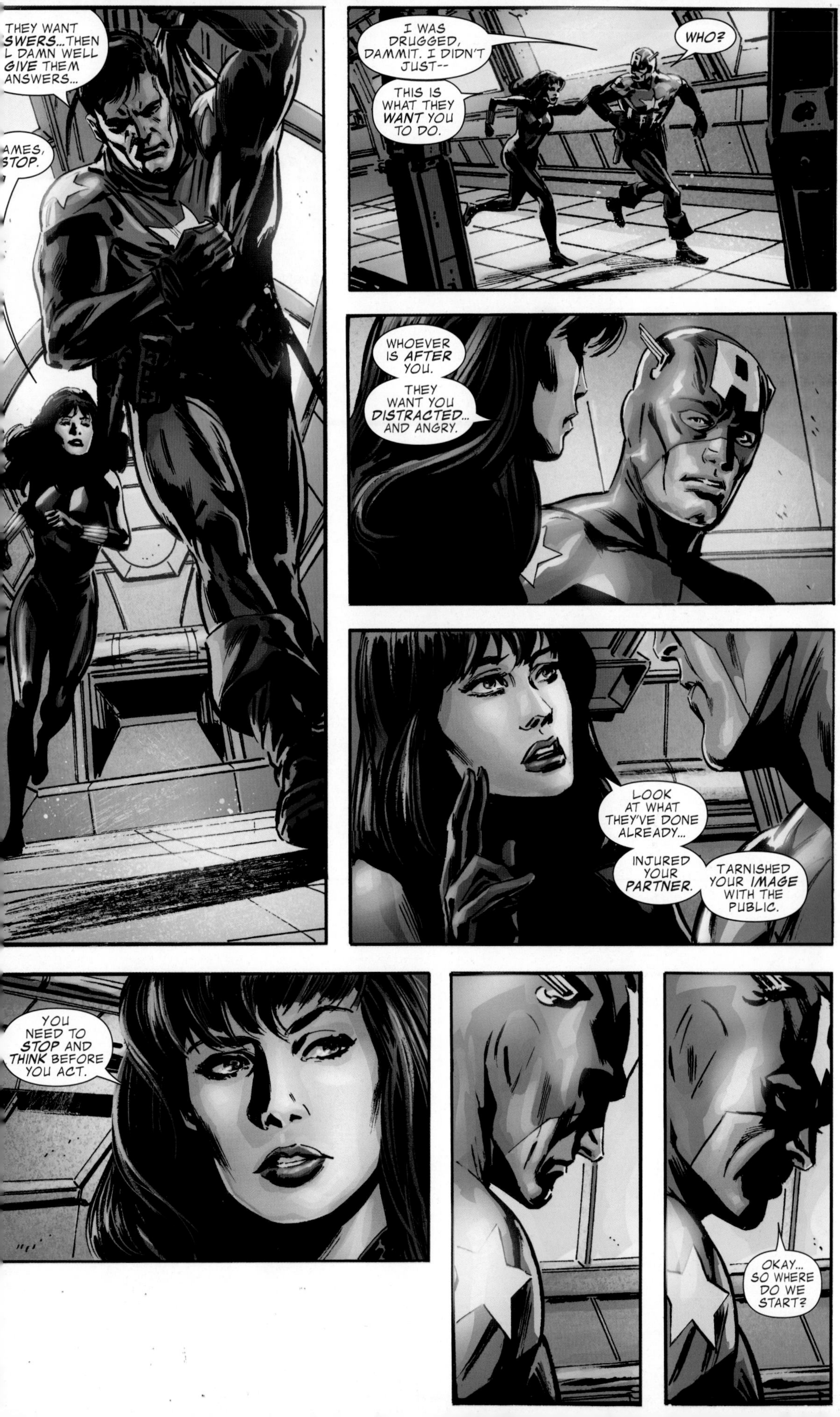
THEY WANT
SWERS...THEN
L DAMN WELL
GIVE THEM
ANSWERS...
AMES,
STOP.
I WAS DRUGGED, DAMMIT. I DIDN'T JUST--
WHO?
THIS IS WHAT THEY WANT YOU TO DO.
WHOEVER IS AFTER YOU.
THEY WANT YOU DISTRACTED... AND ANGRY.
LOOK AT WHAT THEY'VE DONE ALREADY...
INJURED YOUR PARTNER.
TARNISHED YOUR IMAGE WITH THE PUBLIC.
YOU NEED TO STOP AND THINK BEFORE YOU ACT.
OKAY... SO WHERE DO WE START?

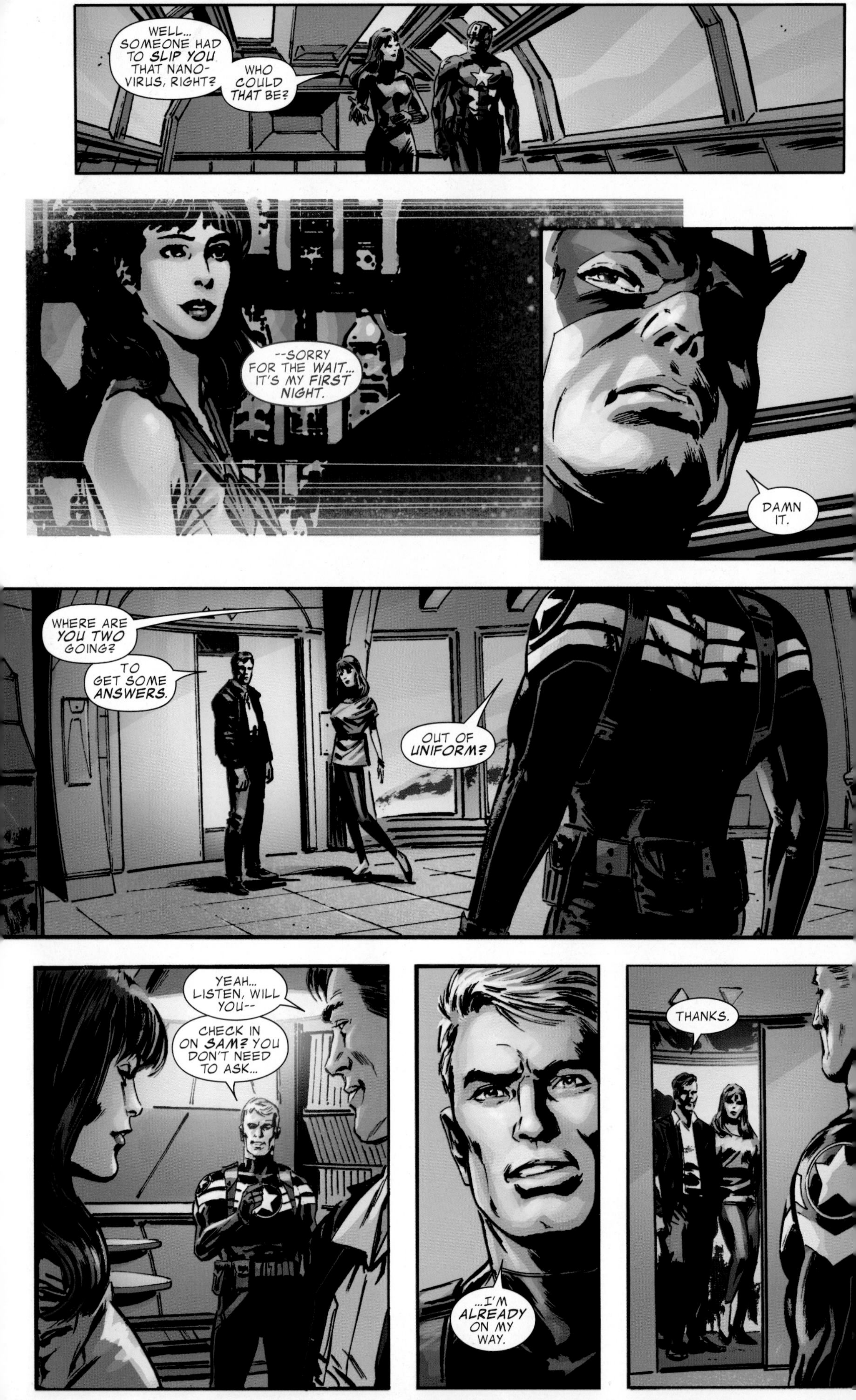
WELL... SOMEONE HAD TO SLIP YOU THAT NANO-VIRUS, RIGHT?
WHO COULD THAT BE?
--SORRY FOR THE WAIT... IT'S MY FIRST NIGHT.
DAMN IT.
WHERE ARE YOU TWO GOING?
TO GET SOME ANSWERS.
OUT OF UNIFORM?
YEAH... LISTEN, WILL YOU--
CHECK IN ON SAM? YOU DON'T NEED TO ASK...
...I'M ALREADY ON MY WAY.
THANKS.

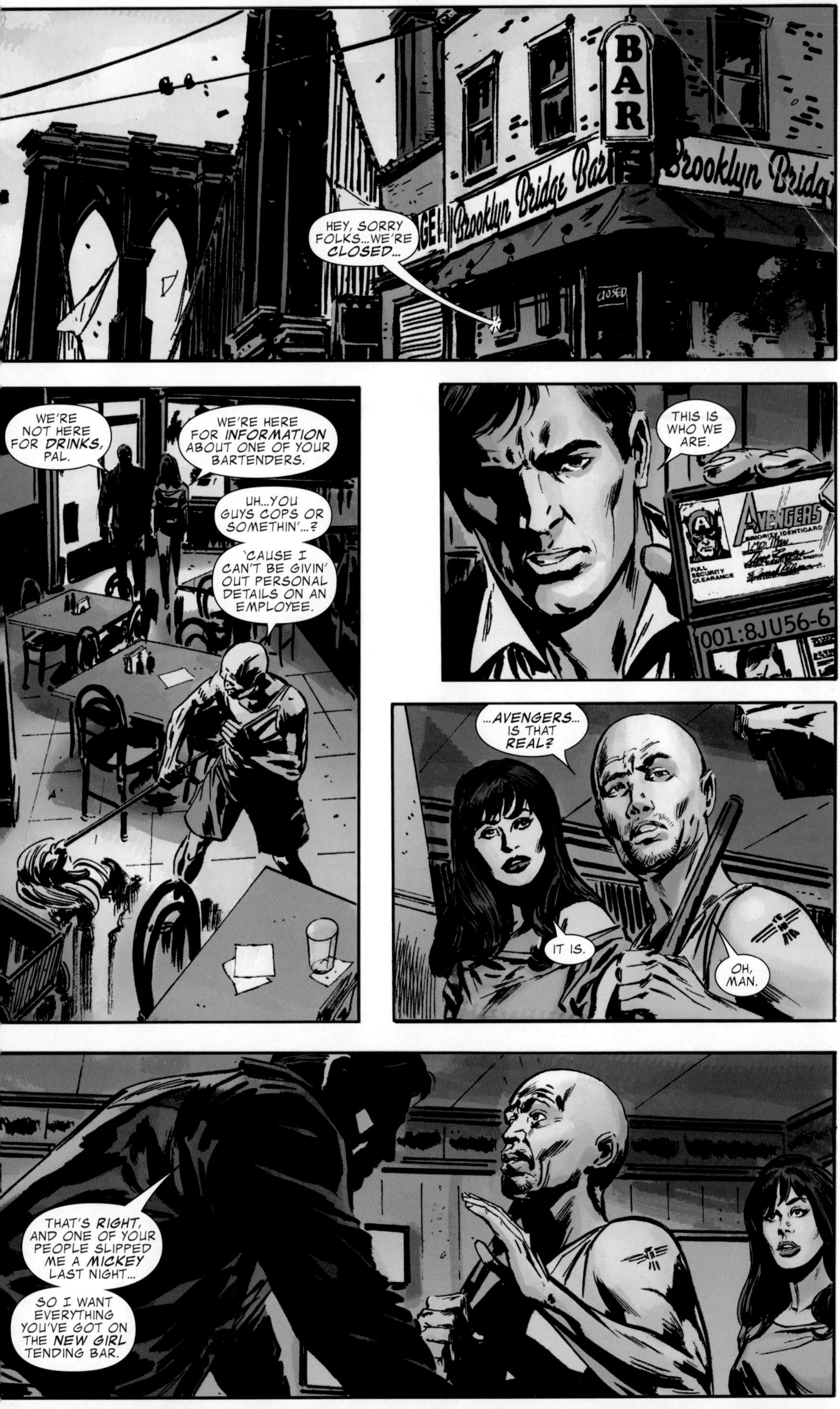

BAR
Brooklyn Bridge Bar
HEY, SORRY FOLKS...WE'RE CLOSED...
CLOSED
WE'RE NOT HERE FOR DRINKS, PAL.
WE'RE HERE FOR INFORMATION ABOUT ONE OF YOUR BARTENDERS.
UH...YOU GUYS COPS OR SOMETHIN'...?
'CAUSE I CAN'T BE GIVIN' OUT PERSONAL DETAILS ON AN EMPLOYEE.
THIS IS WHO WE ARE.
AVENGERS
IDENTICARD
FULL SECURITY CLEARANCE
...AVENGERS... IS THAT REAL?
IT IS.
OH, MAN.
THAT'S RIGHT, AND ONE OF YOUR PEOPLE SLIPPED ME A MICKEY LAST NIGHT...
SO I WANT EVERYTHING YOU'VE GOT ON THE NEW GIRL TENDING BAR.

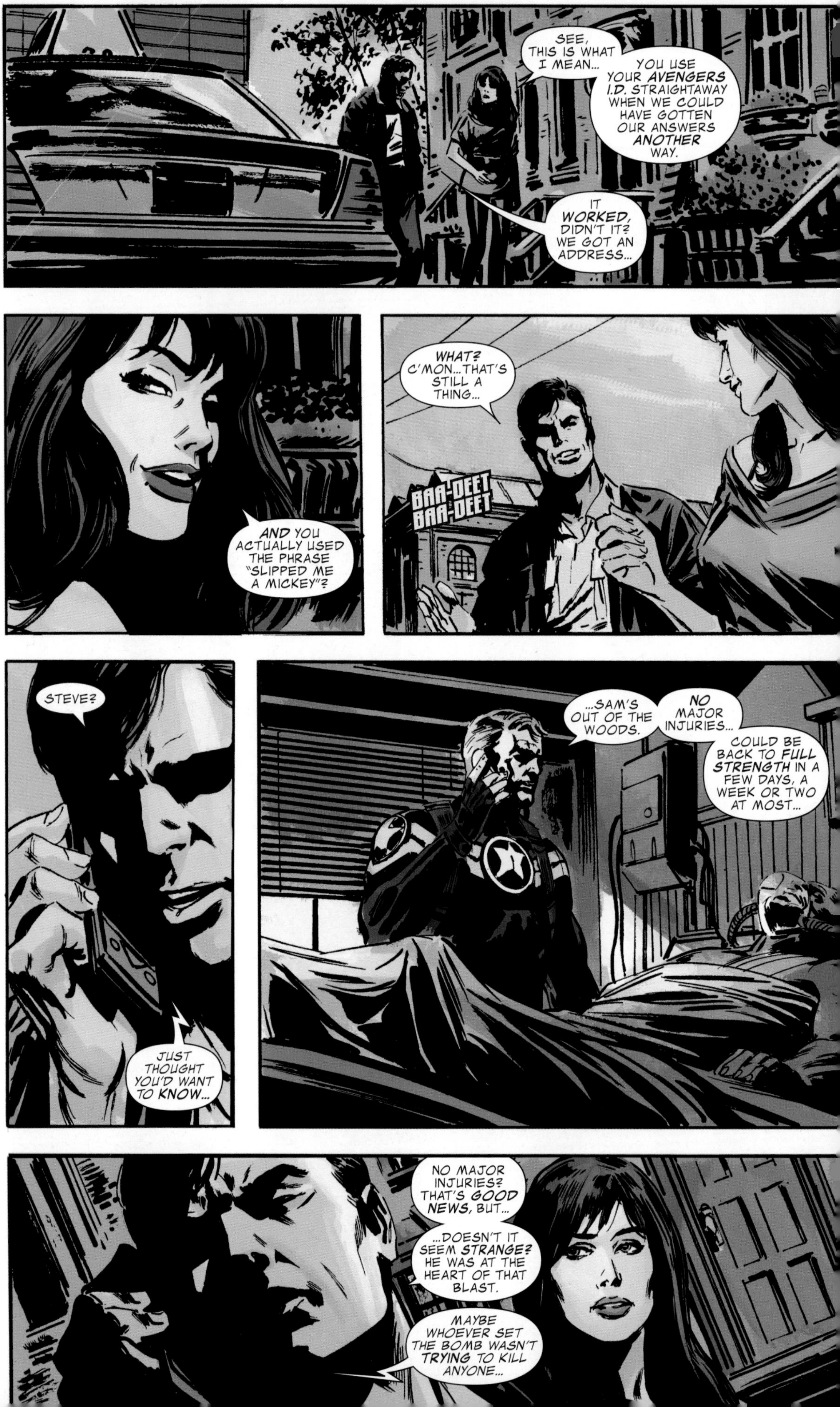

SEE, THIS IS WHAT I MEAN...
YOU USE YOUR AVENGERS I.D. STRAIGHTAWAY WHEN WE COULD HAVE GOTTEN OUR ANSWERS ANOTHER WAY.
IT WORKED, DIDN'T IT? WE GOT AN ADDRESS...
AND YOU ACTUALLY USED THE PHRASE "SLIPPED ME A MICKEY"?
WHAT? C'MON...THAT'S STILL A THING...
BAA-DEET BAA-DEET
STEVE?
...SAM'S OUT OF THE WOODS.
NO MAJOR INJURIES...
COULD BE BACK TO FULL STRENGTH IN A FEW DAYS, A WEEK OR TWO AT MOST...
JUST THOUGHT YOU'D WANT TO KNOW...
NO MAJOR INJURIES? THAT'S GOOD NEWS, BUT...
...DOESN'T IT SEEM STRANGE? HE WAS AT THE HEART OF THAT BLAST.
MAYBE WHOEVER SET THE BOMB WASN'T TRYING TO KILL ANYONE...

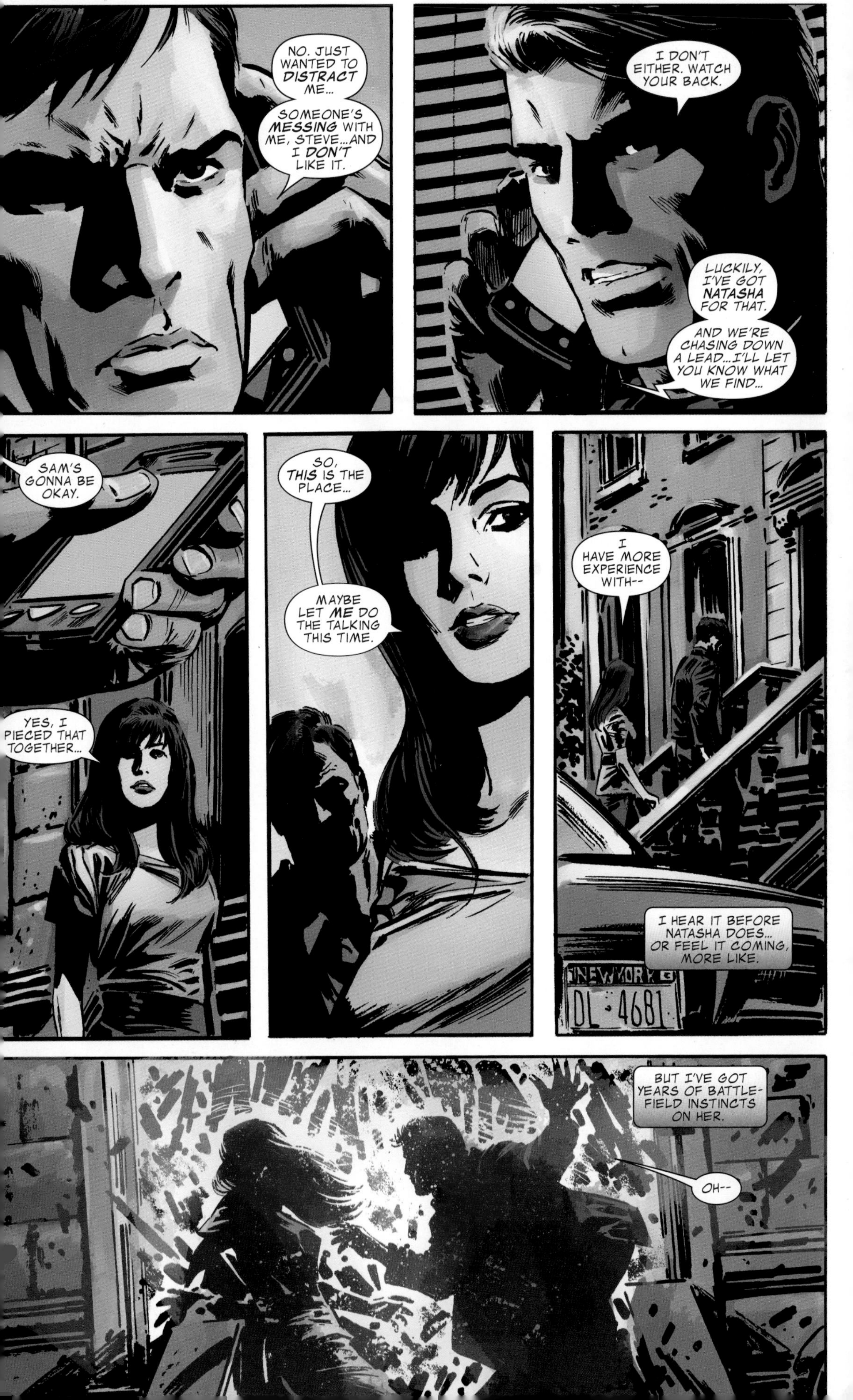
NO. JUST WANTED TO DISTRACT ME...
SOMEONE'S MESSING WITH ME, STEVE...AND I DON'T LIKE IT.
I DON'T EITHER. WATCH YOUR BACK.
LUCKILY, I'VE GOT NATASHA FOR THAT.
AND WE'RE CHASING DOWN A LEAD...I'LL LET YOU KNOW WHAT WE FIND...
SAM'S GONNA BE OKAY.
YES, I PIECED THAT TOGETHER...
SO, THIS IS THE PLACE...
MAYBE LET ME DO THE TALKING THIS TIME.
I HAVE MORE EXPERIENCE WITH--
I HEAR IT BEFORE NATASHA DOES... OR FEEL IT COMING, MORE LIKE.
NEW YORK
DL 4681
BUT I'VE GOT YEARS OF BATTLE-FIELD INSTINCTS ON HER.
OH--

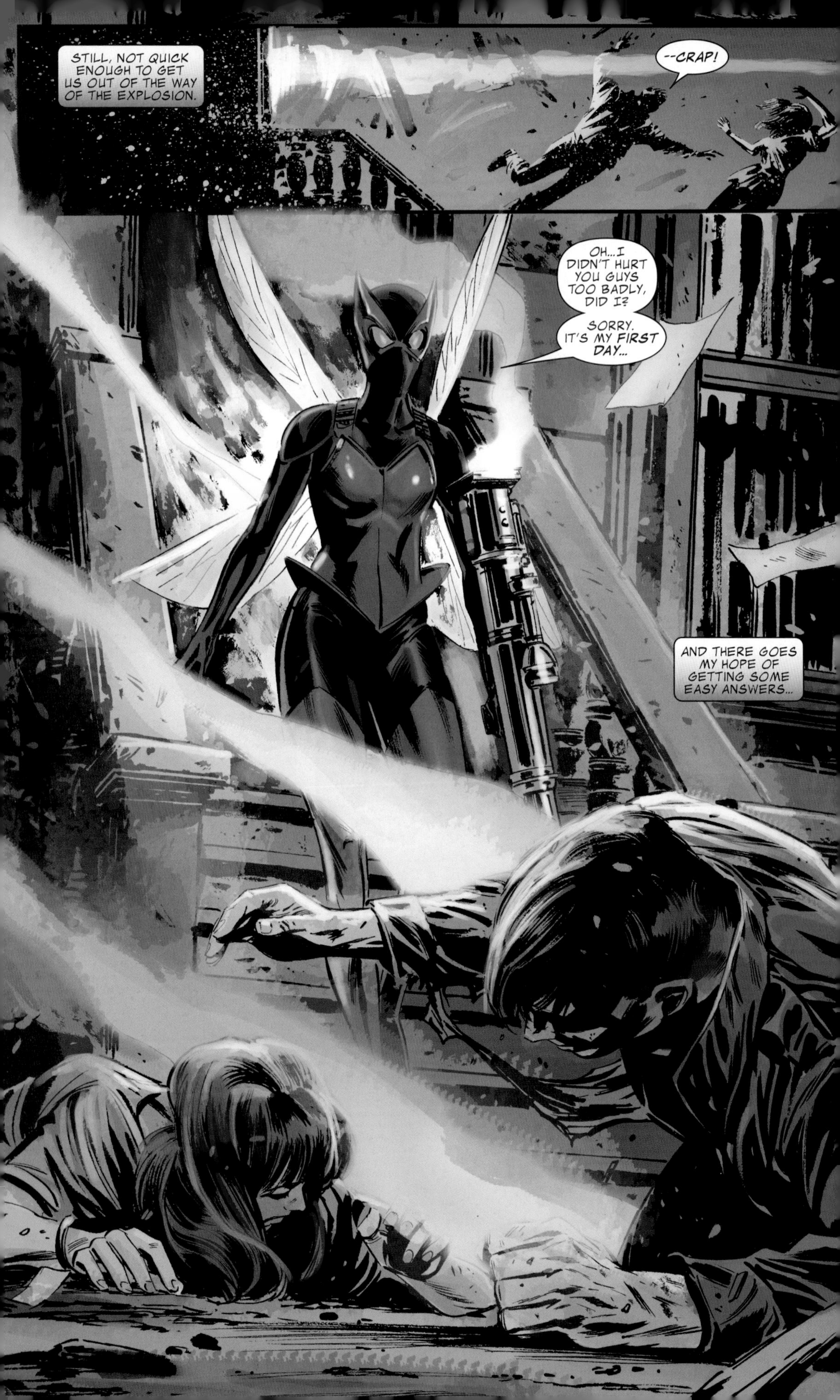
STILL, NOT QUICK ENOUGH TO GET US OUT OF THE WAY OF THE EXPLOSION.
--CRAP!
OH...I DIDN'T HURT YOU GUYS TOO BADLY, DID I?
SORRY. IT'S MY FIRST DAY...
AND THERE GOES MY HOPE OF GETTING SOME EASY ANSWERS...

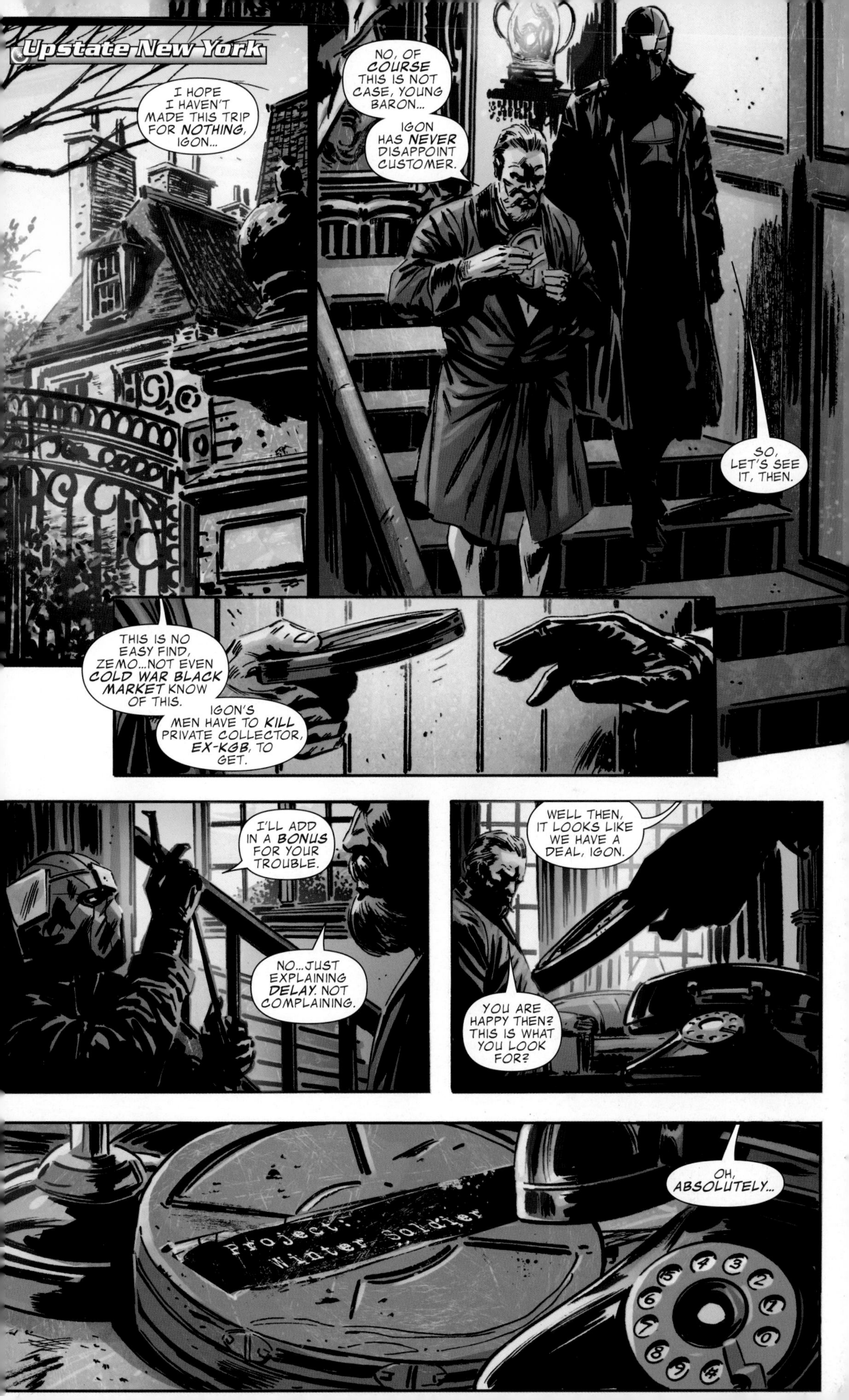
Upstate New York
I HOPE I HAVEN'T MADE THIS TRIP FOR NOTHING, IGON...
NO, OF COURSE THIS IS NOT CASE, YOUNG BARON...
IGON HAS NEVER DISAPPOINT CUSTOMER.
SO, LET'S SEE IT, THEN.
THIS IS NO EASY FIND, ZEMO...NOT EVEN COLD WAR BLACK MARKET KNOW OF THIS.
IGON'S MEN HAVE TO KILL PRIVATE COLLECTOR, EX-KGB, TO GET.
I'LL ADD IN A BONUS FOR YOUR TROUBLE.
NO...JUST EXPLAINING DELAY. NOT COMPLAINING.
WELL THEN, IT LOOKS LIKE WE HAVE A DEAL, IGON.
YOU ARE HAPPY THEN? THIS IS WHAT YOU LOOK FOR?
Project: Winter Soldier
OH, ABSOLUTELY...

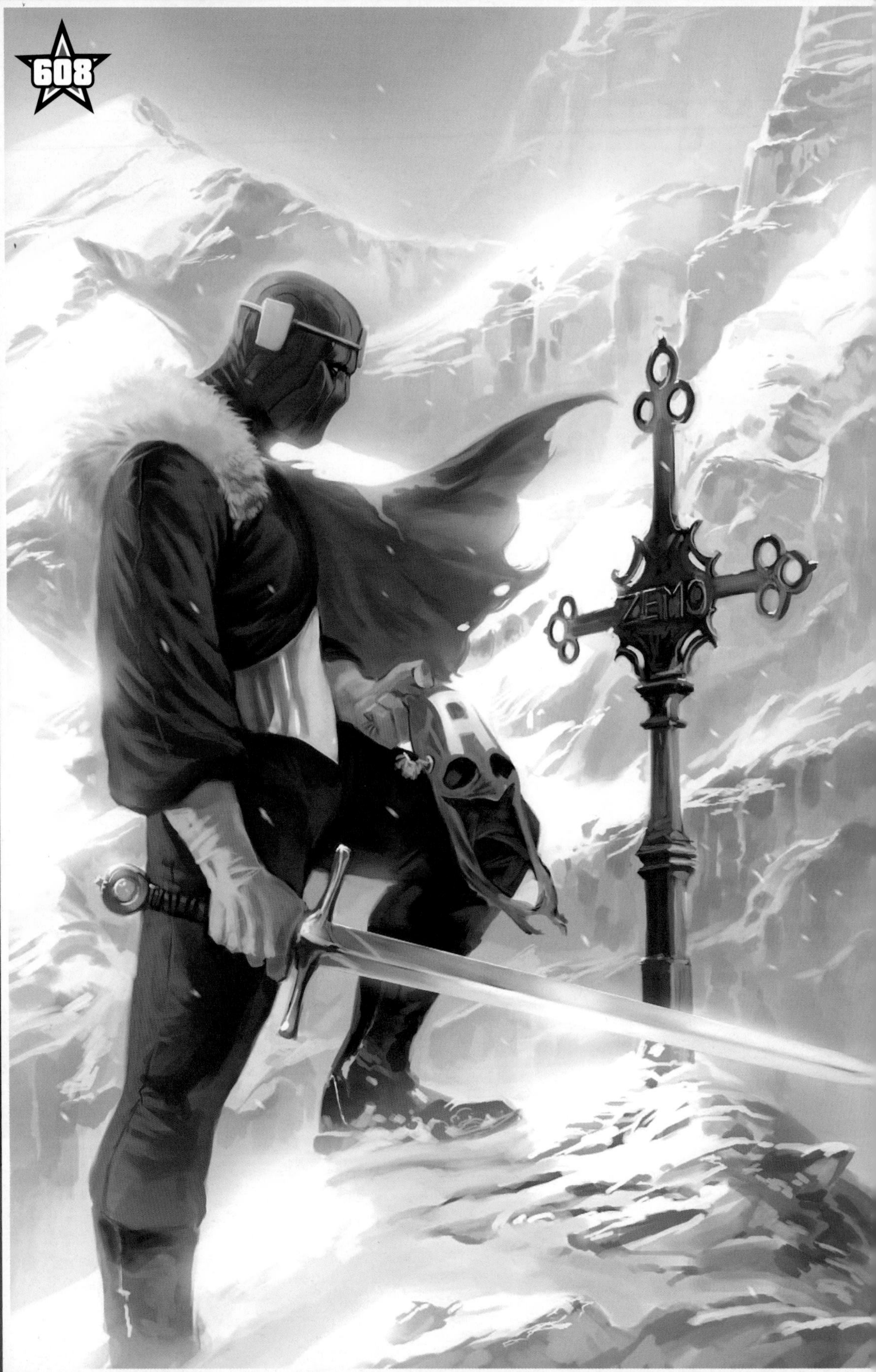
608
ZEMO

NO ESCAPE PART 3

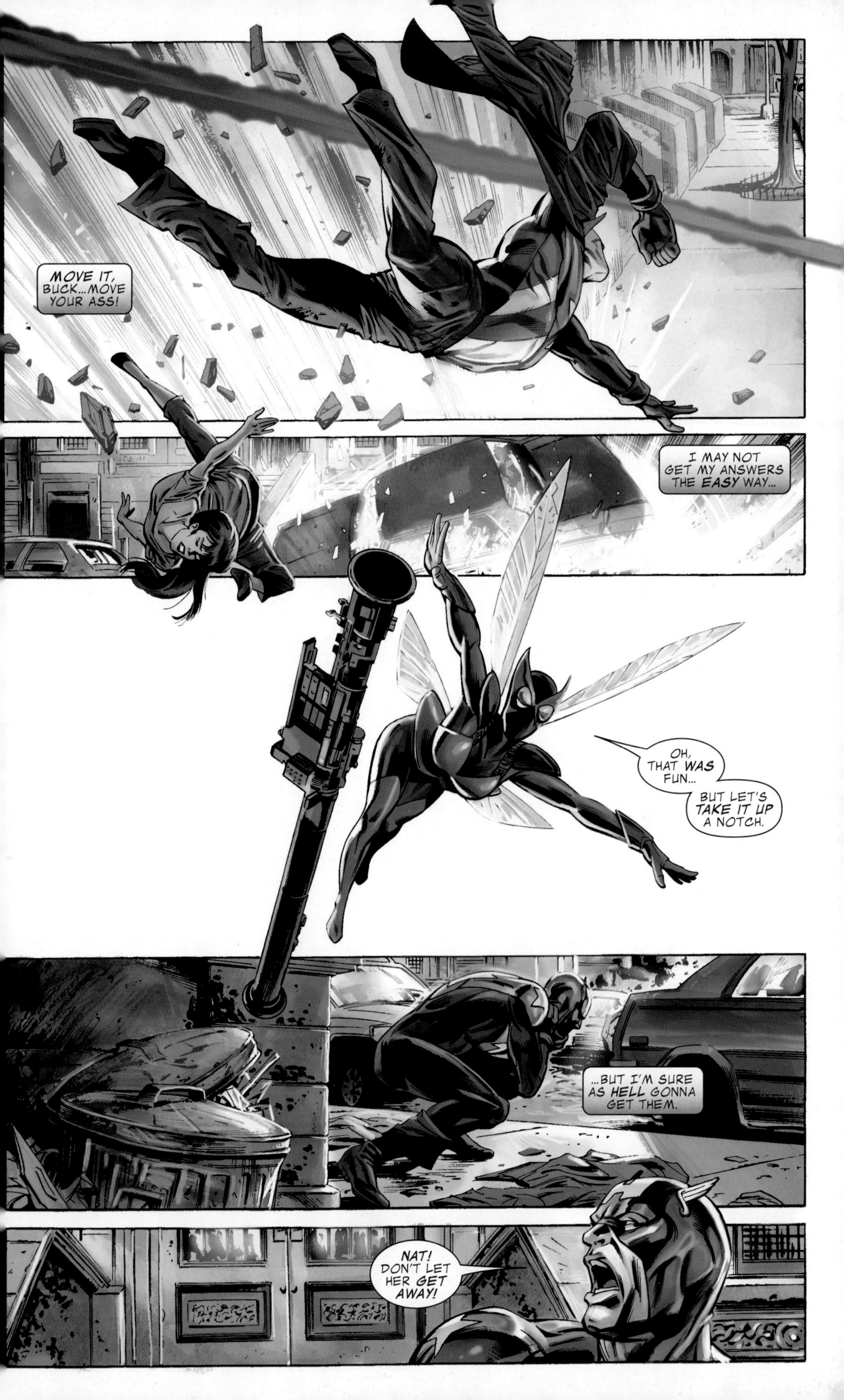
MOVE IT, BUCK...MOVE YOUR ASS!
I MAY NOT GET MY ANSWERS THE EASY WAY...
OH, THAT WAS FUN...
BUT LET'S TAKE IT UP A NOTCH.
...BUT I'M SURE AS HELL GONNA GET THEM.
NAT! DON'T LET HER GET AWAY!

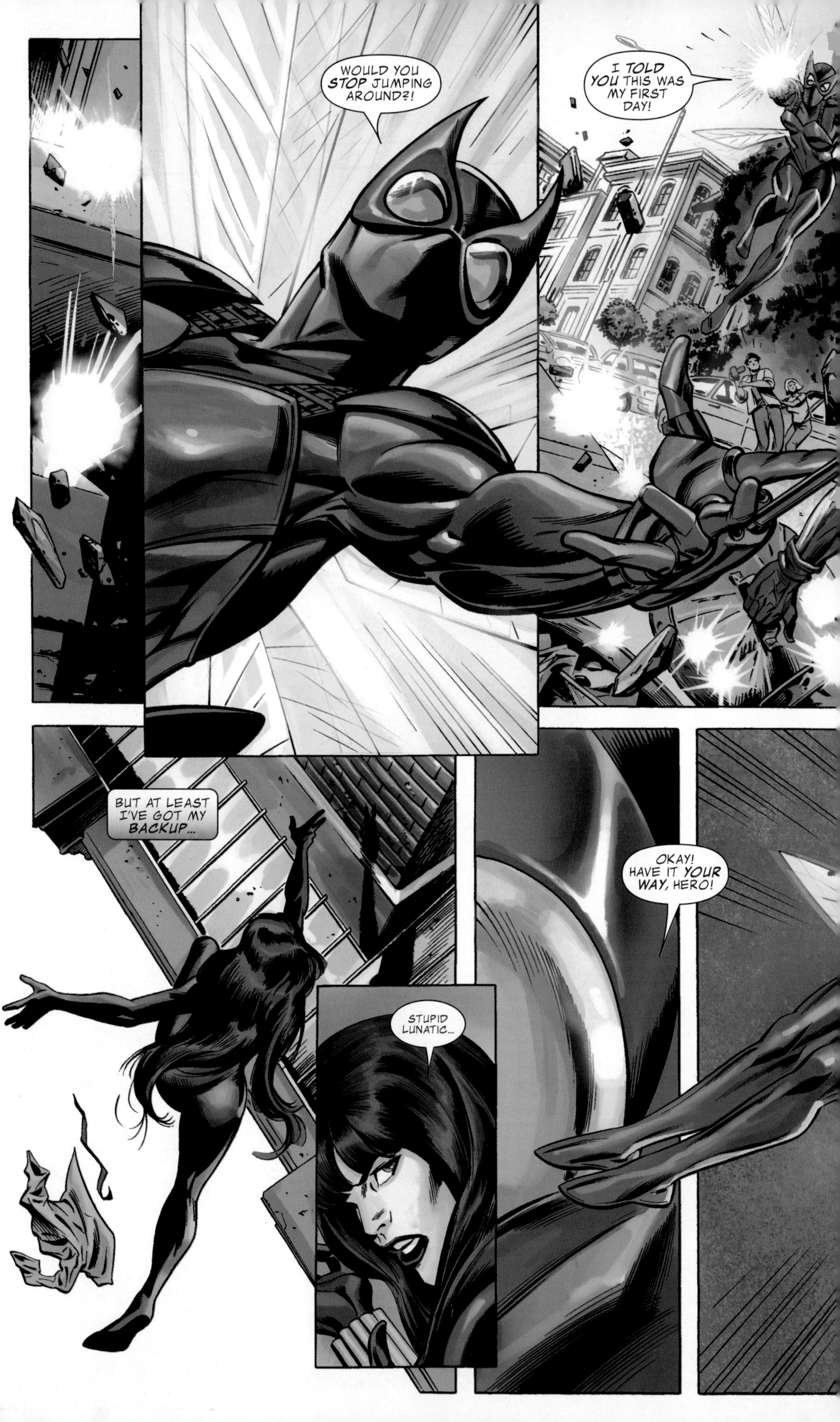

WOULD YOU STOP JUMPING AROUND?!
I TOLD YOU THIS WAS MY FIRST DAY!
BUT AT LEAST I'VE GOT MY BACKUP...
STUPID LUNATIC...
OKAY! HAVE IT YOUR WAY, HERO!

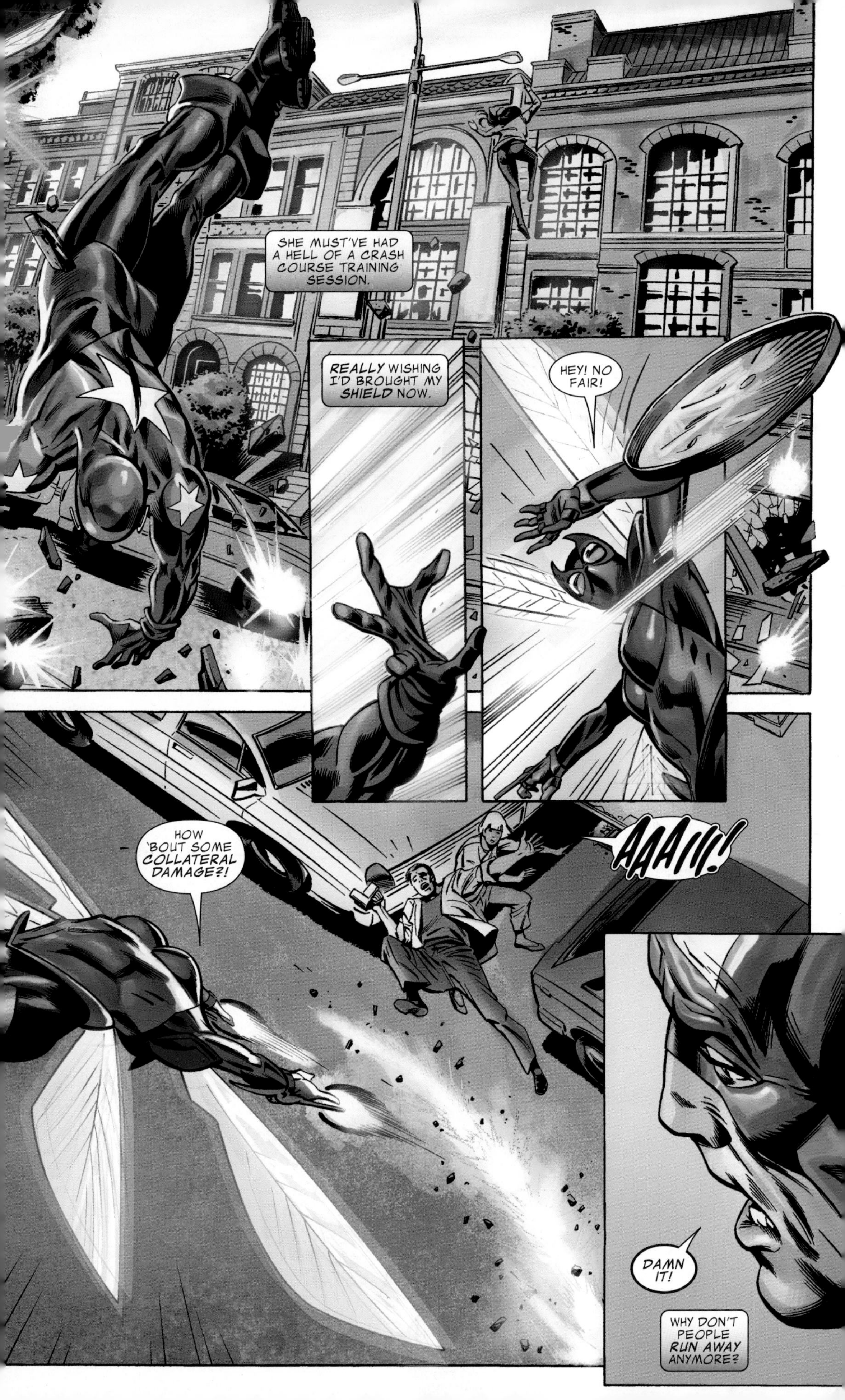

SHE MUST'VE HAD A HELL OF A CRASH COURSE TRAINING SESSION.
REALLY WISHING I'D BROUGHT MY SHIELD NOW.
HEY! NO FAIR!
HOW 'BOUT SOME COLLATERAL DAMAGE?!
AAAIII!
DAMN IT!
WHY DON'T PEOPLE RUN AWAY ANYMORE?

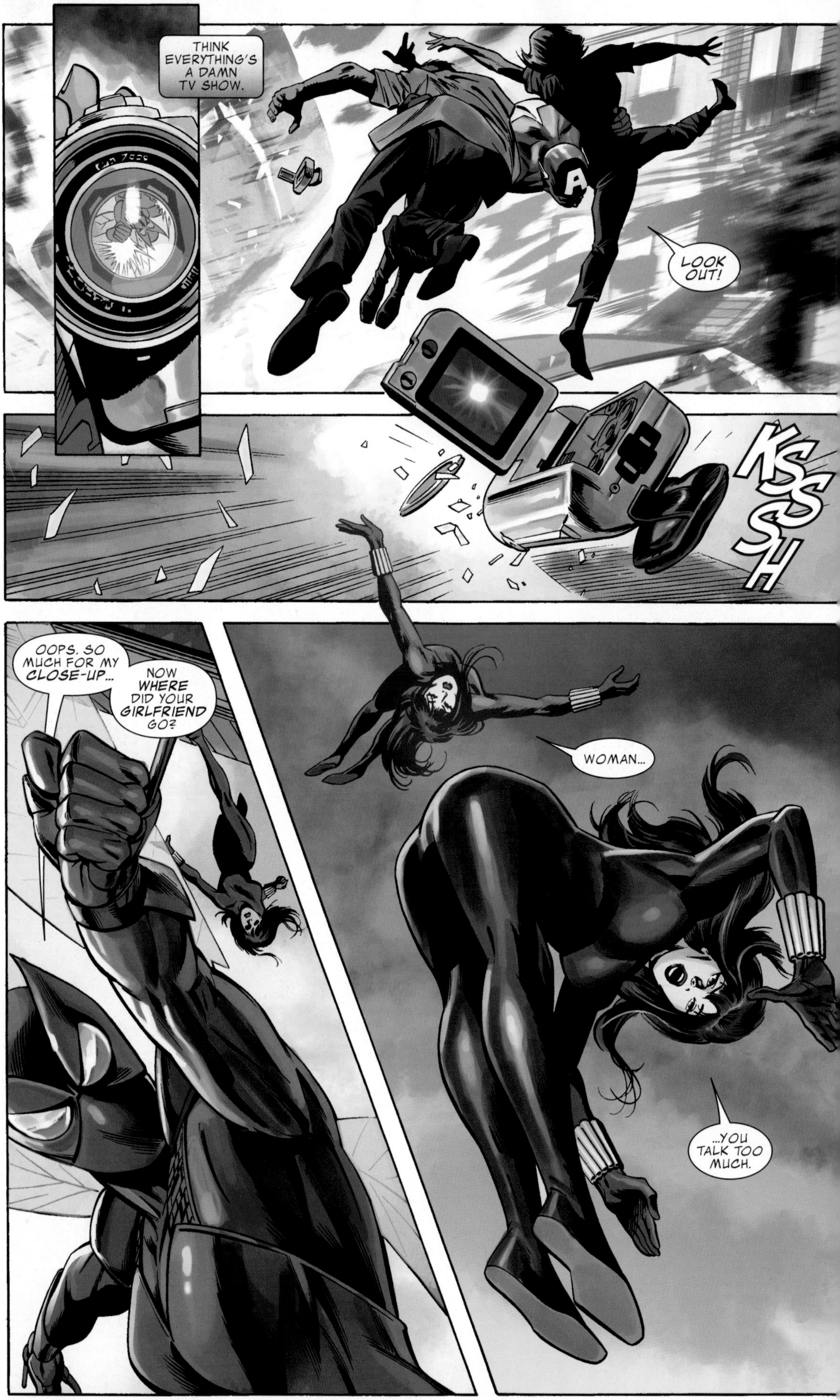
THINK EVERYTHING'S A DAMN TV SHOW.
LOOK OUT!
KSSSH
OOPS. SO MUCH FOR MY CLOSE-UP...
NOW WHERE DID YOUR GIRLFRIEND GO?
WOMAN...
...YOU TALK TOO MUCH.

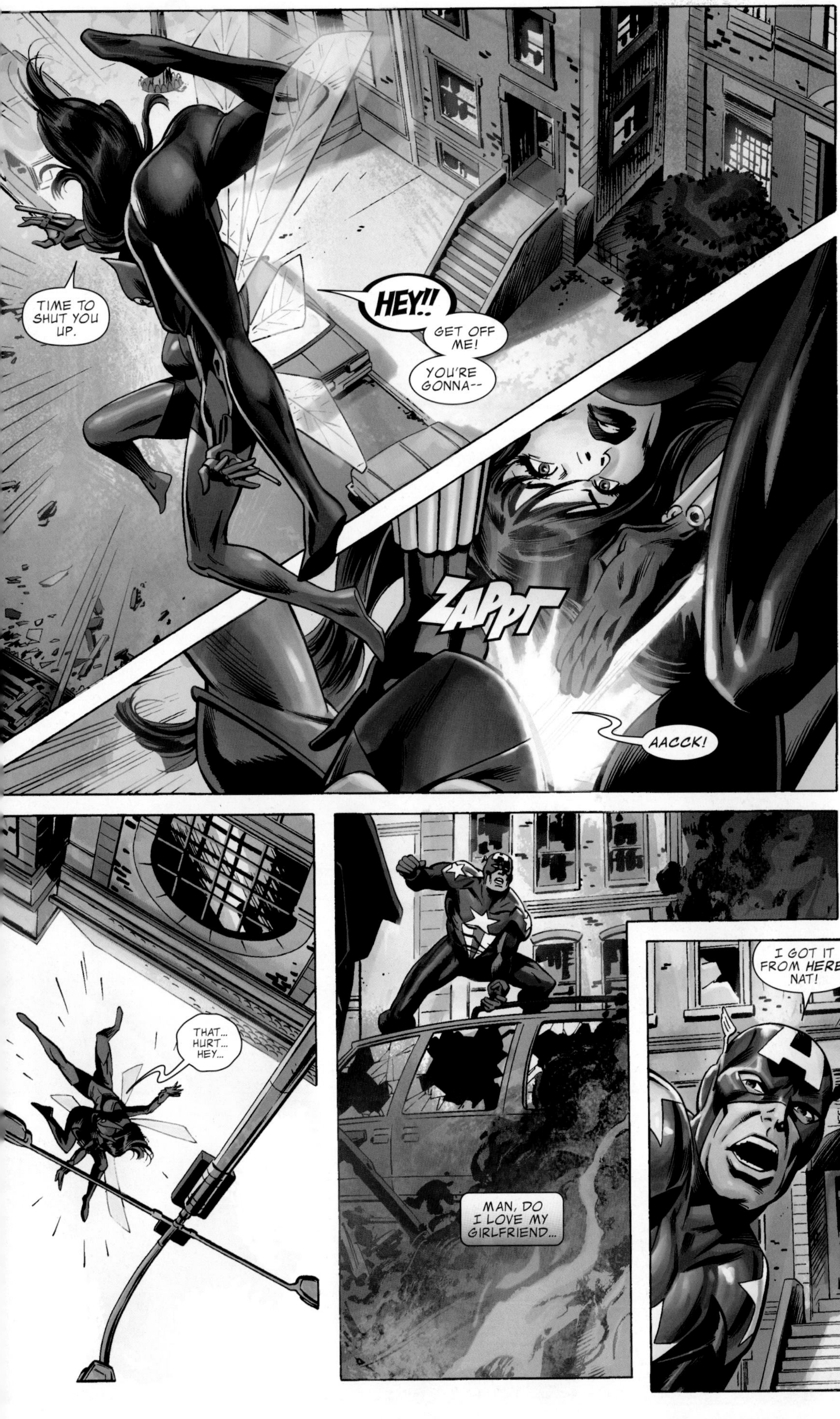
TIME TO SHUT YOU UP.
HEY!!
GET OFF ME!
YOU'RE GONNA--
ZAPPT
AACCK!
THAT... HURT... HEY...
MAN, DO I LOVE MY GIRLFRIEND...
I GOT IT FROM HERE, NAT!

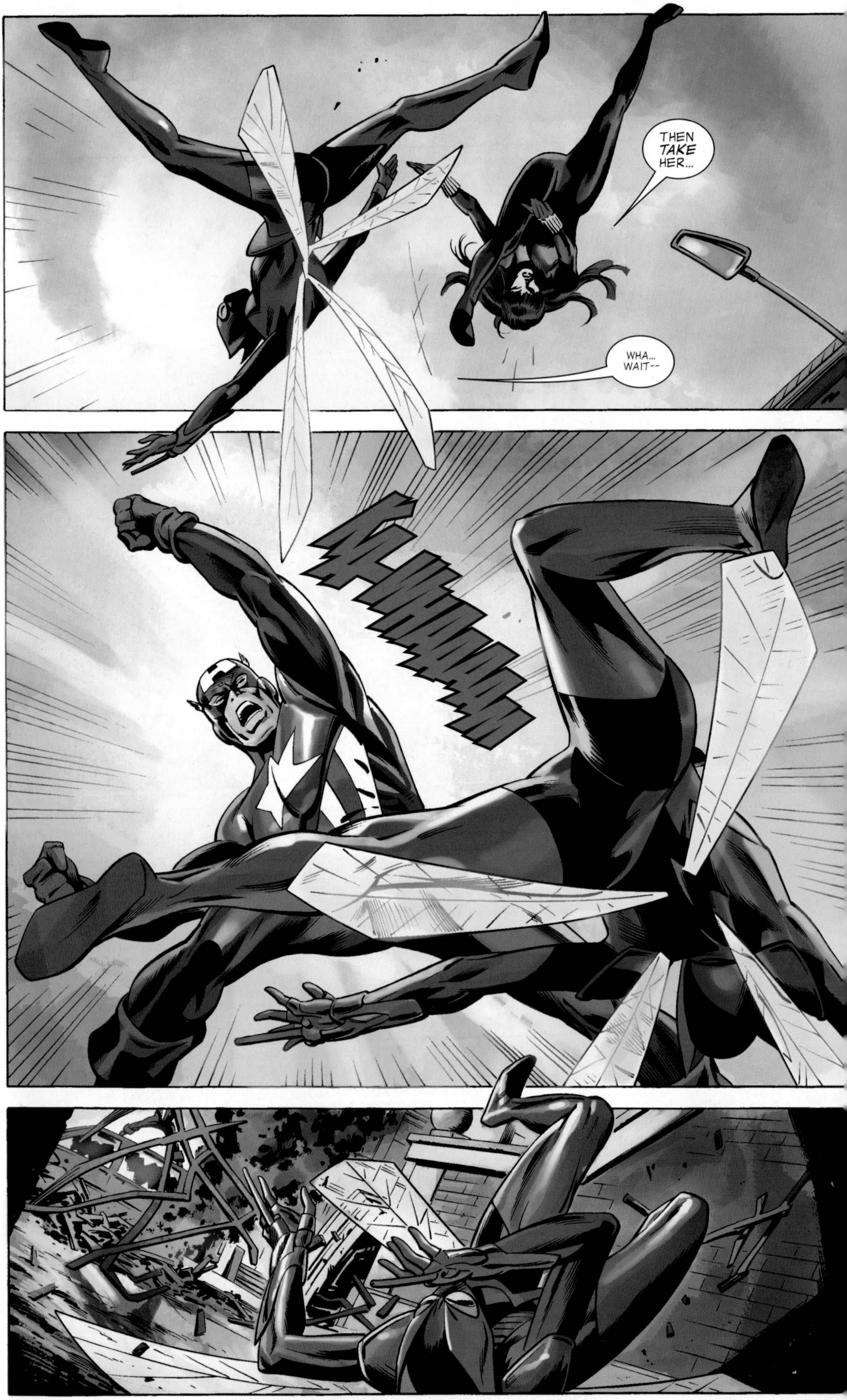
THEN TAKE HER...
WHA... WAIT--

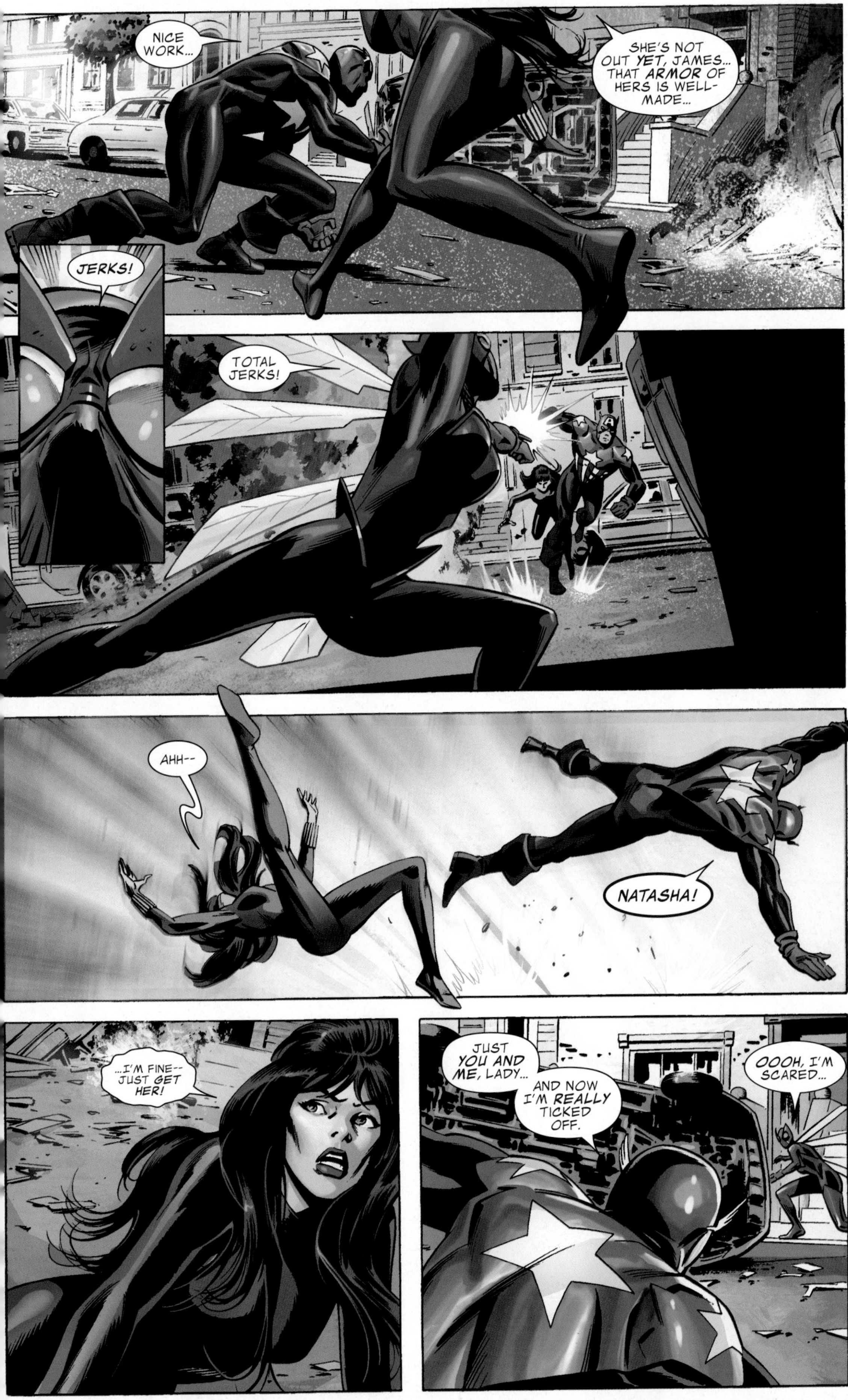
NICE WORK...
SHE'S NOT OUT YET, JAMES... THAT ARMOR OF HERS IS WELL-MADE...
JERKS!
TOTAL JERKS!
AHH--
NATASHA!
...I'M FINE-- JUST GET HER!
JUST YOU AND ME, LADY...
AND NOW I'M REALLY TICKED OFF.
OOOH, I'M SCARED...

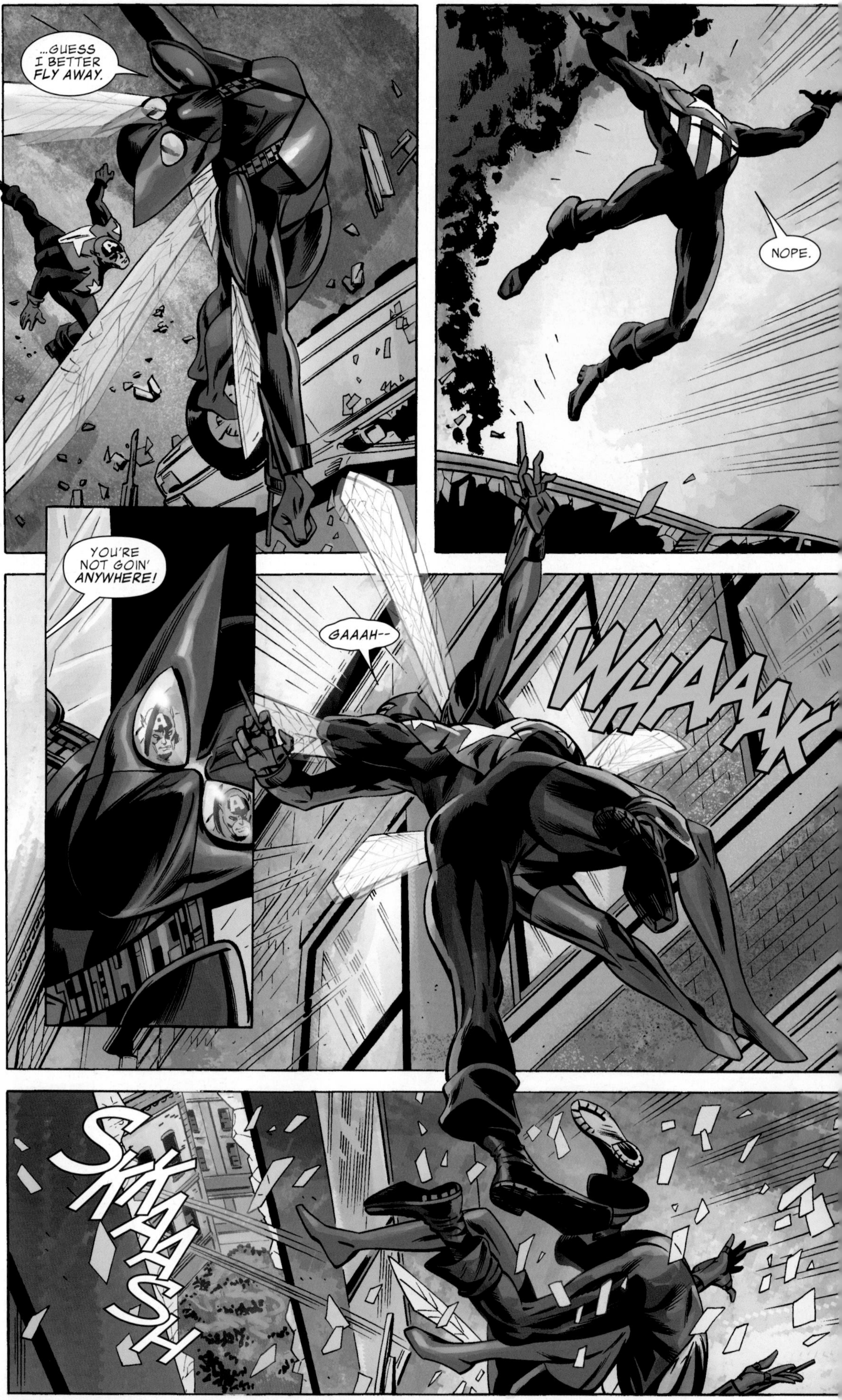
...GUESS I BETTER FLY AWAY.
NOPE.
YOU'RE NOT GOIN' ANYWHERE!
GAAAH--
WHAAAK
SKKAAASH

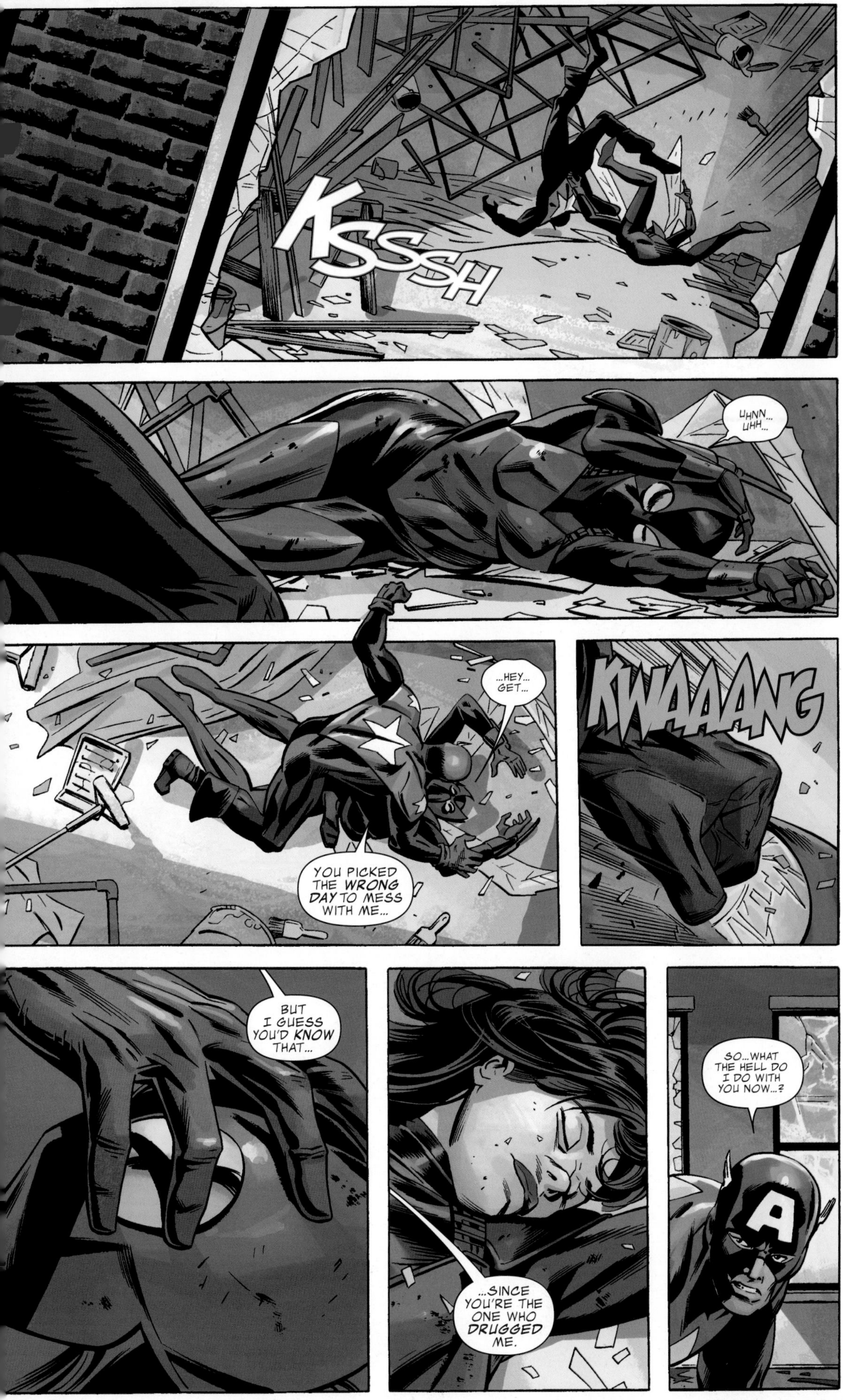
KSSSH
UHNN... UHH...
...HEY... GET...
YOU PICKED THE WRONG DAY TO MESS WITH ME...
KWAAAANG
BUT I GUESS YOU'D KNOW THAT...
...SINCE YOU'RE THE ONE WHO DRUGGED ME.
SO...WHAT THE HELL DO I DO WITH YOU NOW...?

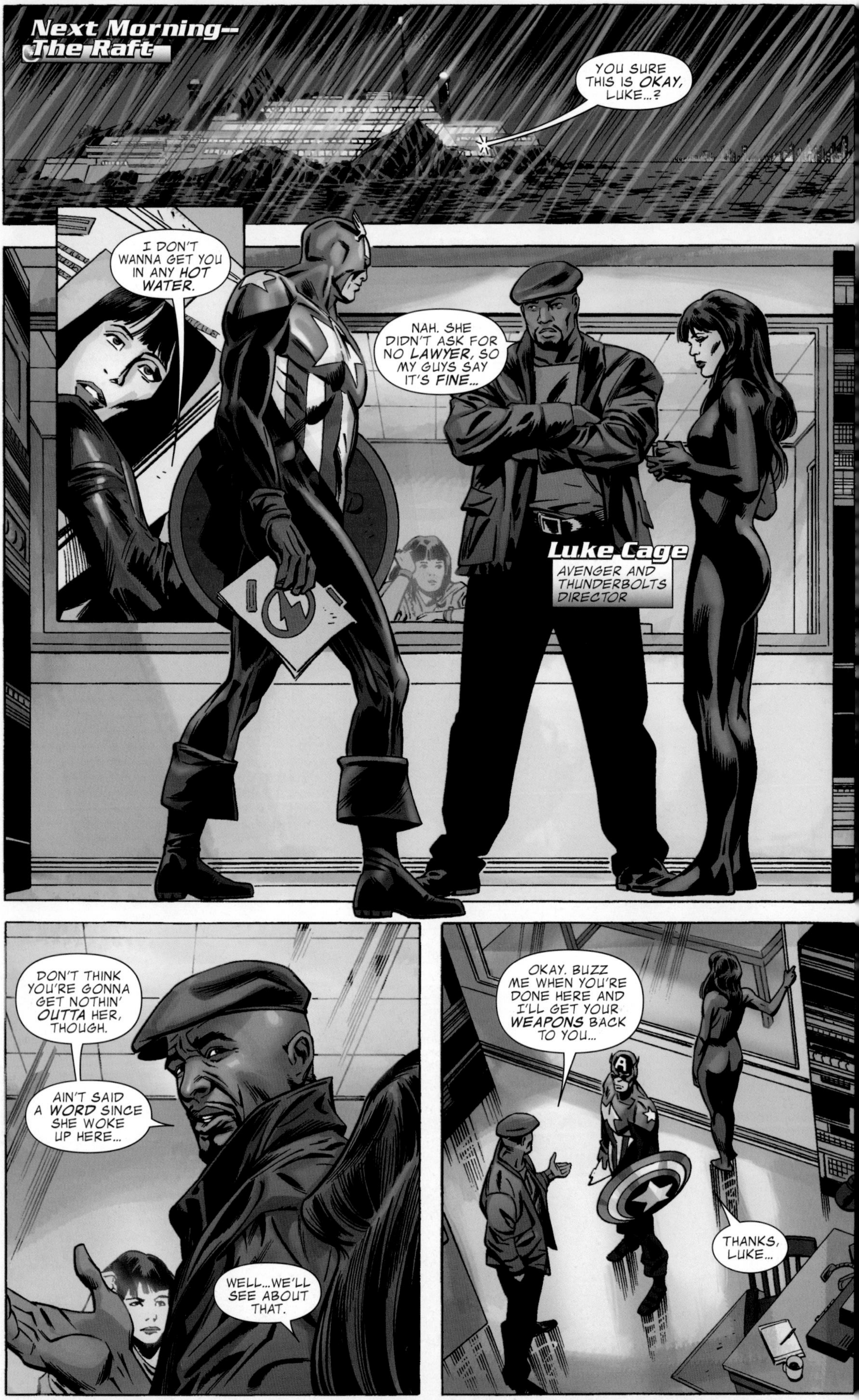

Next Morning— The Raft
YOU SURE THIS IS OKAY, LUKE...?
I DON'T WANNA GET YOU IN ANY HOT WATER.
NAH. SHE DIDN'T ASK FOR NO LAWYER, SO MY GUYS SAY IT'S FINE...
Luke Cage
AVENGER AND THUNDERBOLTS DIRECTOR
DON'T THINK YOU'RE GONNA GET NOTHIN' OUTTA HER, THOUGH.
AIN'T SAID A WORD SINCE SHE WOKE UP HERE...
WELL...WE'LL SEE ABOUT THAT.
OKAY. BUZZ ME WHEN YOU'RE DONE HERE AND I'LL GET YOUR WEAPONS BACK TO YOU...
THANKS, LUKE...

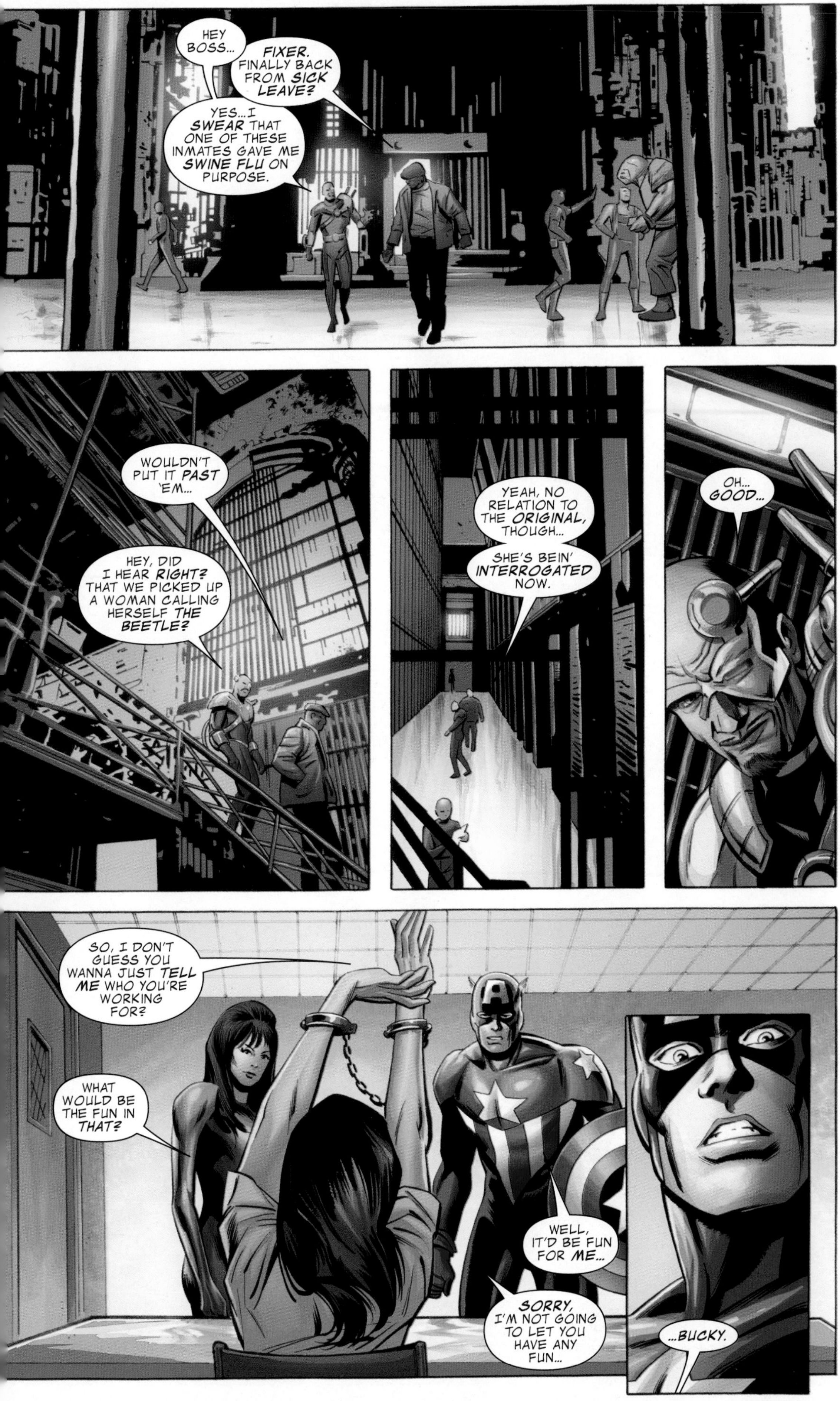
HEY BOSS...
FIXER. FINALLY BACK FROM SICK LEAVE?
YES...I SWEAR THAT ONE OF THESE INMATES GAVE ME SWINE FLU ON PURPOSE.
WOULDN'T PUT IT PAST 'EM...
HEY, DID I HEAR RIGHT? THAT WE PICKED UP A WOMAN CALLING HERSELF THE BEETLE?
YEAH, NO RELATION TO THE ORIGINAL, THOUGH...
SHE'S BEIN' INTERROGATED NOW.
OH... GOOD...
SO, I DON'T GUESS YOU WANNA JUST TELL ME WHO YOU'RE WORKING FOR?
WHAT WOULD BE THE FUN IN THAT?
WELL, IT'D BE FUN FOR ME...
SORRY, I'M NOT GOING TO LET YOU HAVE ANY FUN...
...BUCKY.

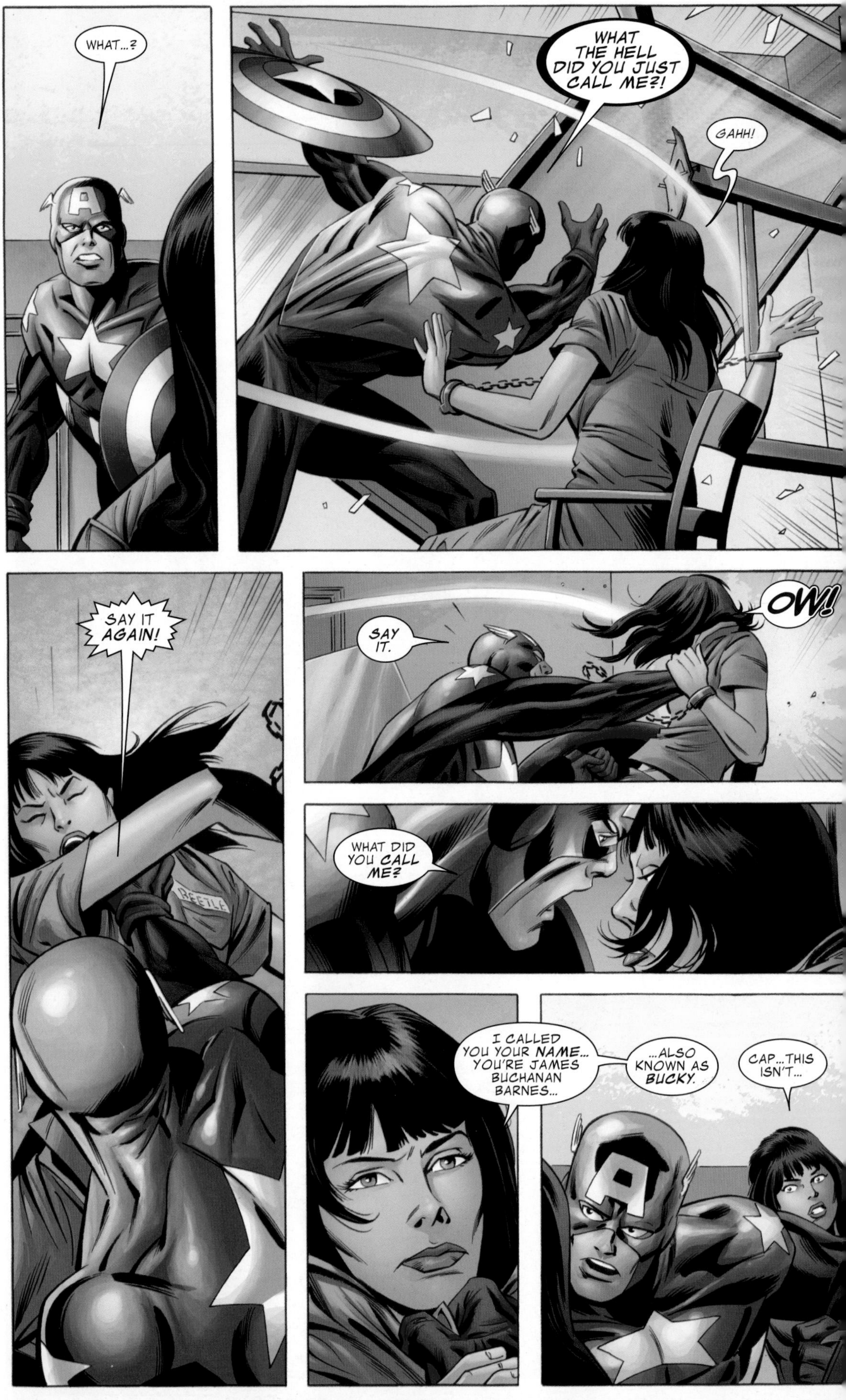
WHAT...?
WHAT THE HELL DID YOU JUST CALL ME?!
GAHH!
SAY IT AGAIN!
SAY IT.
OW!
WHAT DID YOU CALL ME?
I CALLED YOU YOUR NAME... YOU'RE JAMES BUCHANAN BARNES...
...ALSO KNOWN AS BUCKY.
CAP...THIS ISN'T...

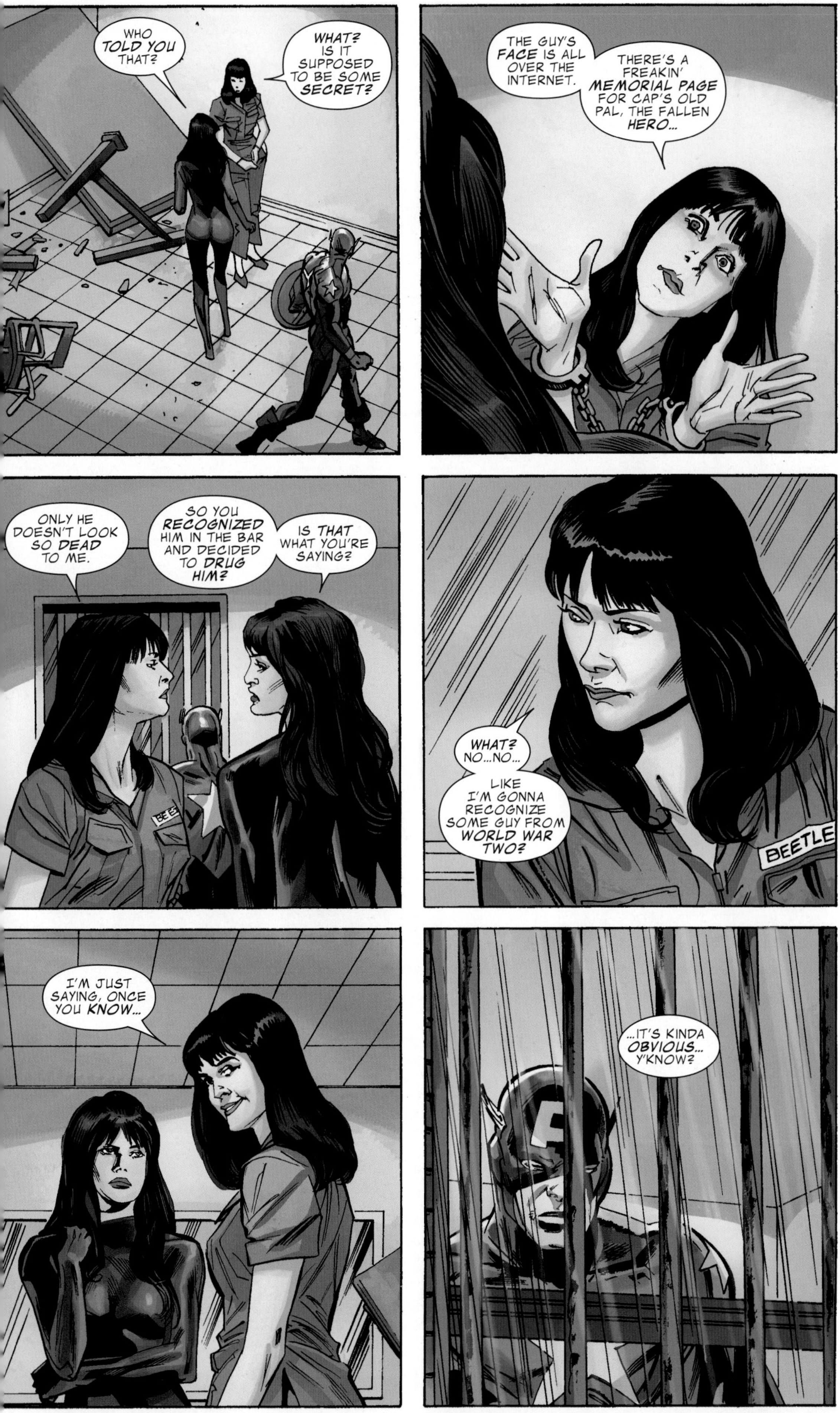
WHO TOLD YOU THAT?
WHAT? IS IT SUPPOSED TO BE SOME SECRET?
THE GUY'S FACE IS ALL OVER THE INTERNET.
THERE'S A FREAKIN' MEMORIAL PAGE FOR CAP'S OLD PAL, THE FALLEN HERO...
ONLY HE DOESN'T LOOK SO DEAD TO ME.
SO YOU RECOGNIZED HIM IN THE BAR AND DECIDED TO DRUG HIM?
IS THAT WHAT YOU'RE SAYING?
WHAT? NO...NO...
LIKE I'M GONNA RECOGNIZE SOME GUY FROM WORLD WAR TWO?
BEETLE
I'M JUST SAYING, ONCE YOU KNOW...
...IT'S KINDA OBVIOUS... Y'KNOW?

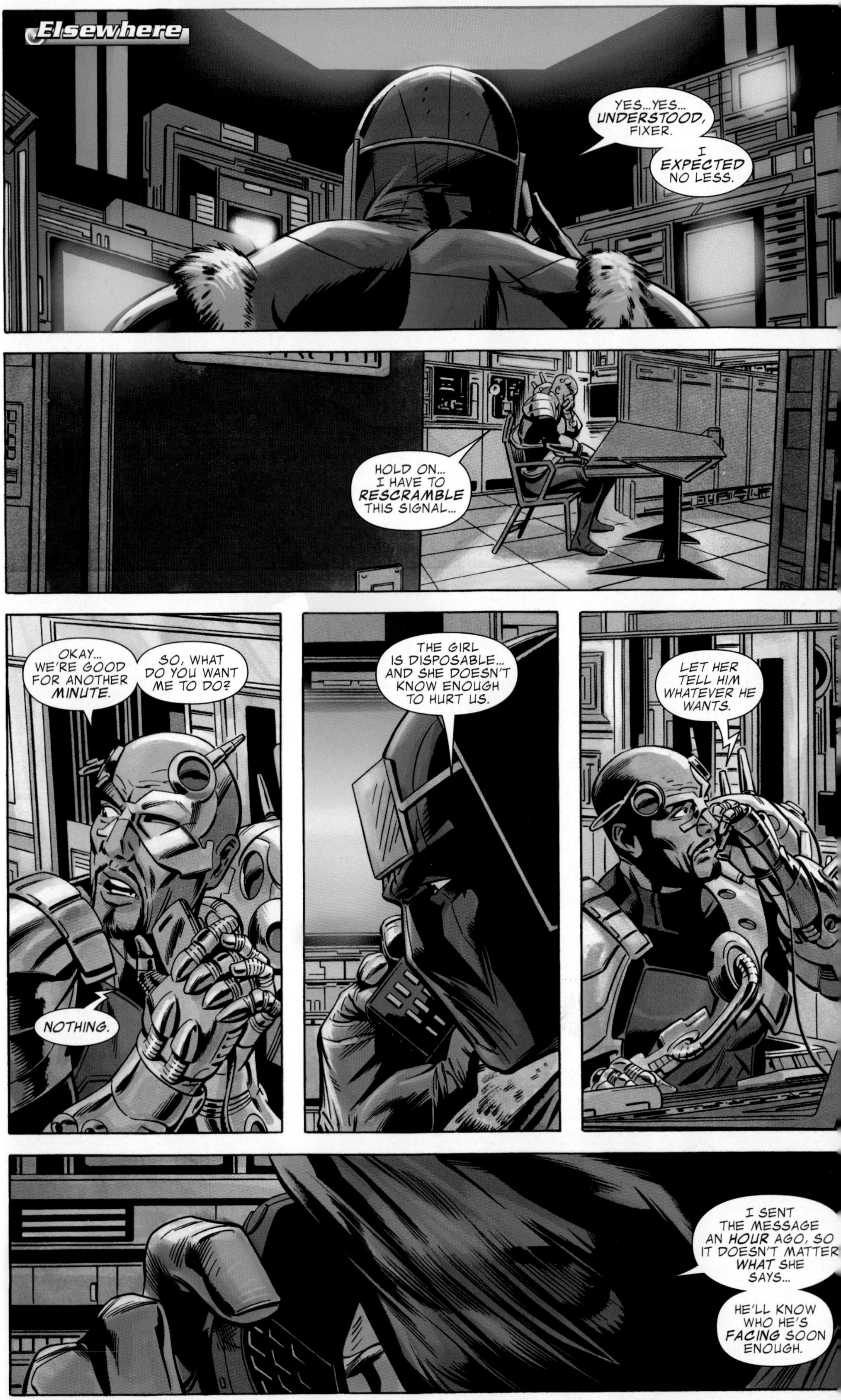
Elsewhere
YES...YES... UNDERSTOOD, FIXER.
I EXPECTED NO LESS.
HOLD ON... I HAVE TO RESCRAMBLE THIS SIGNAL...
OKAY... WE'RE GOOD FOR ANOTHER MINUTE.
SO, WHAT DO YOU WANT ME TO DO?
NOTHING.
THE GIRL IS DISPOSABLE... AND SHE DOESN'T KNOW ENOUGH TO HURT US.
LET HER TELL HIM WHATEVER HE WANTS.
I SENT THE MESSAGE AN HOUR AGO, SO IT DOESN'T MATTER WHAT SHE SAYS...
HE'LL KNOW WHO HE'S FACING SOON ENOUGH.

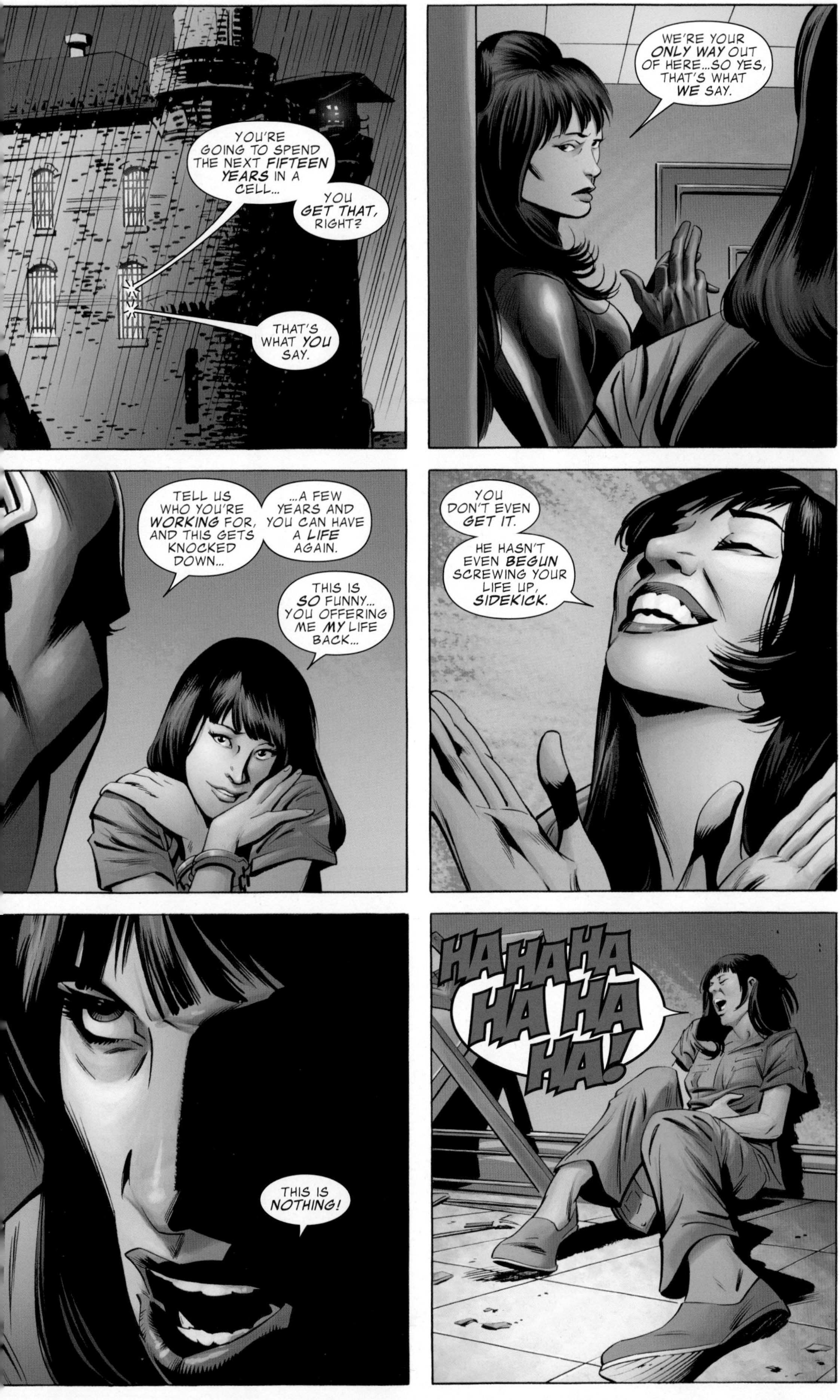
YOU'RE GOING TO SPEND THE NEXT FIFTEEN YEARS IN A CELL...
YOU GET THAT, RIGHT?
THAT'S WHAT YOU SAY.
WE'RE YOUR ONLY WAY OUT OF HERE...SO YES, THAT'S WHAT WE SAY.
TELL US WHO YOU'RE WORKING FOR, AND THIS GETS KNOCKED DOWN...
...A FEW YEARS AND YOU CAN HAVE A LIFE AGAIN.
THIS IS SO FUNNY... YOU OFFERING ME MY LIFE BACK...
YOU DON'T EVEN GET IT.
HE HASN'T EVEN BEGUN SCREWING YOUR LIFE UP, SIDEKICK.
THIS IS NOTHING!
HA HA HA HA HA HA HA!

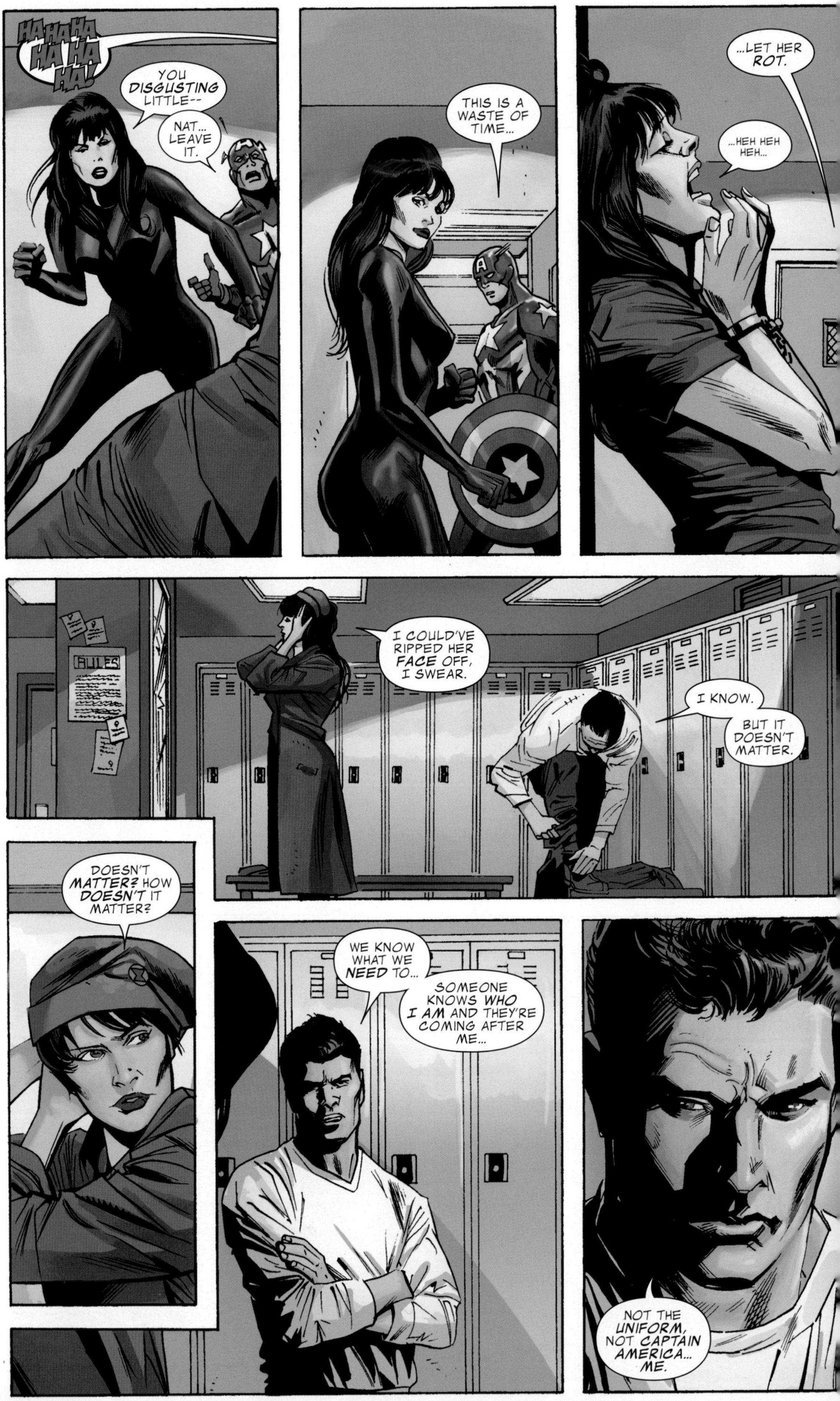
HA HA HA HA HA HA!
YOU DISGUSTING LITTLE--
NAT... LEAVE IT.
THIS IS A WASTE OF TIME...
...LET HER ROT.
...HEH HEH HEH...
RULES
I COULD'VE RIPPED HER FACE OFF, I SWEAR.
I KNOW.
BUT IT DOESN'T MATTER.
DOESN'T MATTER? HOW DOESN'T IT MATTER?
WE KNOW WHAT WE NEED TO...
SOMEONE KNOWS WHO I AM AND THEY'RE COMING AFTER ME...
NOT THE UNIFORM, NOT CAPTAIN AMERICA... ME.

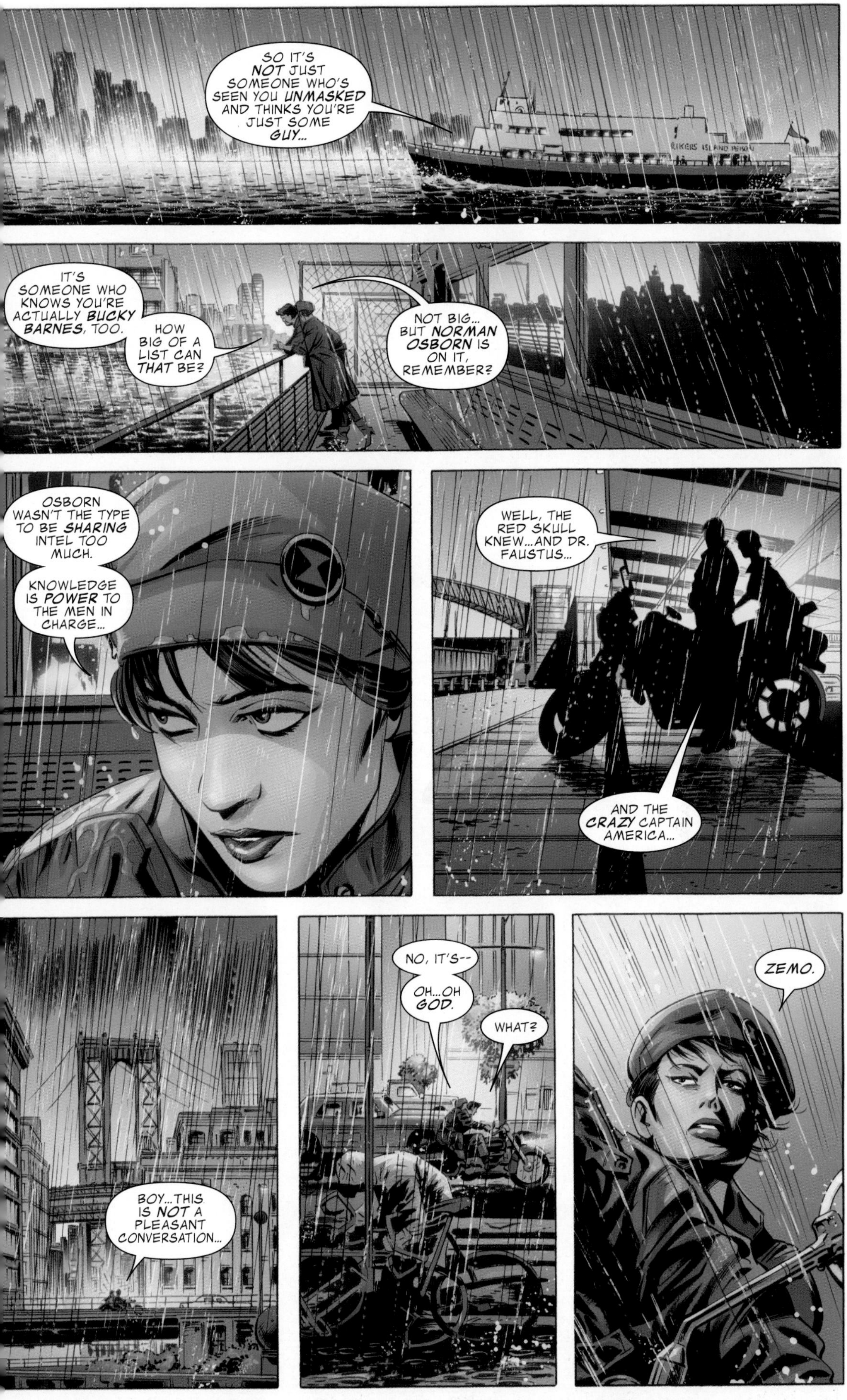
SO IT'S NOT JUST SOMEONE WHO'S SEEN YOU UNMASKED AND THINKS YOU'RE JUST SOME GUY...
IT'S SOMEONE WHO KNOWS YOU'RE ACTUALLY BUCKY BARNES, TOO.
HOW BIG OF A LIST CAN THAT BE?
NOT BIG... BUT NORMAN OSBORN IS ON IT, REMEMBER?
OSBORN WASN'T THE TYPE TO BE SHARING INTEL TOO MUCH.
KNOWLEDGE IS POWER TO THE MEN IN CHARGE...
WELL, THE RED SKULL KNEW...AND DR. FAUSTUS...
AND THE CRAZY CAPTAIN AMERICA...
BOY...THIS IS NOT A PLEASANT CONVERSATION...
NO, IT'S--
OH...OH GOD.
WHAT?
ZEMO.

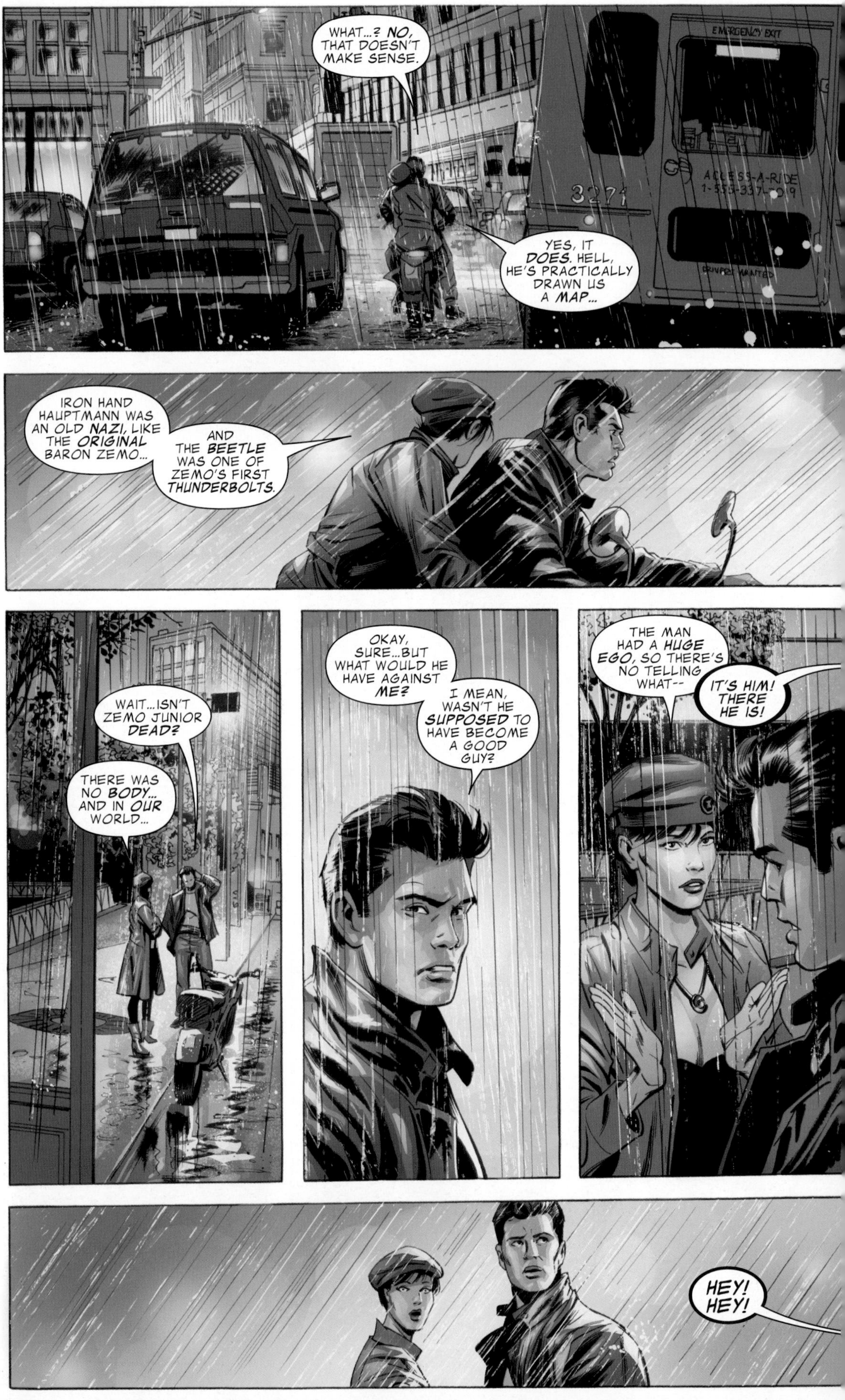
WHAT...? NO, THAT DOESN'T MAKE SENSE.
YES, IT DOES. HELL, HE'S PRACTICALLY DRAWN US A MAP...
EMERGENCY EXIT
ACCESS-A-RIDE
3271
IRON HAND HAUPTMANN WAS AN OLD NAZI, LIKE THE ORIGINAL BARON ZEMO...
AND THE BEETLE WAS ONE OF ZEMO'S FIRST THUNDERBOLTS.
WAIT...ISN'T ZEMO JUNIOR DEAD?
THERE WAS NO BODY... AND IN OUR WORLD...
OKAY, SURE...BUT WHAT WOULD HE HAVE AGAINST ME?
I MEAN, WASN'T HE SUPPOSED TO HAVE BECOME A GOOD GUY?
THE MAN HAD A HUGE EGO, SO THERE'S NO TELLING WHAT--
IT'S HIM! THERE HE IS!
HEY! HEY!

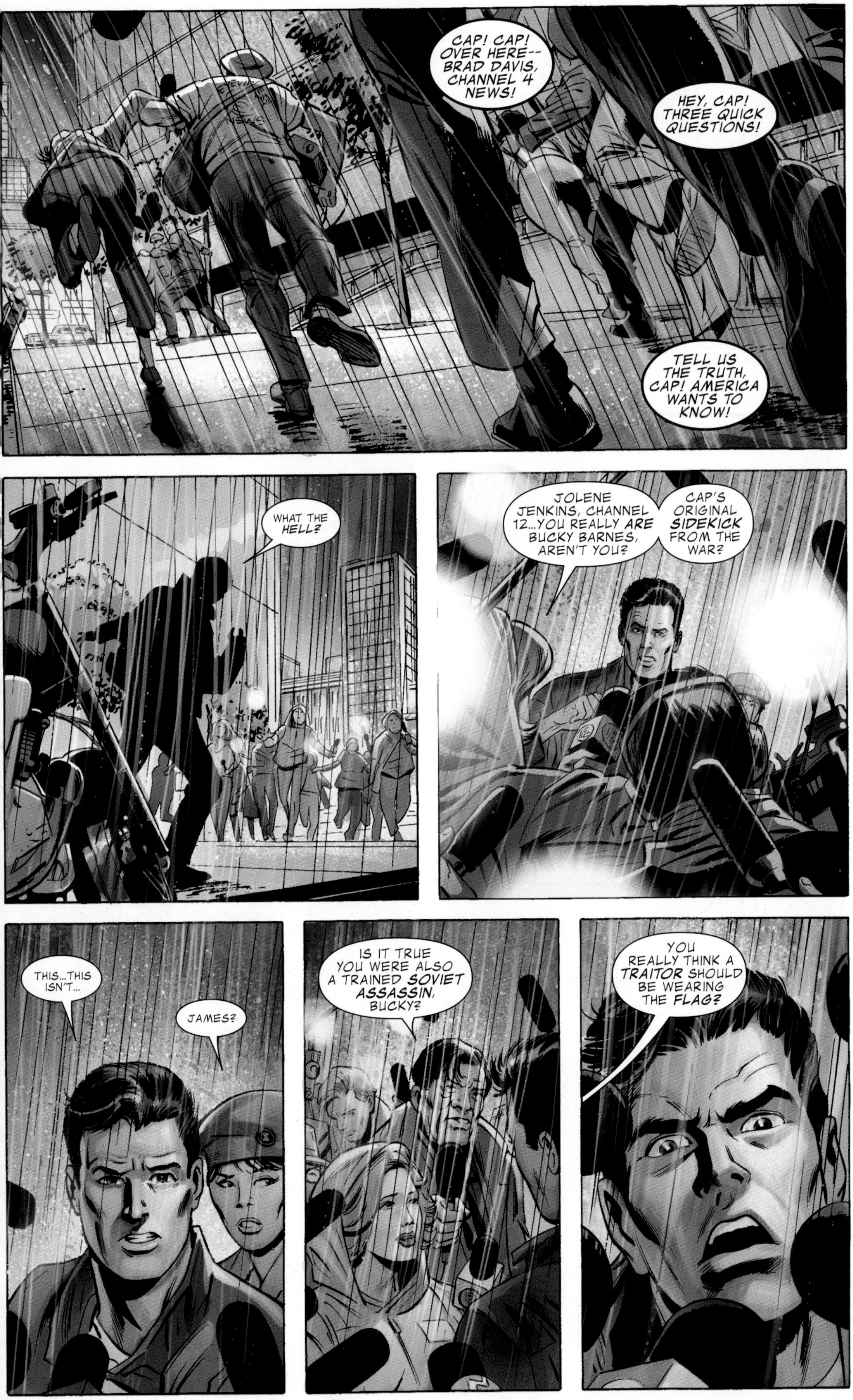
CAP! CAP! OVER HERE-- BRAD DAVIS, CHANNEL 4 NEWS!
HEY, CAP! THREE QUICK QUESTIONS!
TELL US THE TRUTH, CAP! AMERICA WANTS TO KNOW!
WHAT THE HELL?
JOLENE JENKINS, CHANNEL 12...YOU REALLY ARE BUCKY BARNES, AREN'T YOU?
CAP'S ORIGINAL SIDEKICK FROM THE WAR?
THIS...THIS ISN'T...
JAMES?
IS IT TRUE YOU WERE ALSO A TRAINED SOVIET ASSASSIN, BUCKY?
YOU REALLY THINK A TRAITOR SHOULD BE WEARING THE FLAG?

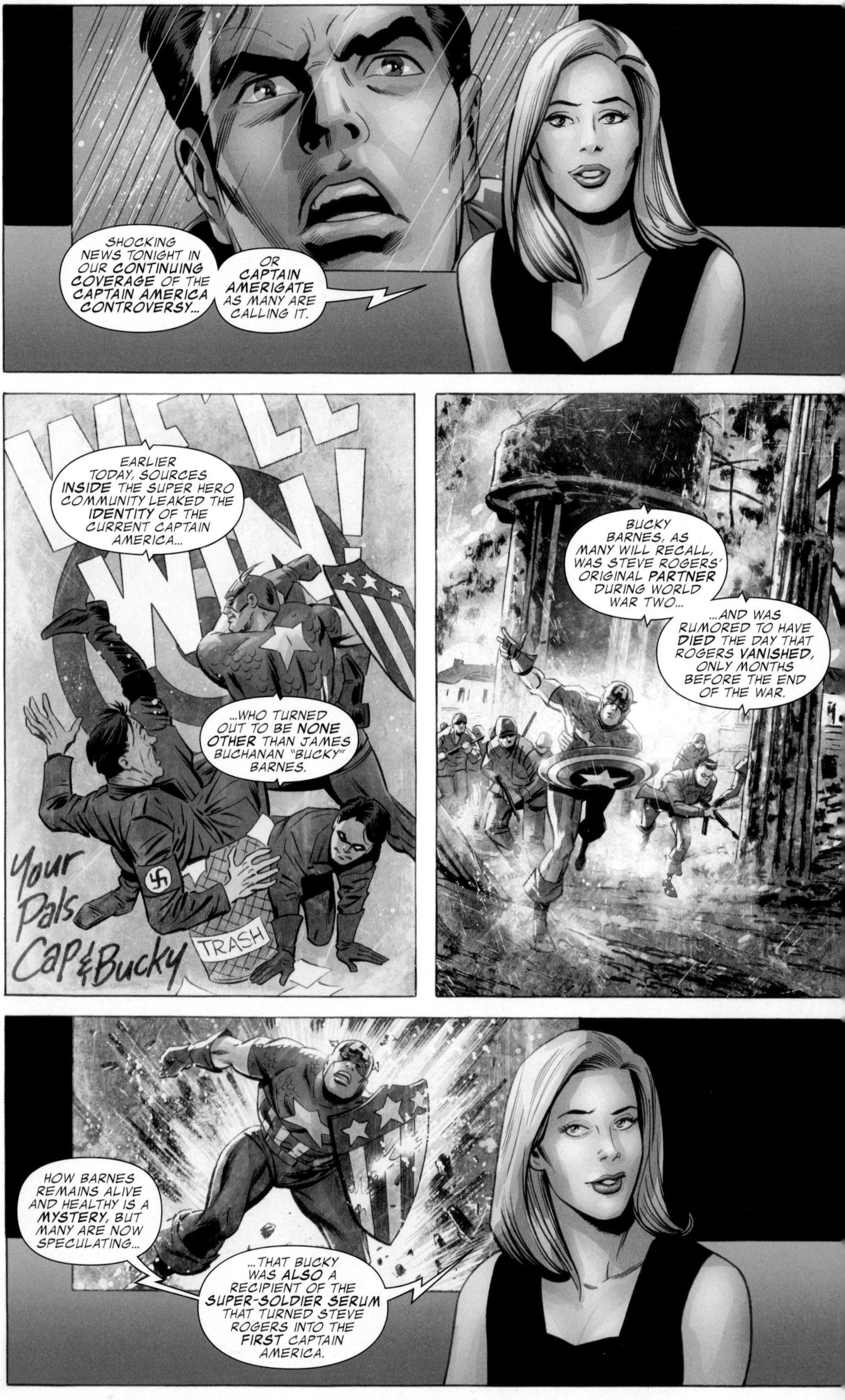
SHOCKING NEWS TONIGHT IN OUR CONTINUING COVERAGE OF THE CAPTAIN AMERICA CONTROVERSY...
OR CAPTAIN AMERIGATE AS MANY ARE CALLING IT.
EARLIER TODAY, SOURCES INSIDE THE SUPER HERO COMMUNITY LEAKED THE IDENTITY OF THE CURRENT CAPTAIN AMERICA...
...WHO TURNED OUT TO BE NONE OTHER THAN JAMES BUCHANAN "BUCKY" BARNES.
Your Pals Cap & Bucky
TRASH
BUCKY BARNES, AS MANY WILL RECALL, WAS STEVE ROGERS' ORIGINAL PARTNER DURING WORLD WAR TWO...
...AND WAS RUMORED TO HAVE DIED THE DAY THAT ROGERS VANISHED, ONLY MONTHS BEFORE THE END OF THE WAR.
HOW BARNES REMAINS ALIVE AND HEALTHY IS A MYSTERY, BUT MANY ARE NOW SPECULATING...
...THAT BUCKY WAS ALSO A RECIPIENT OF THE SUPER-SOLDIER SERUM THAT TURNED STEVE ROGERS INTO THE FIRST CAPTAIN AMERICA.

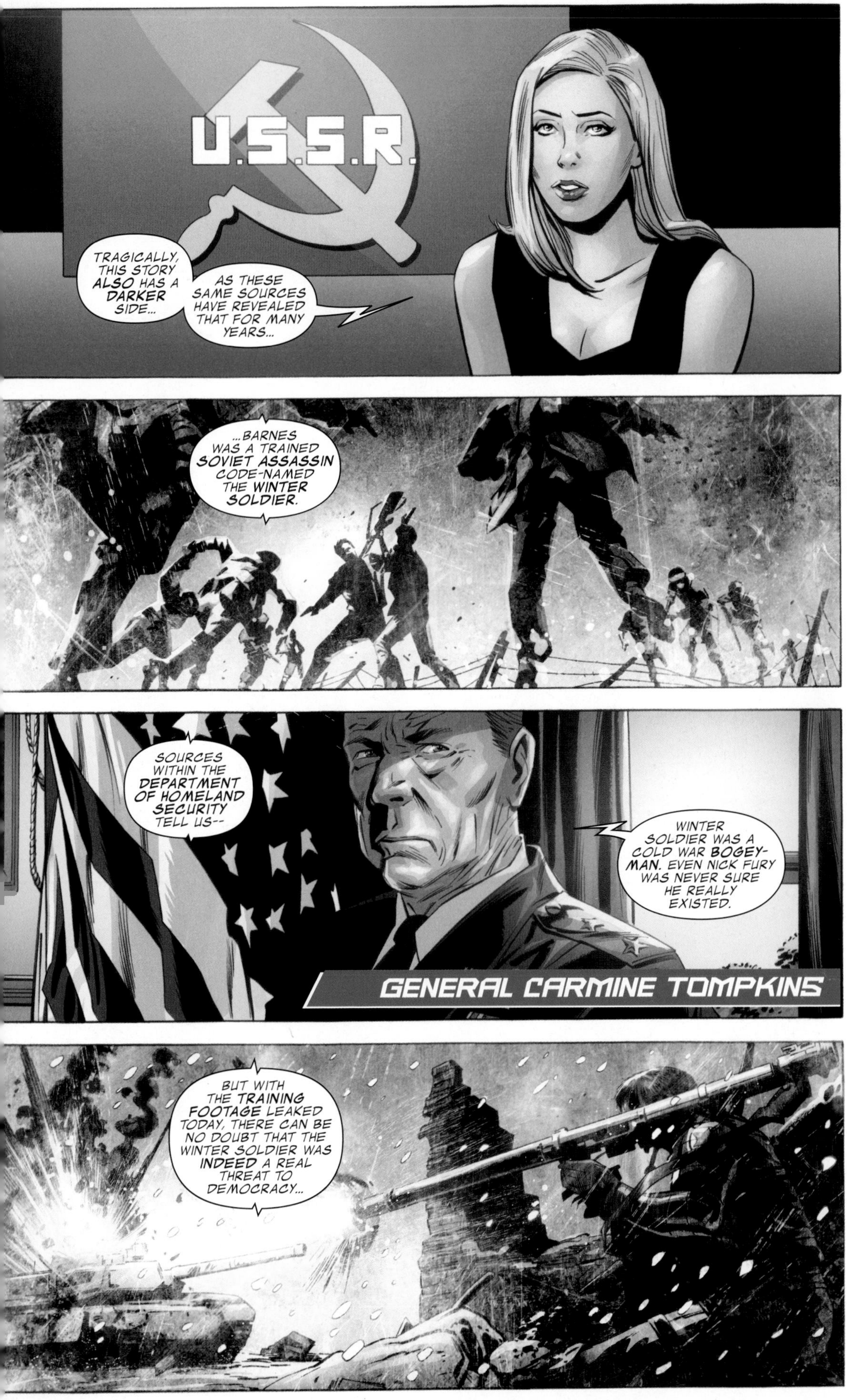
U.S.S.R.
TRAGICALLY, THIS STORY ALSO HAS A DARKER SIDE...
AS THESE SAME SOURCES HAVE REVEALED THAT FOR MANY YEARS...
...BARNES WAS A TRAINED SOVIET ASSASSIN CODE-NAMED THE WINTER SOLDIER.
SOURCES WITHIN THE DEPARTMENT OF HOMELAND SECURITY TELL US--
WINTER SOLDIER WAS A COLD WAR BOGEY-MAN. EVEN NICK FURY WAS NEVER SURE HE REALLY EXISTED.
GENERAL CARMINE TOMPKINS
BUT WITH THE TRAINING FOOTAGE LEAKED TODAY, THERE CAN BE NO DOUBT THAT THE WINTER SOLDIER WAS INDEED A REAL THREAT TO DEMOCRACY...

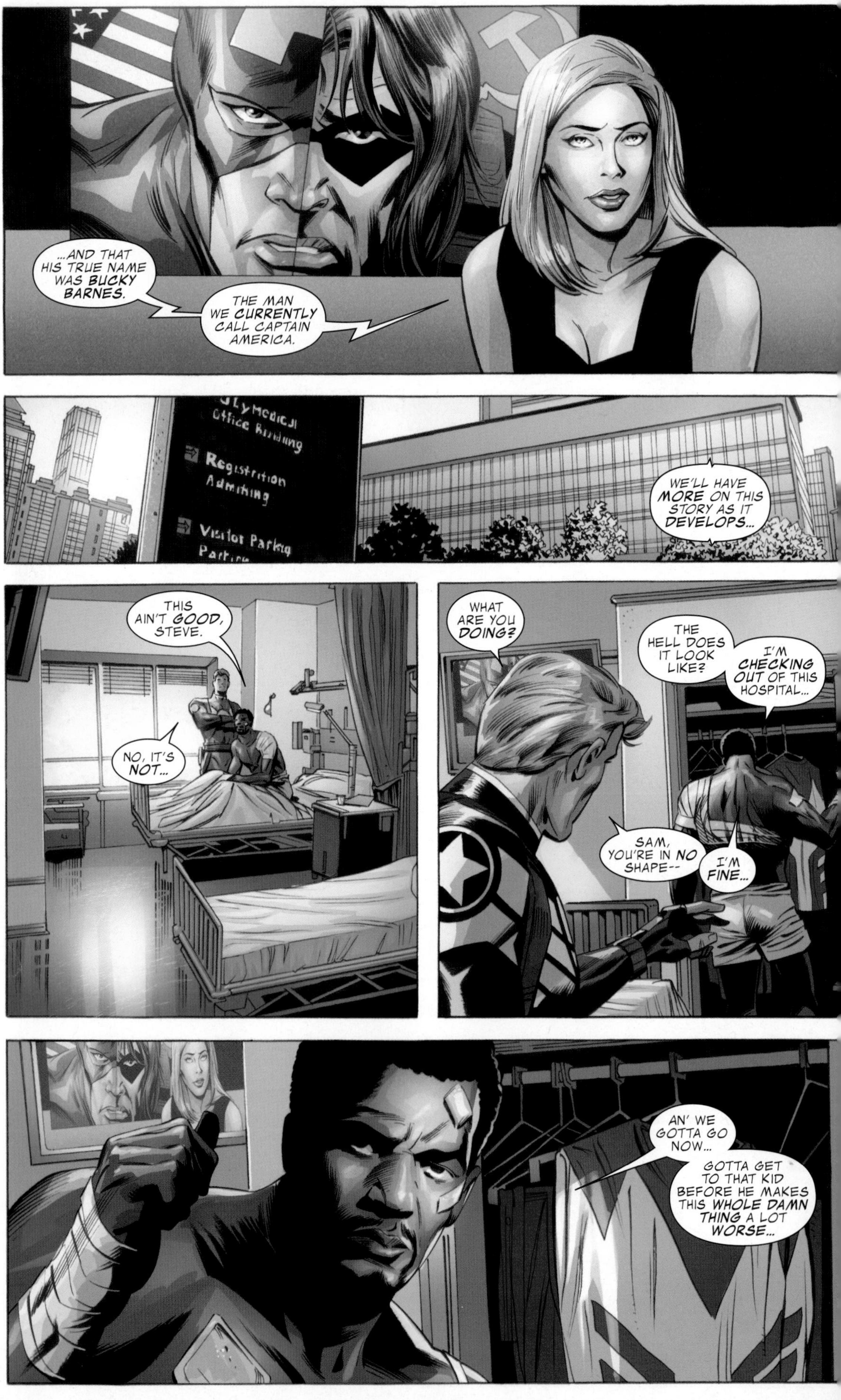
...AND THAT HIS TRUE NAME WAS BUCKY BARNES.
THE MAN WE CURRENTLY CALL CAPTAIN AMERICA.
Medical Office Building
Registration Admitting
Visitor Parking
WE'LL HAVE MORE ON THIS STORY AS IT DEVELOPS...
THIS AIN'T GOOD, STEVE.
NO, IT'S NOT...
WHAT ARE YOU DOING?
THE HELL DOES IT LOOK LIKE?
I'M CHECKING OUT OF THIS HOSPITAL...
SAM, YOU'RE IN NO SHAPE--
I'M FINE...
AN' WE GOTTA GO NOW...
GOTTA GET TO THAT KID BEFORE HE MAKES THIS WHOLE DAMN THING A LOT WORSE...

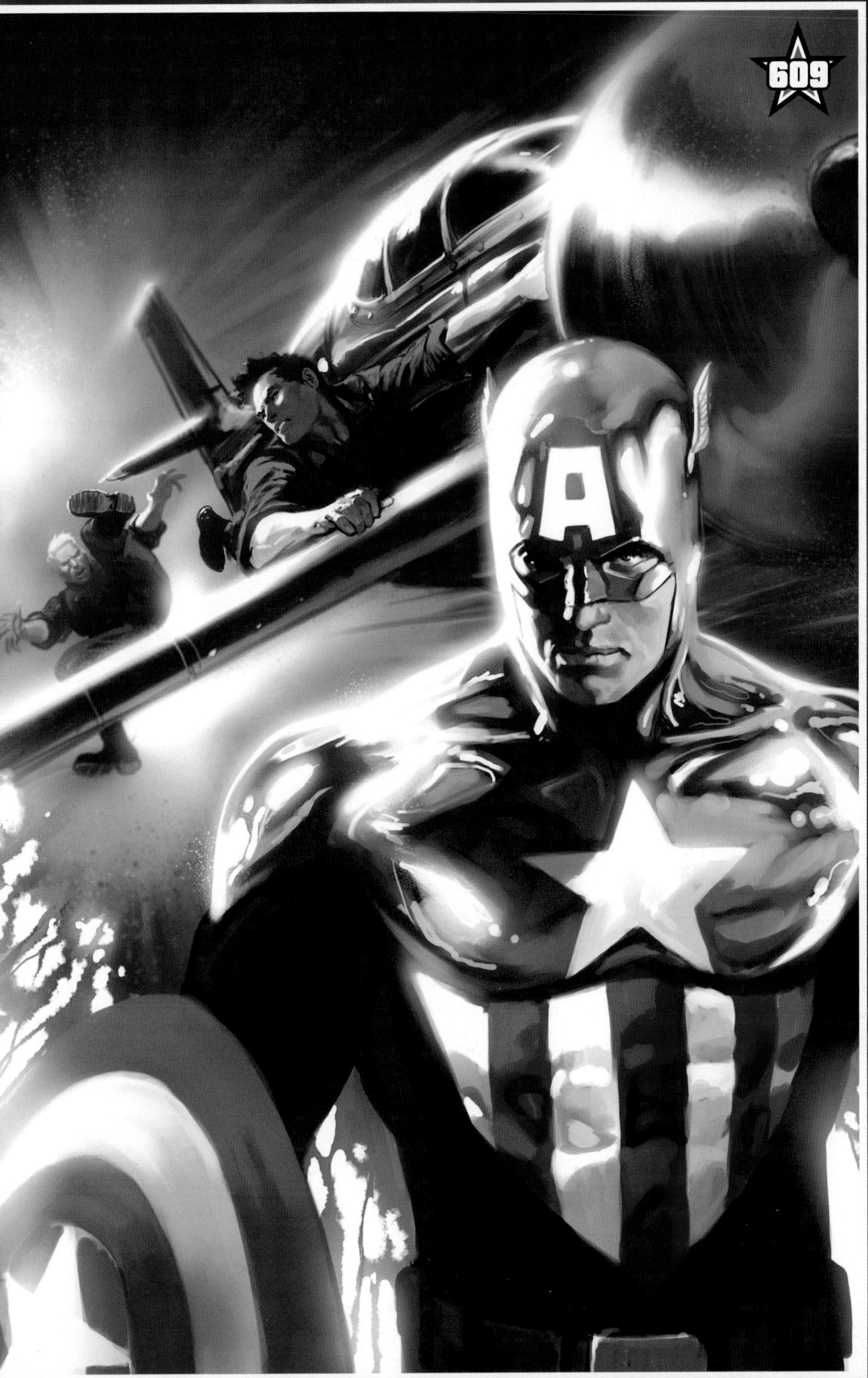
609

NO ESCAPE PART 4

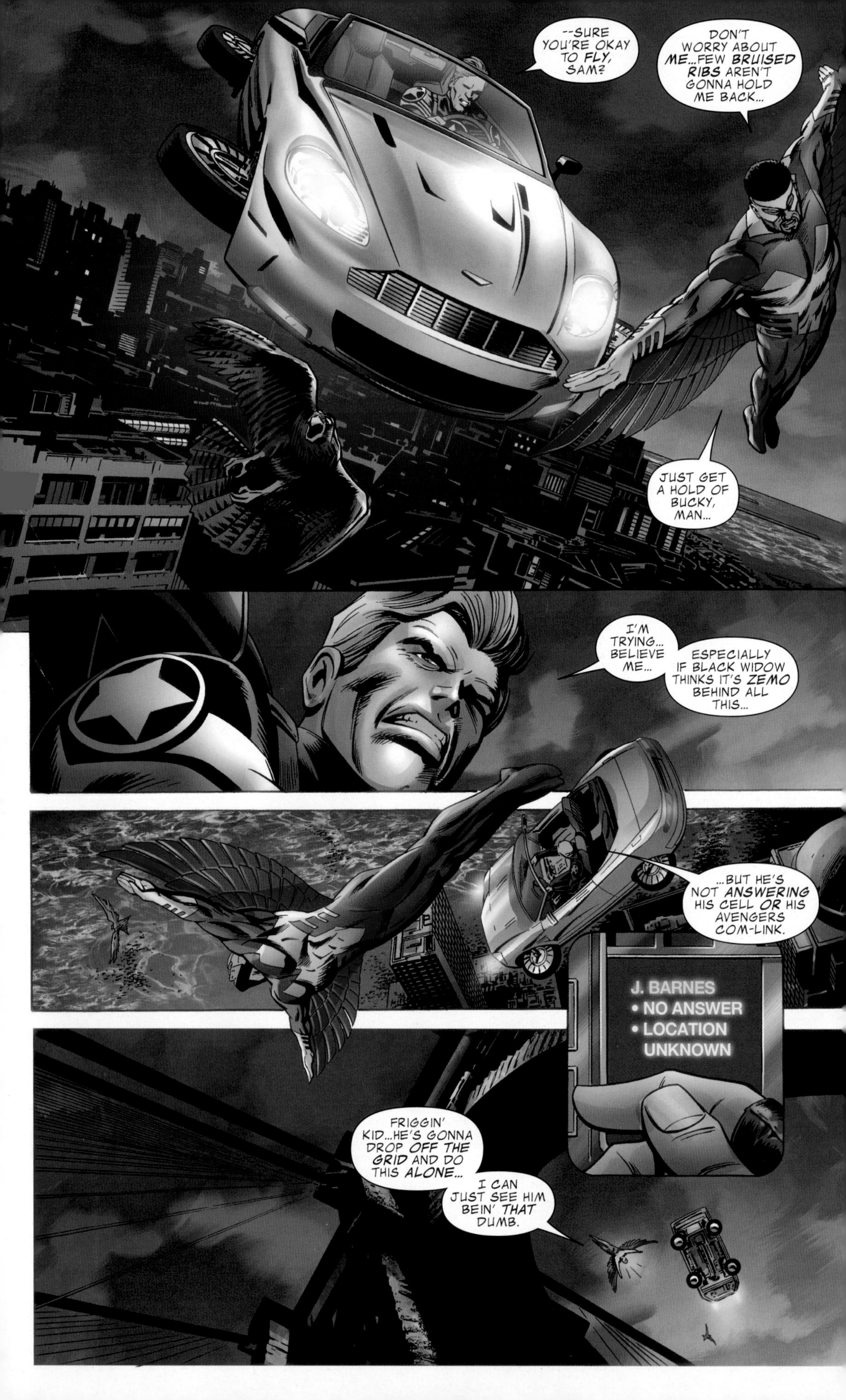
--SURE YOU'RE OKAY TO FLY, SAM?
DON'T WORRY ABOUT ME...FEW BRUISED RIBS AREN'T GONNA HOLD ME BACK...
JUST GET A HOLD OF BUCKY, MAN...
I'M TRYING... BELIEVE ME...
ESPECIALLY IF BLACK WIDOW THINKS IT'S ZEMO BEHIND ALL THIS...
...BUT HE'S NOT ANSWERING HIS CELL OR HIS AVENGERS COM-LINK.
J. BARNES
• NO ANSWER
• LOCATION UNKNOWN
FRIGGIN' KID...HE'S GONNA DROP OFF THE GRID AND DO THIS ALONE...
I CAN JUST SEE HIM BEIN' THAT DUMB.

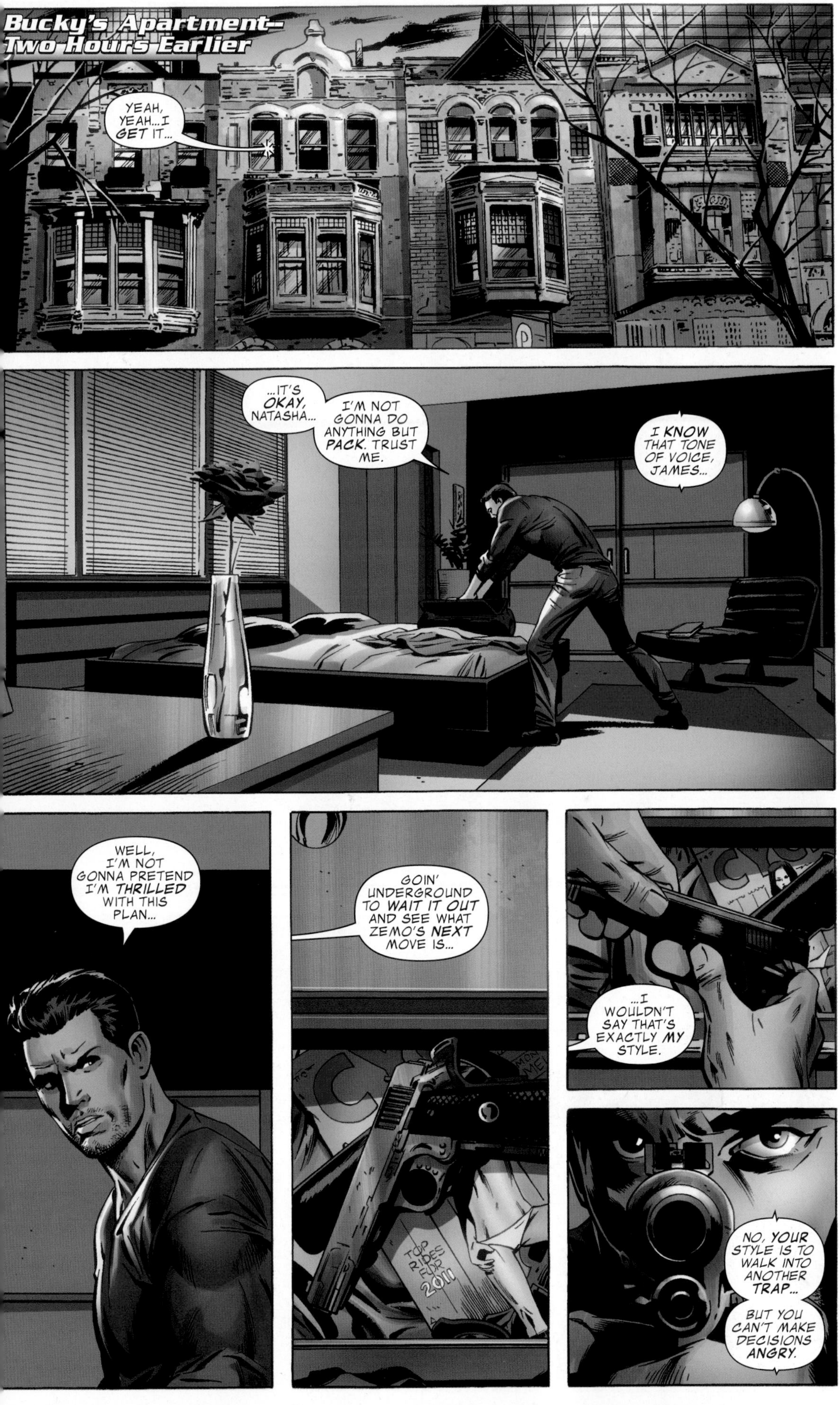
Bucky's Apartment--
Two Hours Earlier
YEAH, YEAH...I GET IT...
...IT'S OKAY, NATASHA...
I'M NOT GONNA DO ANYTHING BUT PACK. TRUST ME.
I KNOW THAT TONE OF VOICE, JAMES...
WELL, I'M NOT GONNA PRETEND I'M THRILLED WITH THIS PLAN...
GOIN' UNDERGROUND TO WAIT IT OUT AND SEE WHAT ZEMO'S NEXT MOVE IS...
...I WOULDN'T SAY THAT'S EXACTLY MY STYLE.
NO, YOUR STYLE IS TO WALK INTO ANOTHER TRAP...
BUT YOU CAN'T MAKE DECISIONS ANGRY.
TOP RIDES FOR 2011

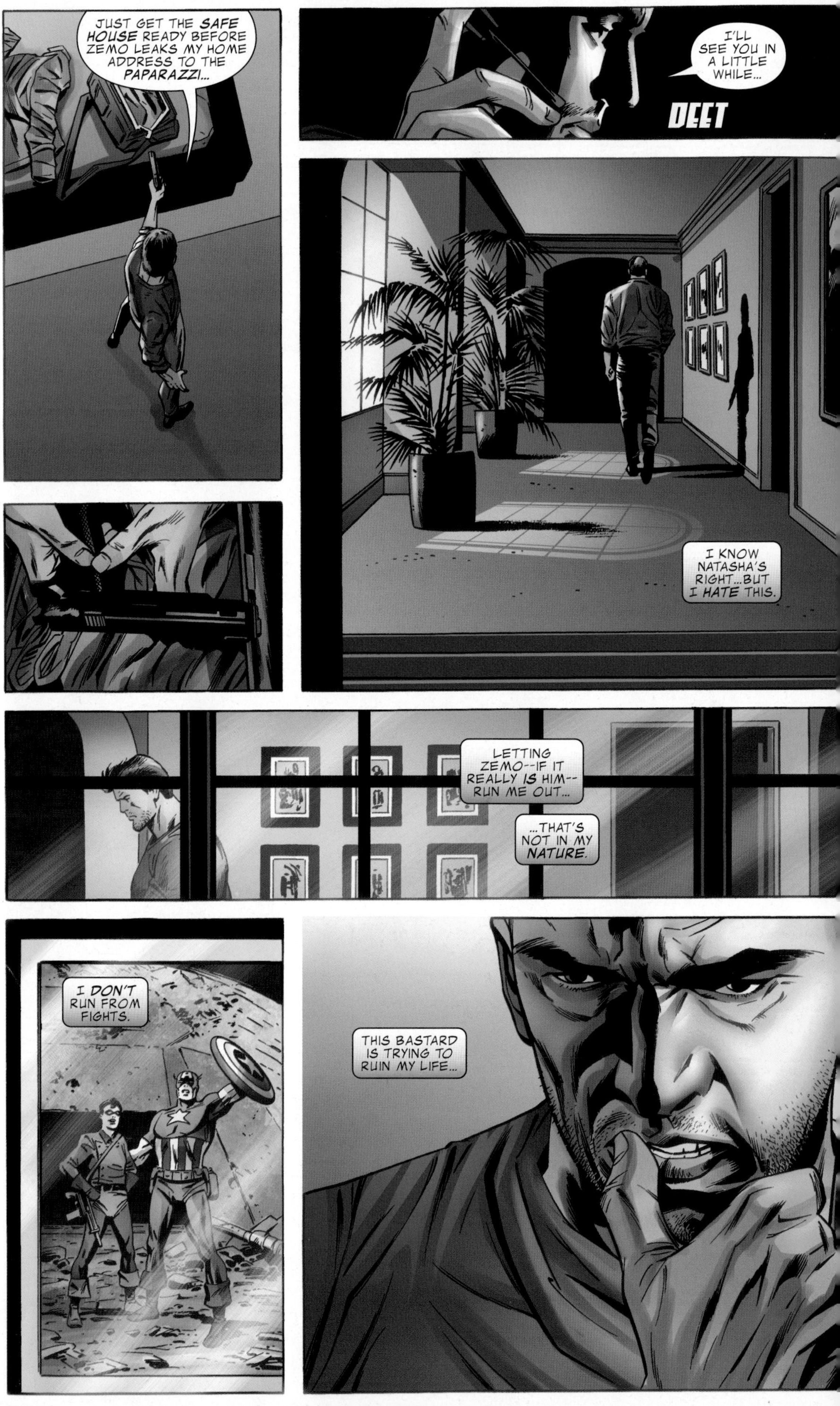
JUST GET THE SAFE HOUSE READY BEFORE ZEMO LEAKS MY HOME ADDRESS TO THE PAPARAZZI...
I'LL SEE YOU IN A LITTLE WHILE...
DEET
I KNOW NATASHA'S RIGHT...BUT I HATE THIS.
LETTING ZEMO--IF IT REALLY IS HIM--RUN ME OUT...
...THAT'S NOT IN MY NATURE.
I DON'T RUN FROM FIGHTS.
THIS BASTARD IS TRYING TO RUIN MY LIFE...

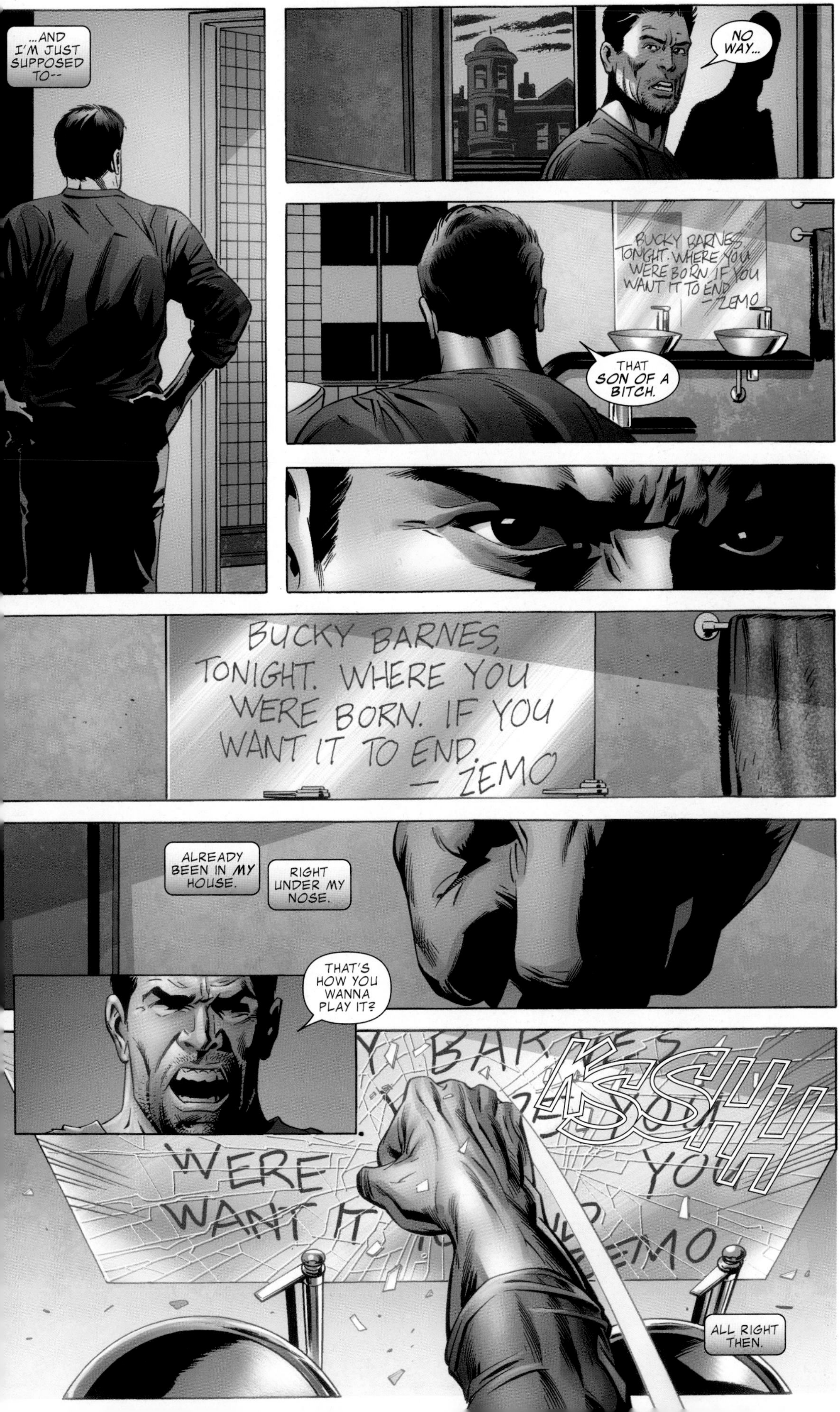
...AND I'M JUST SUPPOSED TO--
NO WAY...
BUCKY BARNES, TONIGHT. WHERE YOU WERE BORN. IF YOU WANT IT TO END. —ZEMO
THAT SON OF A BITCH.
BUCKY BARNES, TONIGHT. WHERE YOU WERE BORN. IF YOU WANT IT TO END. — ZEMO
ALREADY BEEN IN MY HOUSE.
RIGHT UNDER MY NOSE.
THAT'S HOW YOU WANNA PLAY IT?
KSSHH
ALL RIGHT THEN.

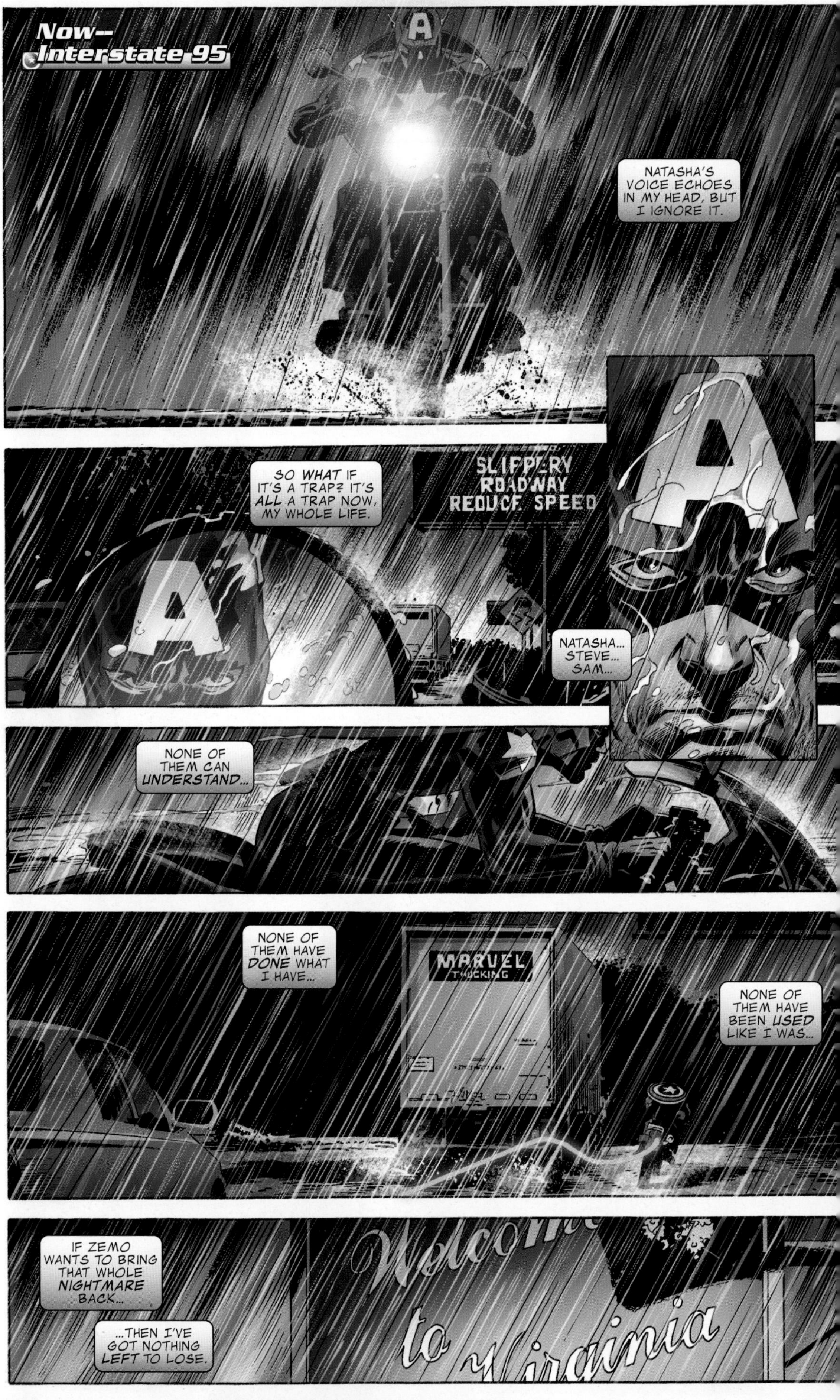
Now--
Interstate 95
NATASHA'S VOICE ECHOES IN MY HEAD, BUT I IGNORE IT.
SO WHAT IF IT'S A TRAP? IT'S ALL A TRAP NOW, MY WHOLE LIFE.
SLIPPERY ROADWAY REDUCE SPEED
NATASHA... STEVE... SAM...
NONE OF THEM CAN UNDERSTAND...
NONE OF THEM HAVE DONE WHAT I HAVE...
MARVEL TRUCKING
NONE OF THEM HAVE BEEN USED LIKE I WAS...
IF ZEMO WANTS TO BRING THAT WHOLE NIGHTMARE BACK...
...THEN I'VE GOT NOTHING LEFT TO LOSE.
to Virginia

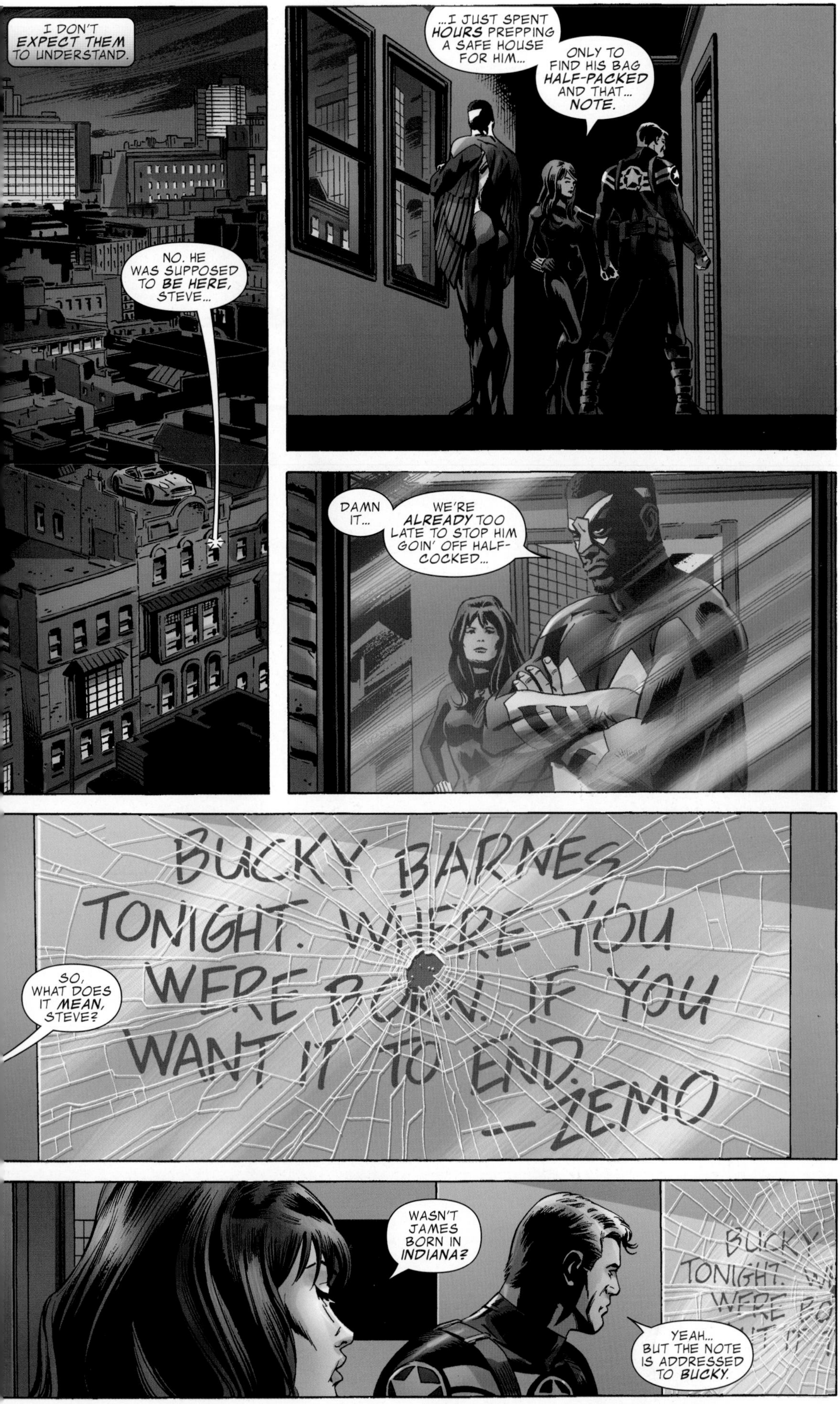
I DON'T EXPECT THEM TO UNDERSTAND.
...I JUST SPENT HOURS PREPPING A SAFE HOUSE FOR HIM...
ONLY TO FIND HIS BAG HALF-PACKED AND THAT... NOTE.
NO. HE WAS SUPPOSED TO BE HERE, STEVE...
DAMN IT...
WE'RE ALREADY TOO LATE TO STOP HIM GOIN' OFF HALF-COCKED...
BUCKY BARNES
TONIGHT. WHERE YOU WERE BORN. IF YOU WANT IT TO END.
—ZEMO
SO, WHAT DOES IT MEAN, STEVE?
WASN'T JAMES BORN IN INDIANA?
YEAH... BUT THE NOTE IS ADDRESSED TO BUCKY.

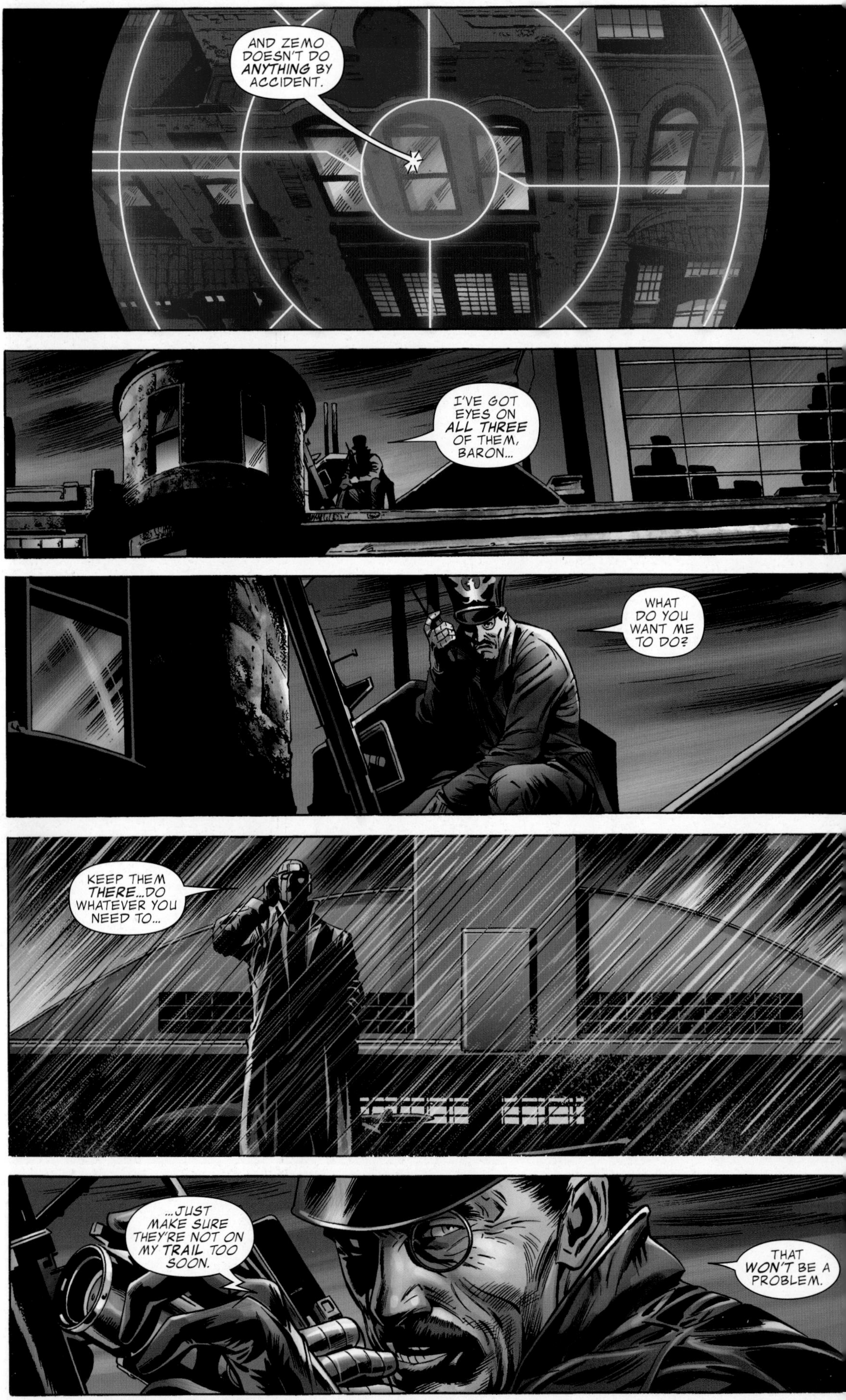
AND ZEMO DOESN'T DO ANYTHING BY ACCIDENT.
I'VE GOT EYES ON ALL THREE OF THEM, BARON...
WHAT DO YOU WANT ME TO DO?
KEEP THEM THERE...DO WHATEVER YOU NEED TO...
...JUST MAKE SURE THEY'RE NOT ON MY TRAIL TOO SOON.
THAT WON'T BE A PROBLEM.

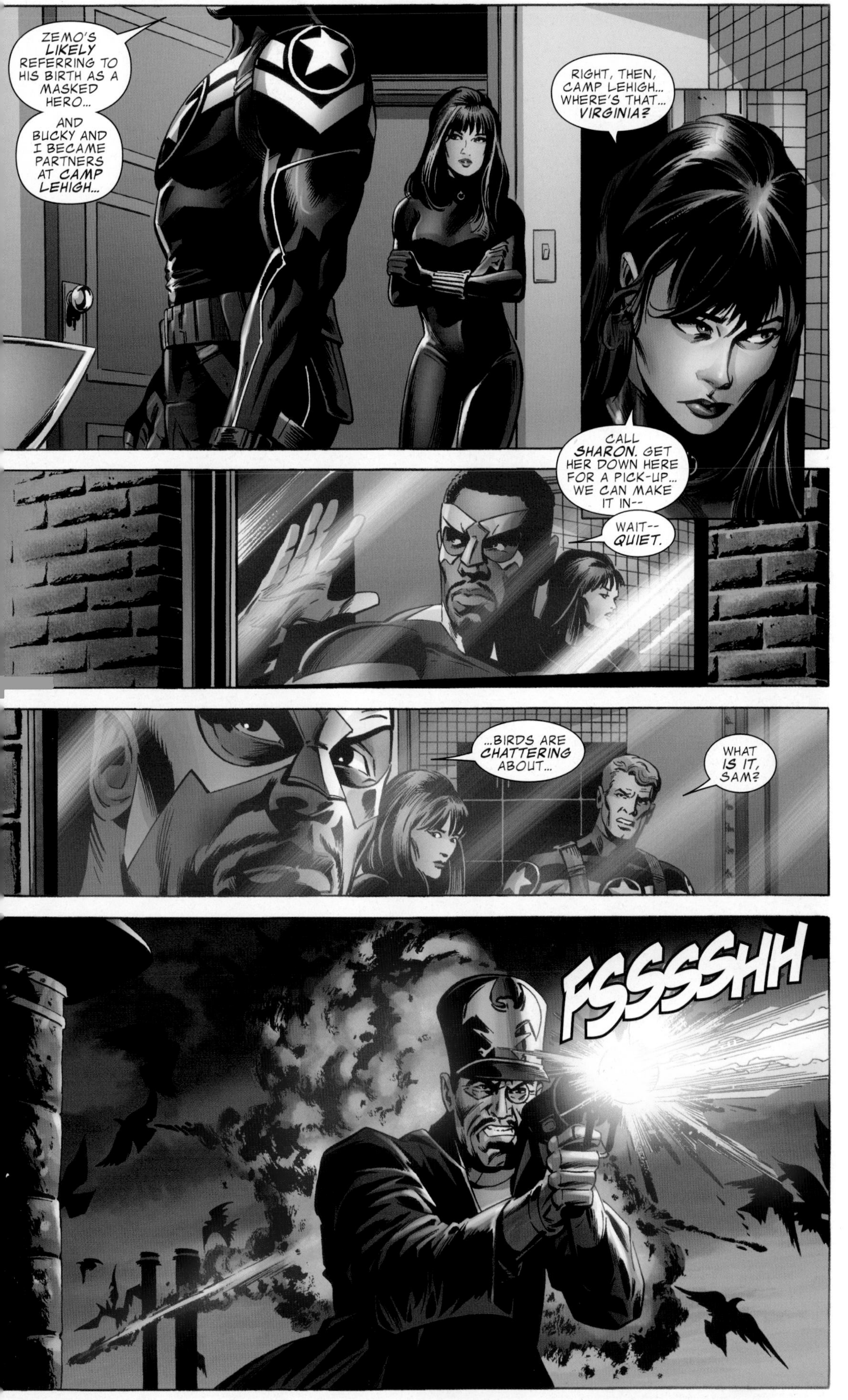
ZEMO'S LIKELY REFERRING TO HIS BIRTH AS A MASKED HERO...
AND BUCKY AND I BECAME PARTNERS AT CAMP LEHIGH...
RIGHT, THEN, CAMP LEHIGH... WHERE'S THAT... VIRGINIA?
CALL SHARON. GET HER DOWN HERE FOR A PICK-UP... WE CAN MAKE IT IN--
WAIT-- QUIET.
...BIRDS ARE CHATTERING ABOUT...
WHAT IS IT, SAM?
FSSSSHH

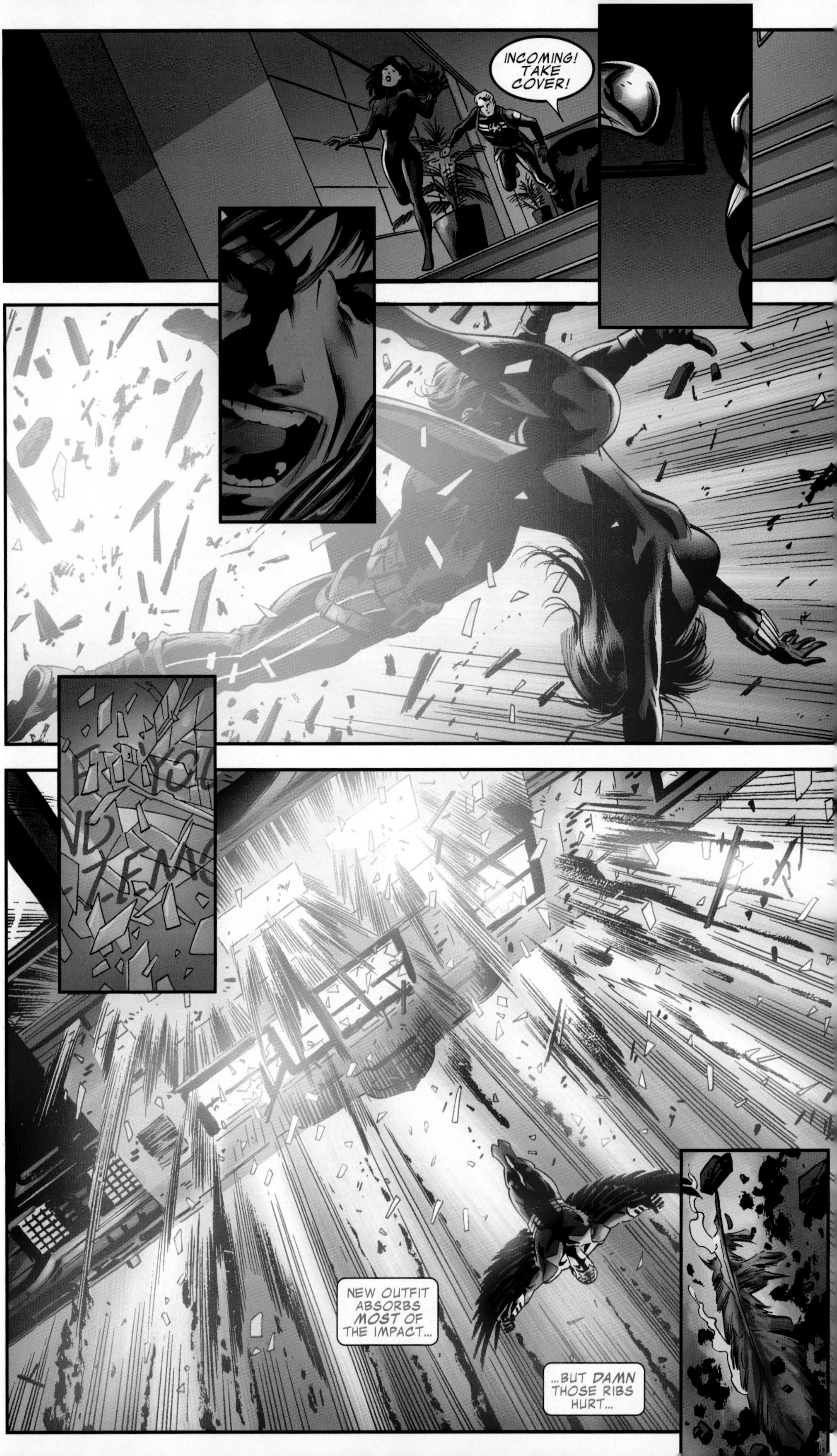
INCOMING! TAKE COVER!
NEW OUTFIT ABSORBS MOST OF THE IMPACT...
...BUT DAMN THOSE RIBS HURT...

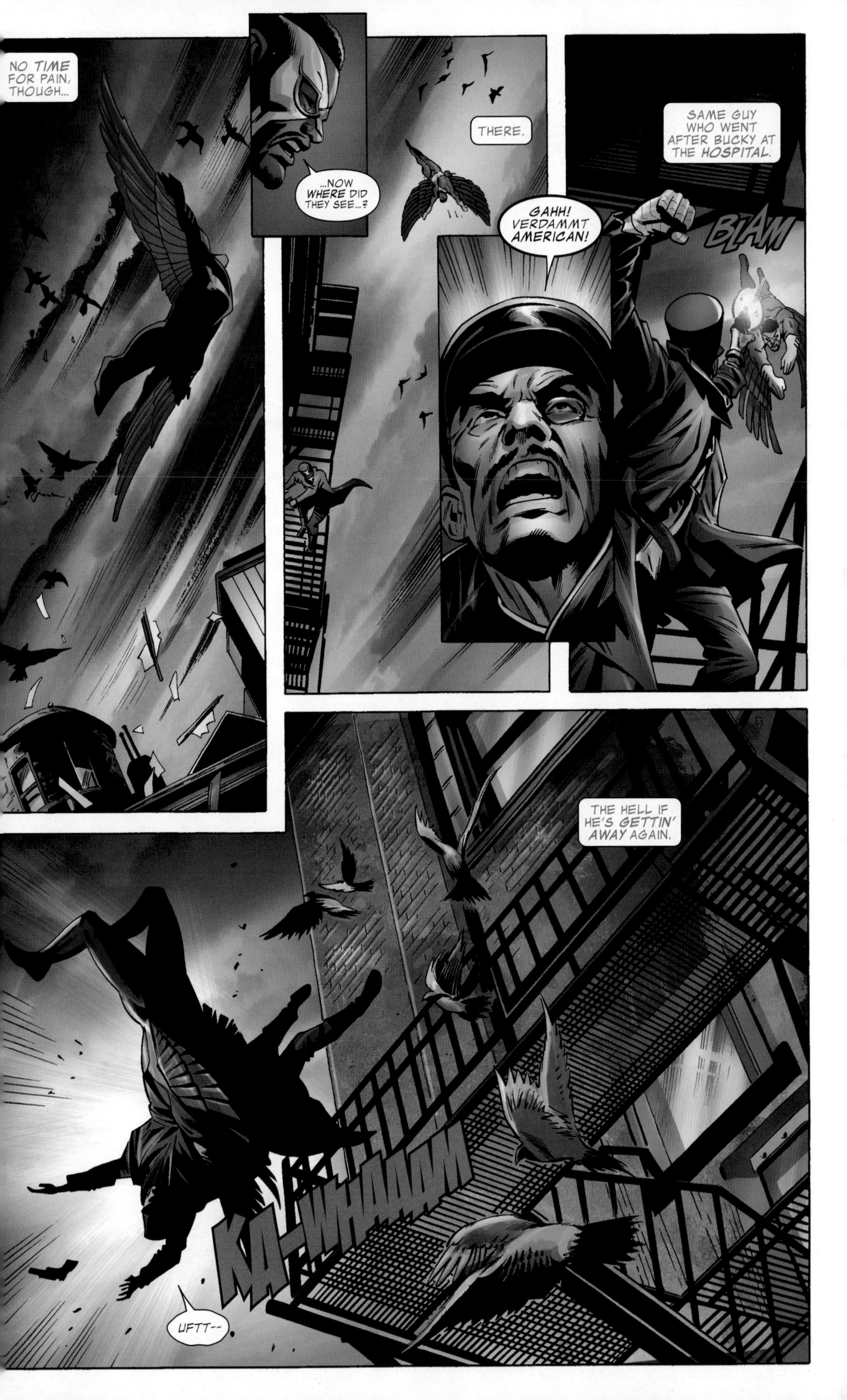
NO TIME FOR PAIN, THOUGH...
...NOW WHERE DID THEY SEE...?
THERE.
SAME GUY WHO WENT AFTER BUCKY AT THE HOSPITAL.
GAHH! VERDAMMT AMERICAN!
BLAM
THE HELL IF HE'S GETTIN' AWAY AGAIN.
KA-WHAAAM
UFTT--

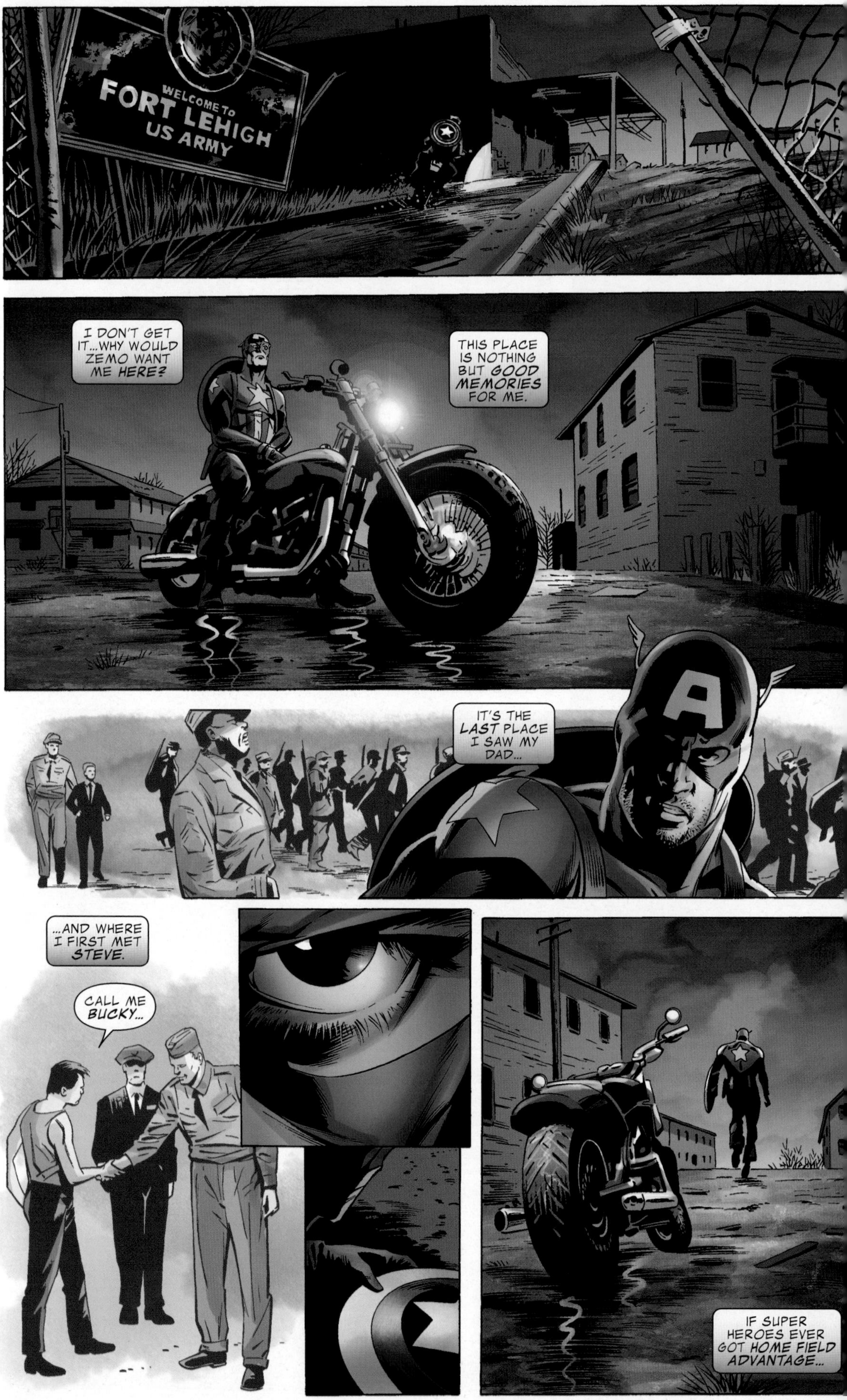
WELCOME TO
FORT LEHIGH
US ARMY
I DON'T GET IT...WHY WOULD ZEMO WANT ME HERE?
THIS PLACE IS NOTHING BUT GOOD MEMORIES FOR ME.
IT'S THE LAST PLACE I SAW MY DAD...
...AND WHERE I FIRST MET STEVE.
CALL ME BUCKY...
IF SUPER HEROES EVER GOT HOME FIELD ADVANTAGE...

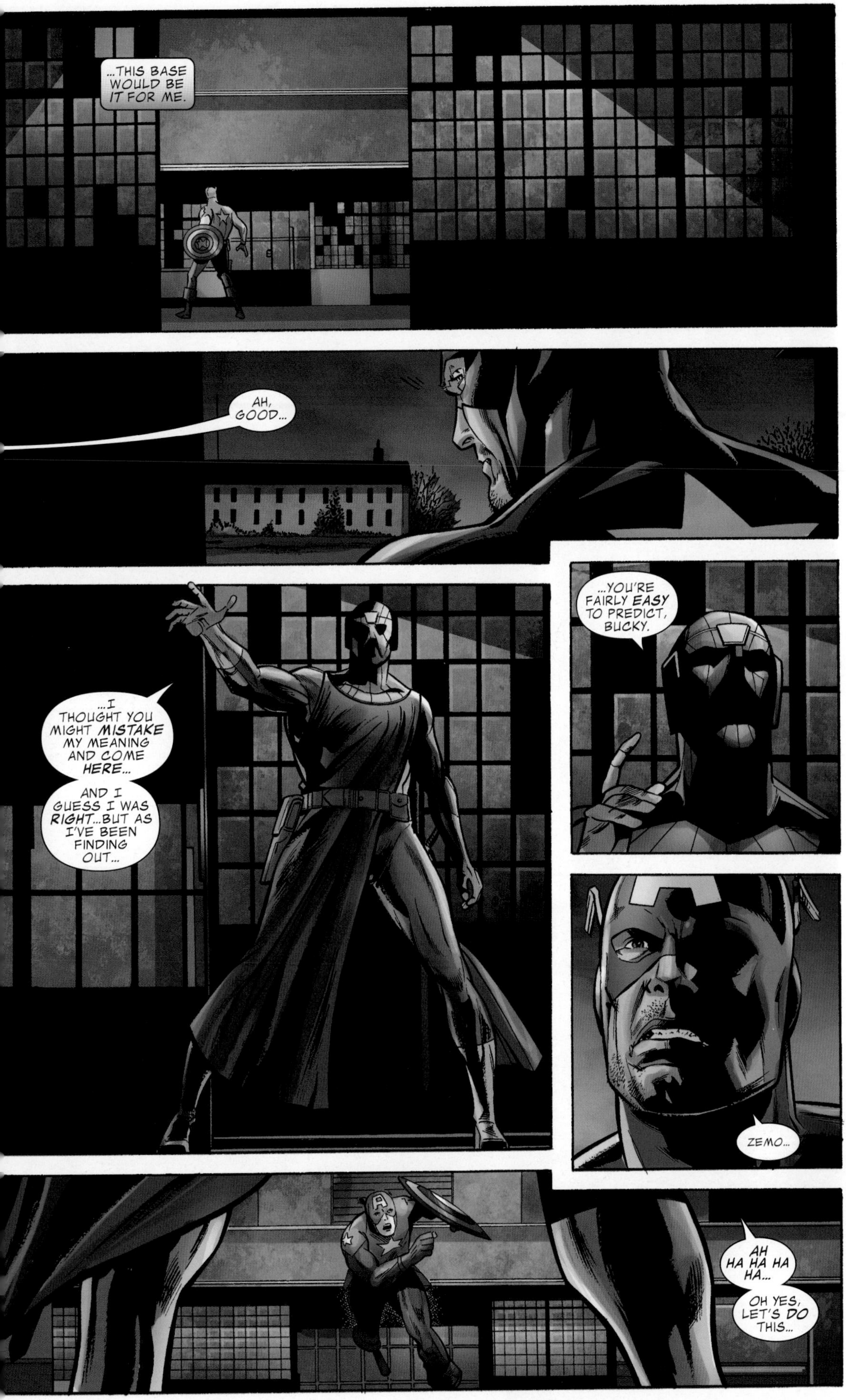
...THIS BASE WOULD BE IT FOR ME.
AH, GOOD...
...I THOUGHT YOU MIGHT MISTAKE MY MEANING AND COME HERE...
AND I GUESS I WAS RIGHT...BUT AS I'VE BEEN FINDING OUT...
...YOU'RE FAIRLY EASY TO PREDICT, BUCKY.
ZEMO...
AH HA HA HA HA...
OH YES, LET'S DO THIS...

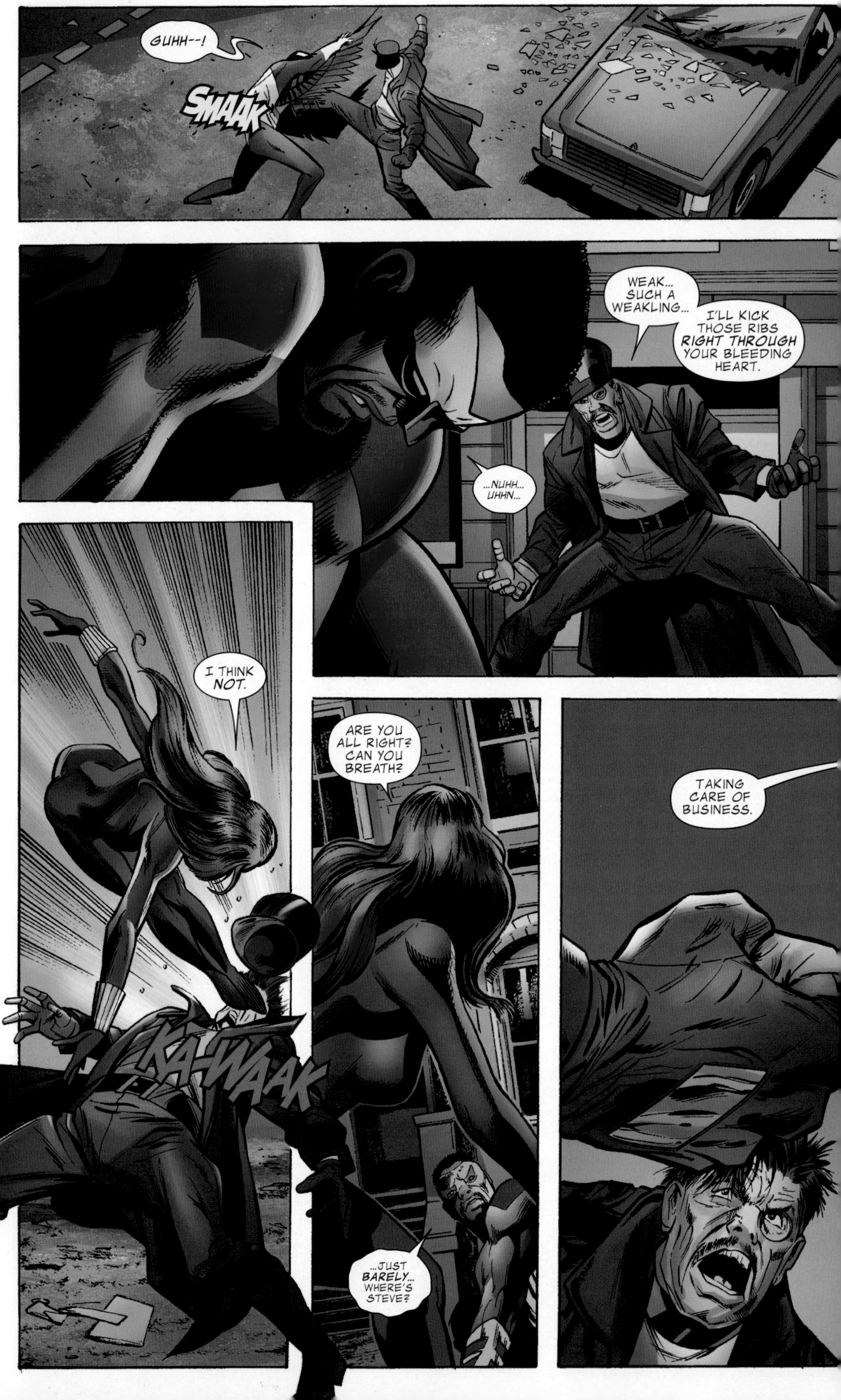
GUHH--!
SMAAK
WEAK... SUCH A WEAKLING...
I'LL KICK THOSE RIBS RIGHT THROUGH YOUR BLEEDING HEART.
...NUHH... UHHN...
I THINK NOT.
KA-WAAK
ARE YOU ALL RIGHT? CAN YOU BREATH?
...JUST BARELY... WHERE'S STEVE?
TAKING CARE OF BUSINESS.

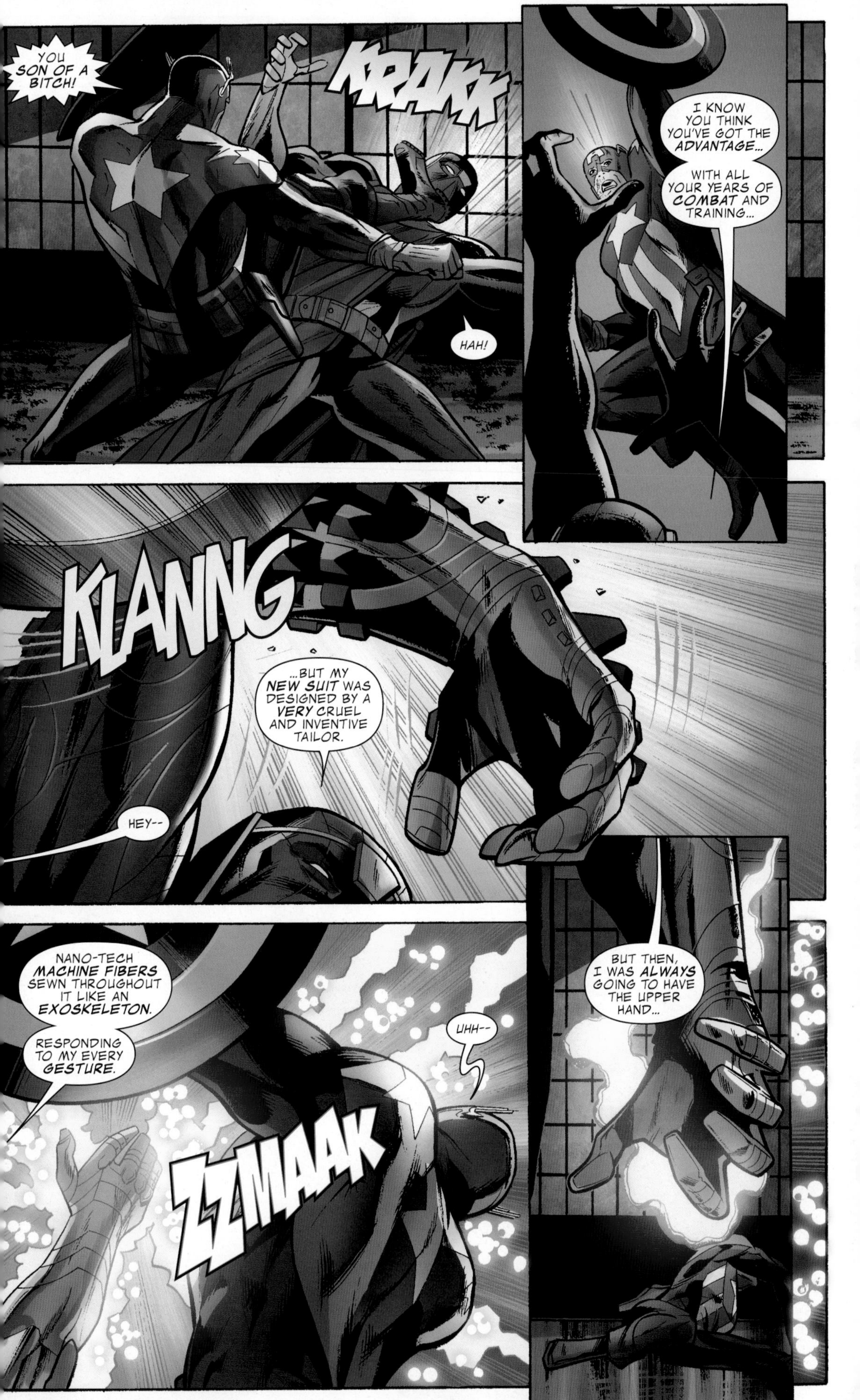
YOU SON OF A BITCH!
KRAKK
HAH!
I KNOW YOU THINK YOU'VE GOT THE ADVANTAGE...
WITH ALL YOUR YEARS OF COMBAT AND TRAINING...
KLANNG
...BUT MY NEW SUIT WAS DESIGNED BY A VERY CRUEL AND INVENTIVE TAILOR.
HEY--
NANO-TECH MACHINE FIBERS SEWN THROUGHOUT IT LIKE AN EXOSKELETON.
RESPONDING TO MY EVERY GESTURE.
UHH--
ZZMAAK
BUT THEN, I WAS ALWAYS GOING TO HAVE THE UPPER HAND...

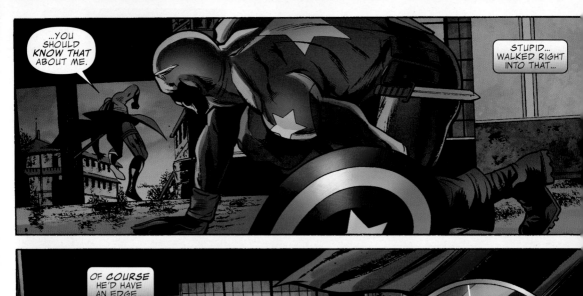

...YOU SHOULD KNOW THAT ABOUT ME.

STUPID... WALKED RIGHT INTO THAT...

OF COURSE HE'D HAVE AN EDGE...

OF COURSE HE'D CHEAT...

BZZAAAM

HE'S A ZEMO.

WHUUK

GUHH--

I MEAN, YOU DIDN'T THINK THIS WAS GOING TO BE EASY, DID YOU?

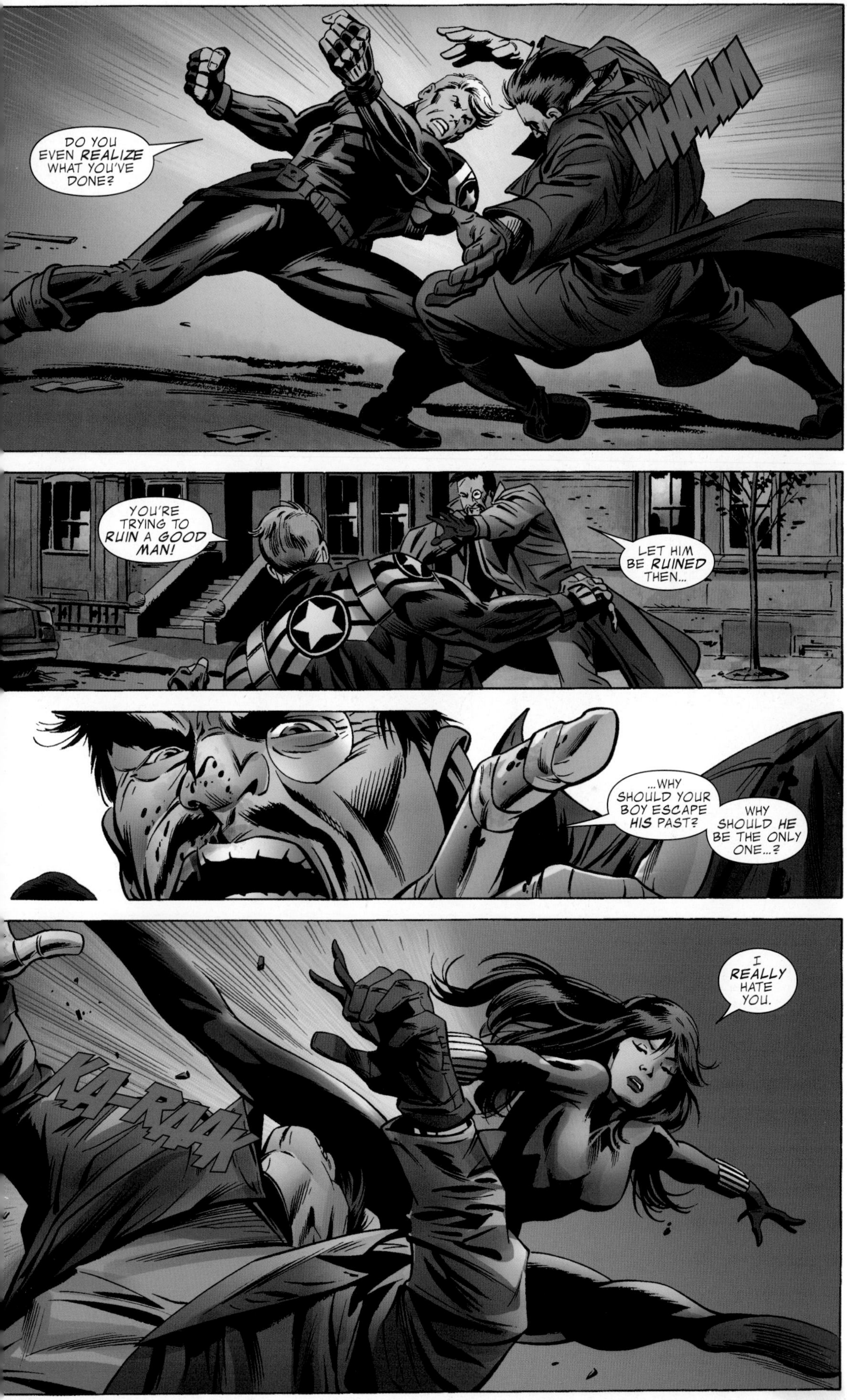
DO YOU EVEN REALIZE WHAT YOU'VE DONE?
WHAAM
YOU'RE TRYING TO RUIN A GOOD MAN!
LET HIM BE RUINED THEN...
...WHY SHOULD YOUR BOY ESCAPE HIS PAST?
WHY SHOULD HE BE THE ONLY ONE...?
I REALLY HATE YOU.
KA-RAAK

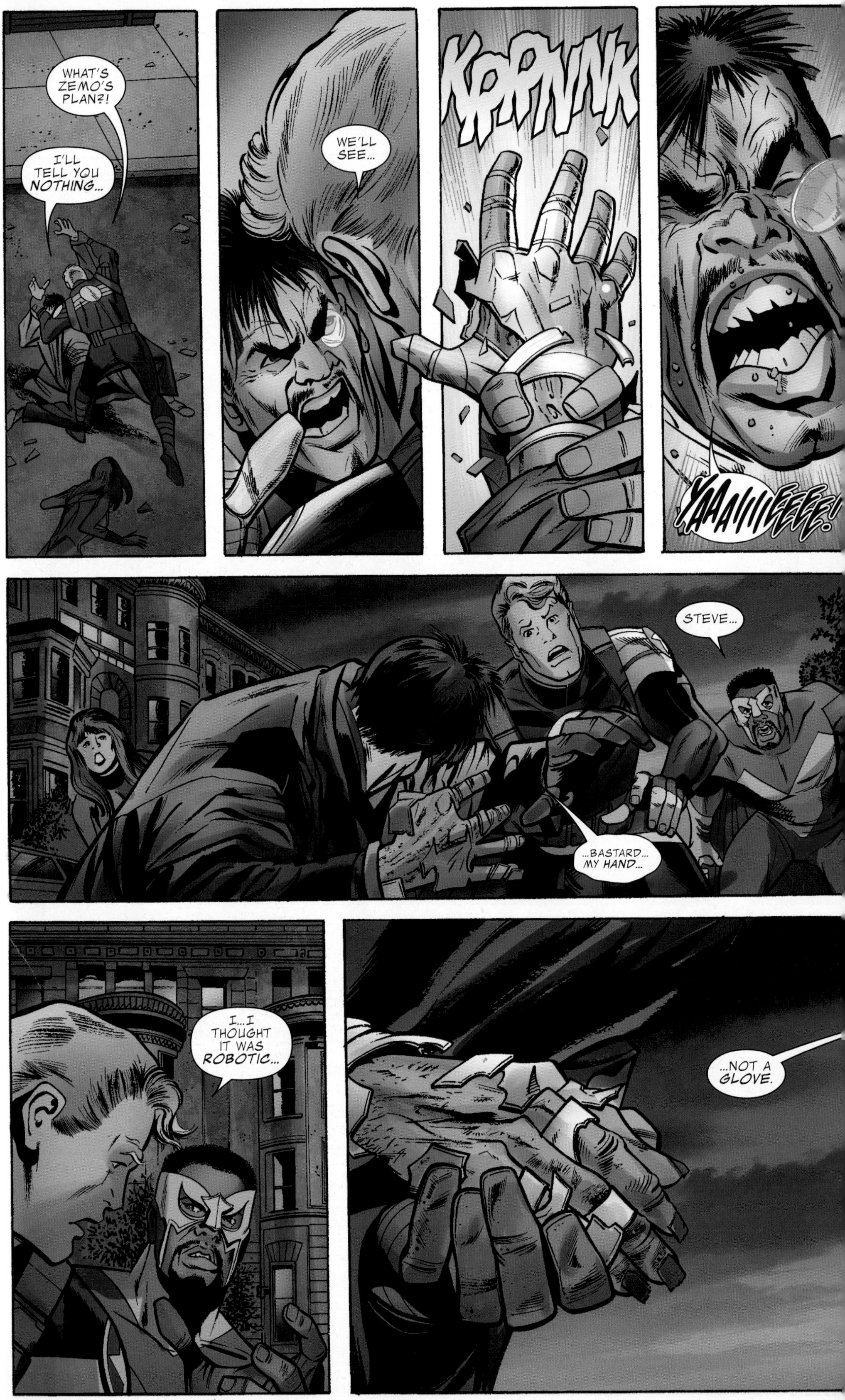
WHAT'S ZEMO'S PLAN?!
I'LL TELL YOU NOTHING...
WE'LL SEE...
KRRNNK
YAAAIIIIEEEE!
STEVE...
...BASTARD... MY HAND...
I...I THOUGHT IT WAS ROBOTIC...
...NOT A GLOVE.

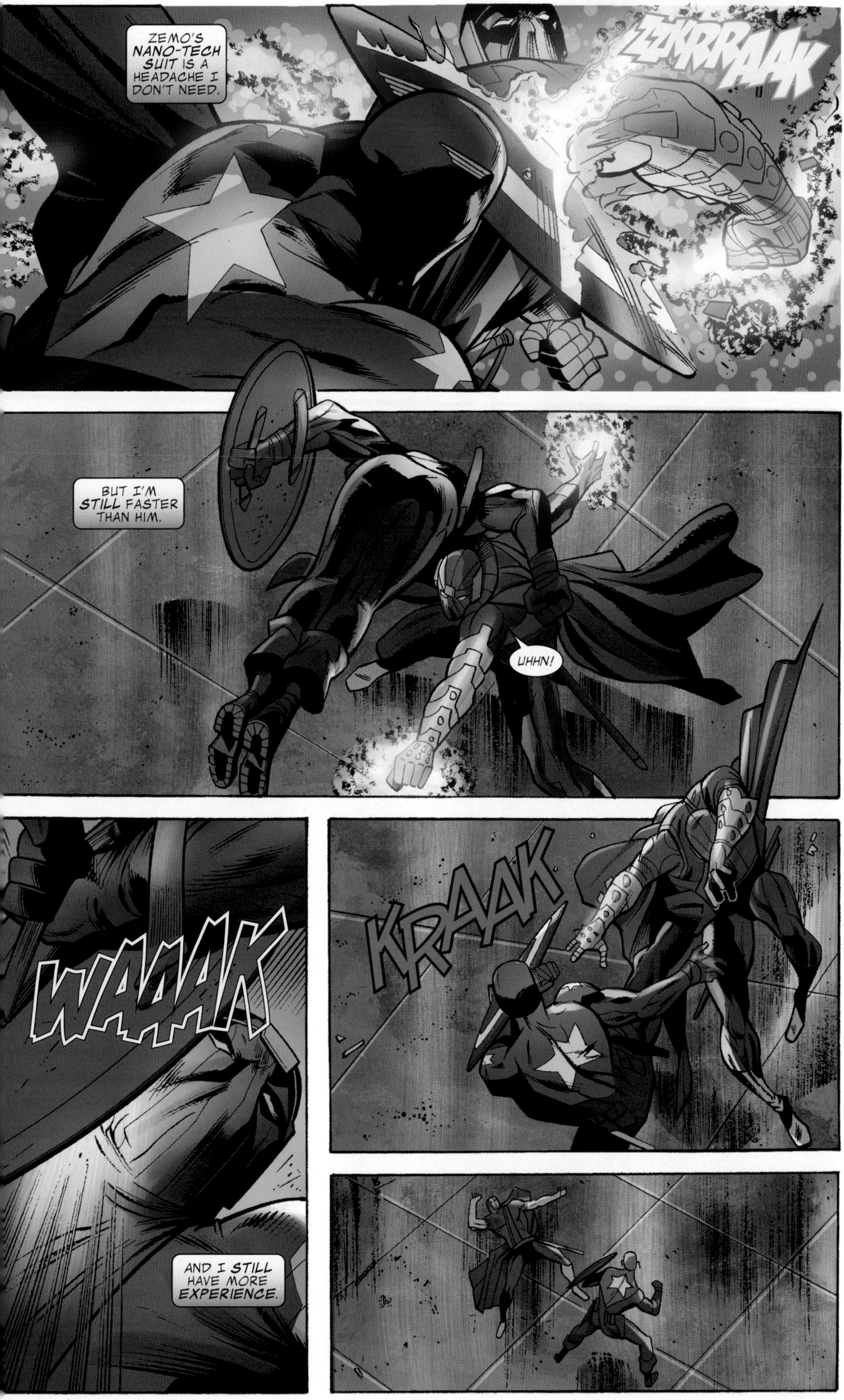
ZEMO'S NANO-TECH SUIT IS A HEADACHE I DON'T NEED.
ZZKRRAAK
BUT I'M STILL FASTER THAN HIM.
UHHN!
WAAAK
KRAAK
AND I STILL HAVE MORE EXPERIENCE.

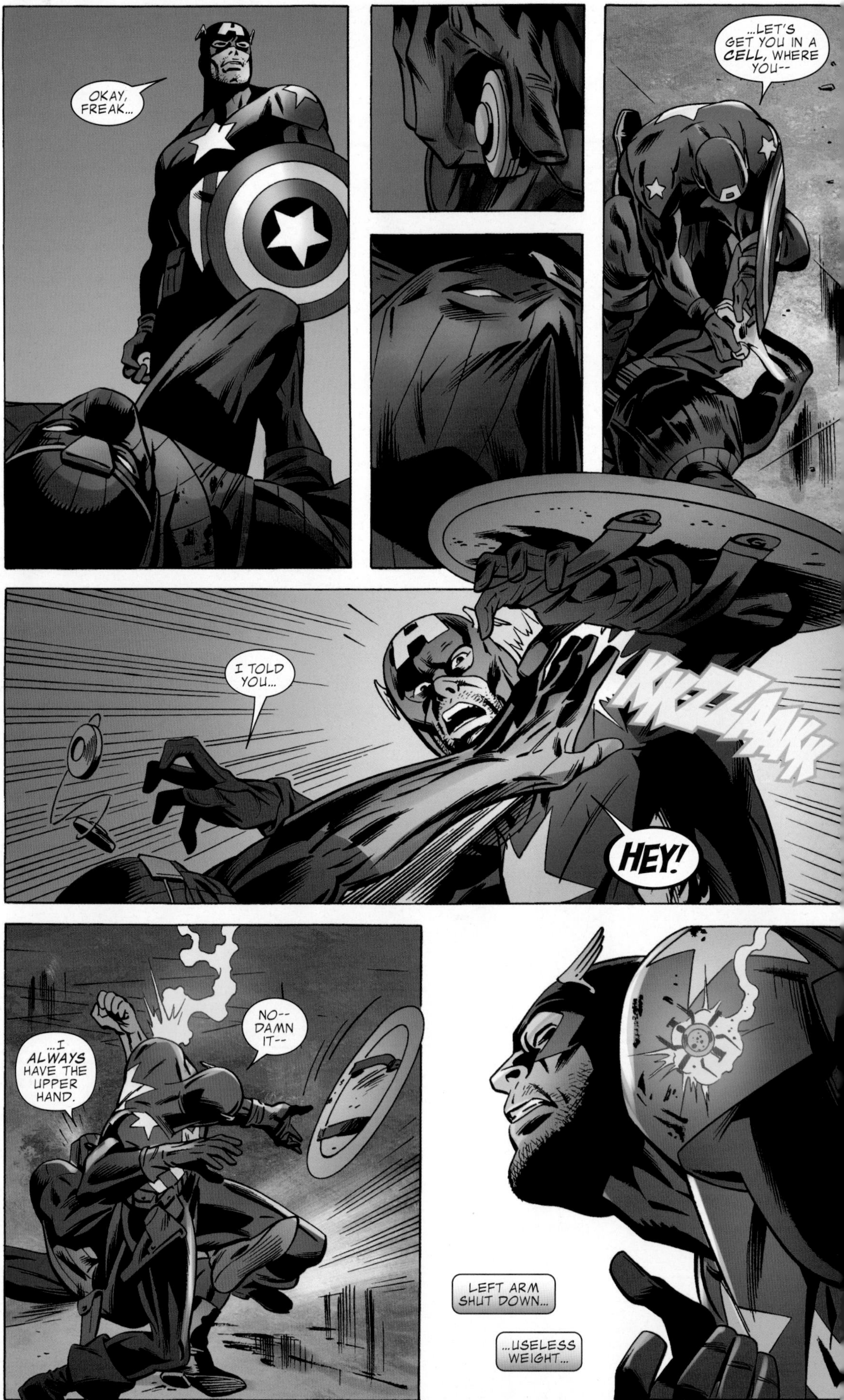
OKAY, FREAK...
...LET'S GET YOU IN A CELL, WHERE YOU--
I TOLD YOU...
KKZZAAKK
HEY!
...I ALWAYS HAVE THE UPPER HAND.
NO-- DAMN IT--
LEFT ARM SHUT DOWN...
...USELESS WEIGHT...

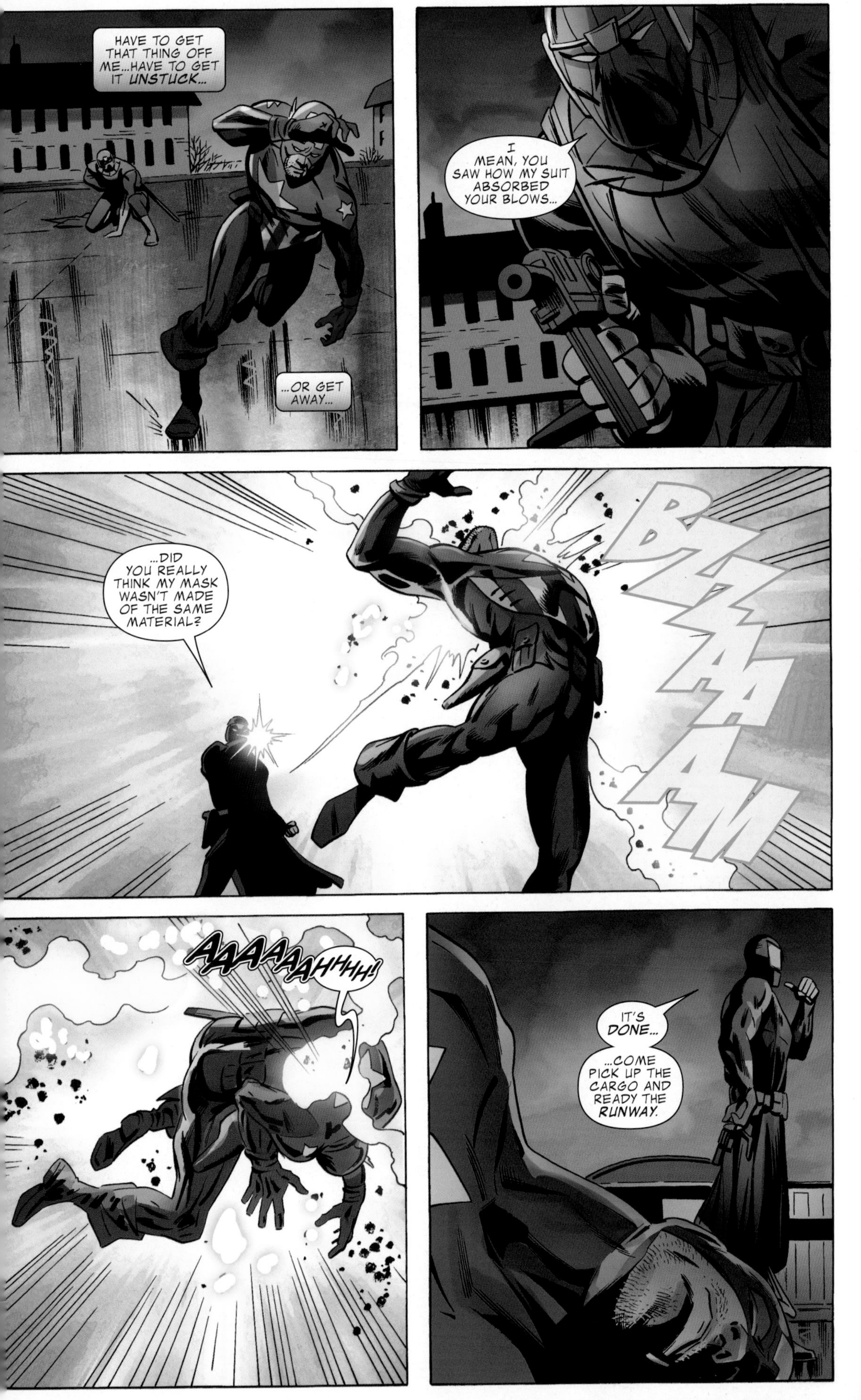
HAVE TO GET THAT THING OFF ME...HAVE TO GET IT UNSTUCK...
...OR GET AWAY...
I MEAN, YOU SAW HOW MY SUIT ABSORBED YOUR BLOWS...
...DID YOU REALLY THINK MY MASK WASN'T MADE OF THE SAME MATERIAL?
BZZAAAM
AAAAAAAHHHH!
IT'S DONE...
...COME PICK UP THE CARGO AND READY THE RUNWAY.

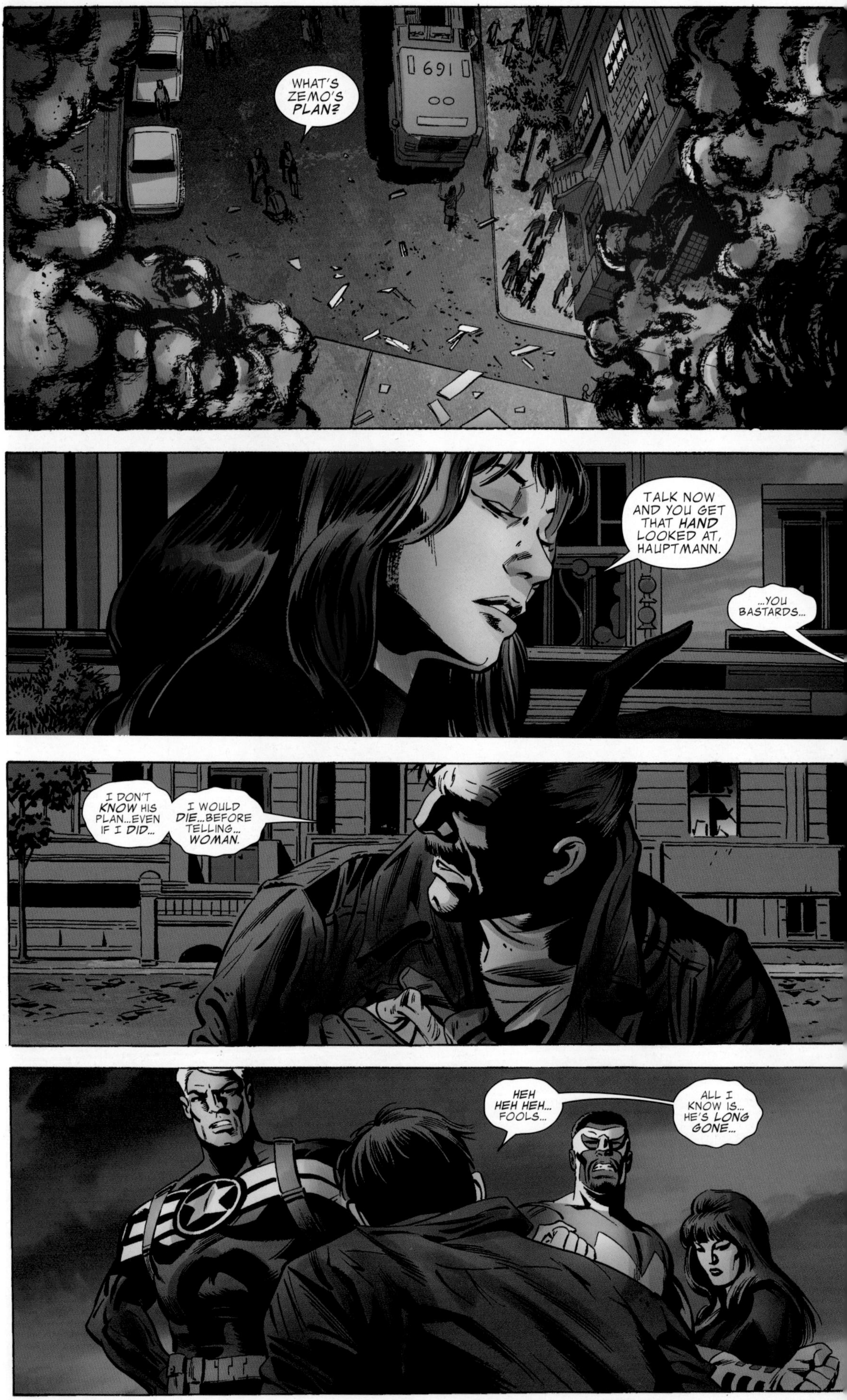
WHAT'S ZEMO'S PLAN?
TALK NOW AND YOU GET THAT HAND LOOKED AT, HAUPTMANN.
...YOU BASTARDS...
I DON'T KNOW HIS PLAN...EVEN IF I DID...
I WOULD DIE...BEFORE TELLING... WOMAN.
HEH HEH HEH... FOOLS...
ALL I KNOW IS... HE'S LONG GONE...

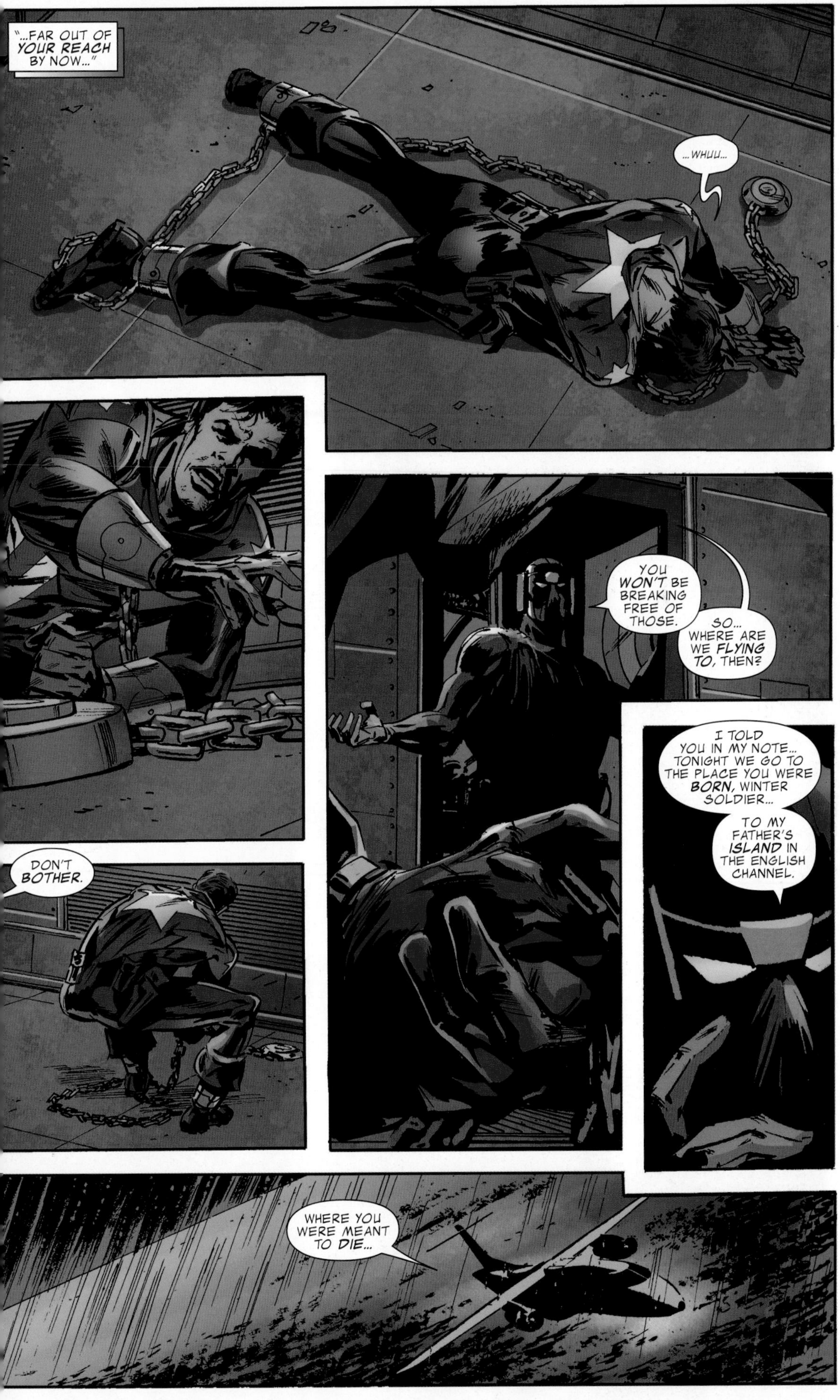
"...FAR OUT OF YOUR REACH BY NOW..."
...WHUU...
DON'T BOTHER.
YOU WON'T BE BREAKING FREE OF THOSE.
SO... WHERE ARE WE FLYING TO, THEN?
I TOLD YOU IN MY NOTE... TONIGHT WE GO TO THE PLACE YOU WERE BORN, WINTER SOLDIER...
TO MY FATHER'S ISLAND IN THE ENGLISH CHANNEL.
WHERE YOU WERE MEANT TO DIE...

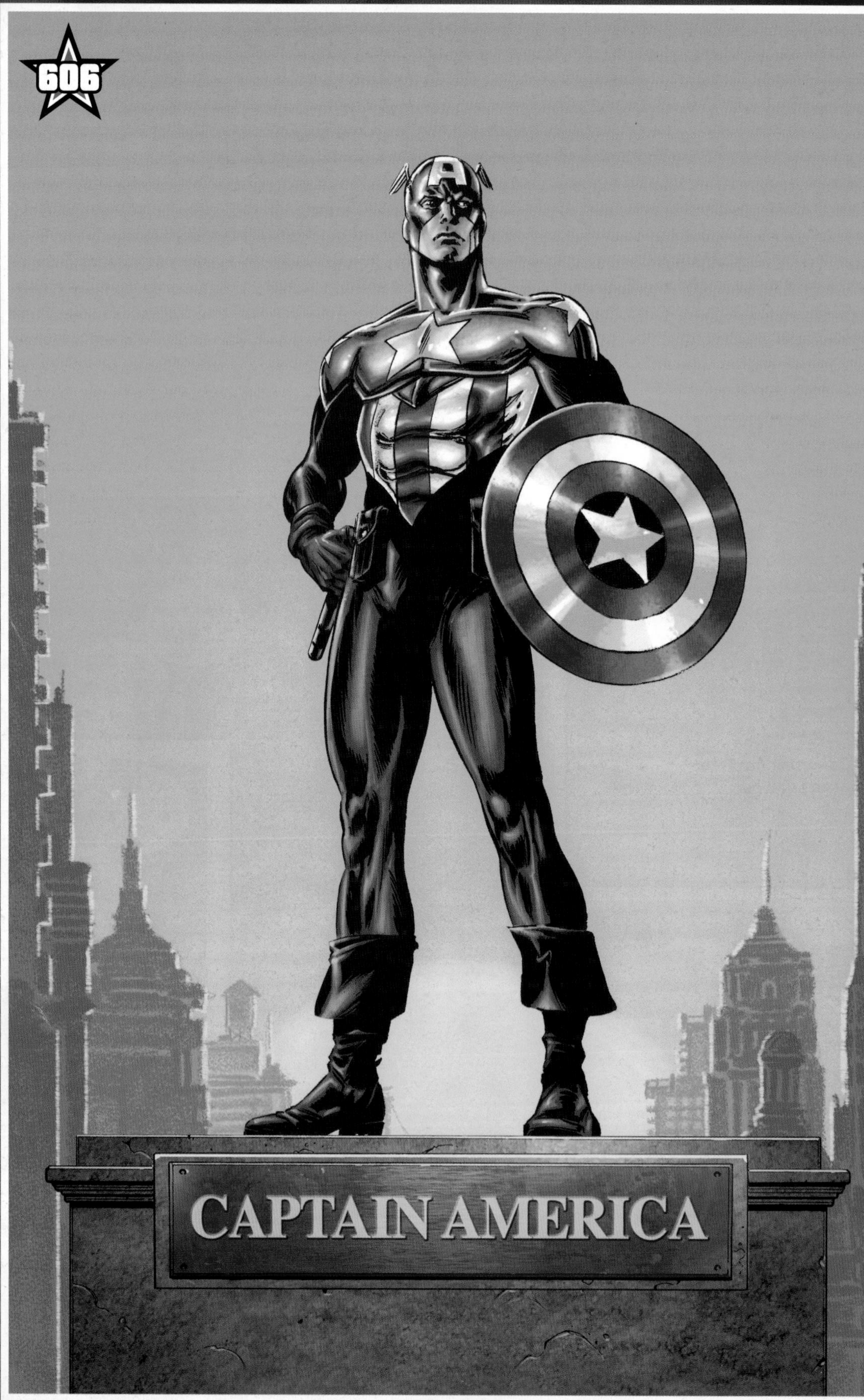
606
CAPTAIN AMERICA

HEROIC AGE VARIANT BY
BUTCH GUICE & MORRY HOLLOWELL

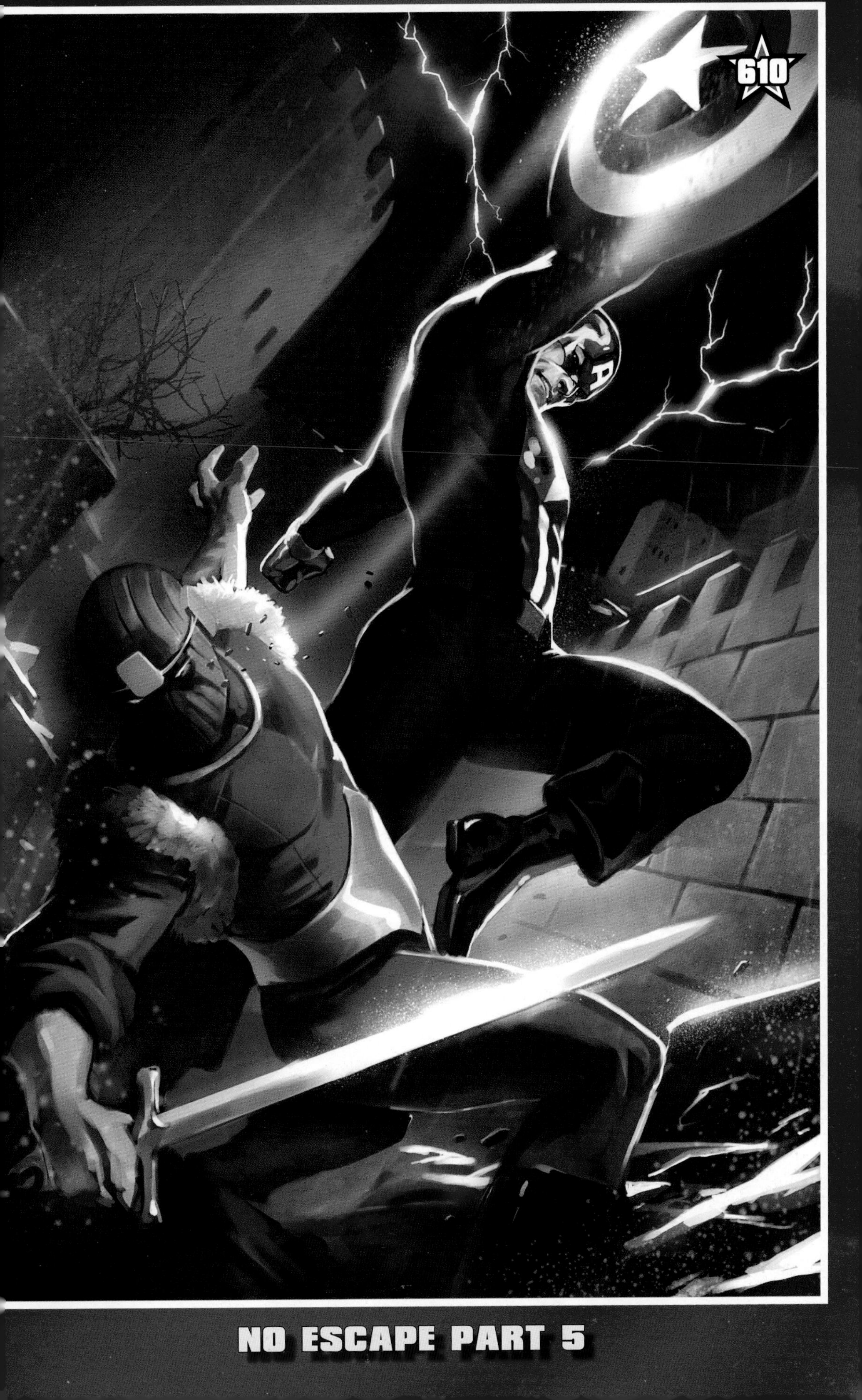
610

NO ESCAPE PART 5

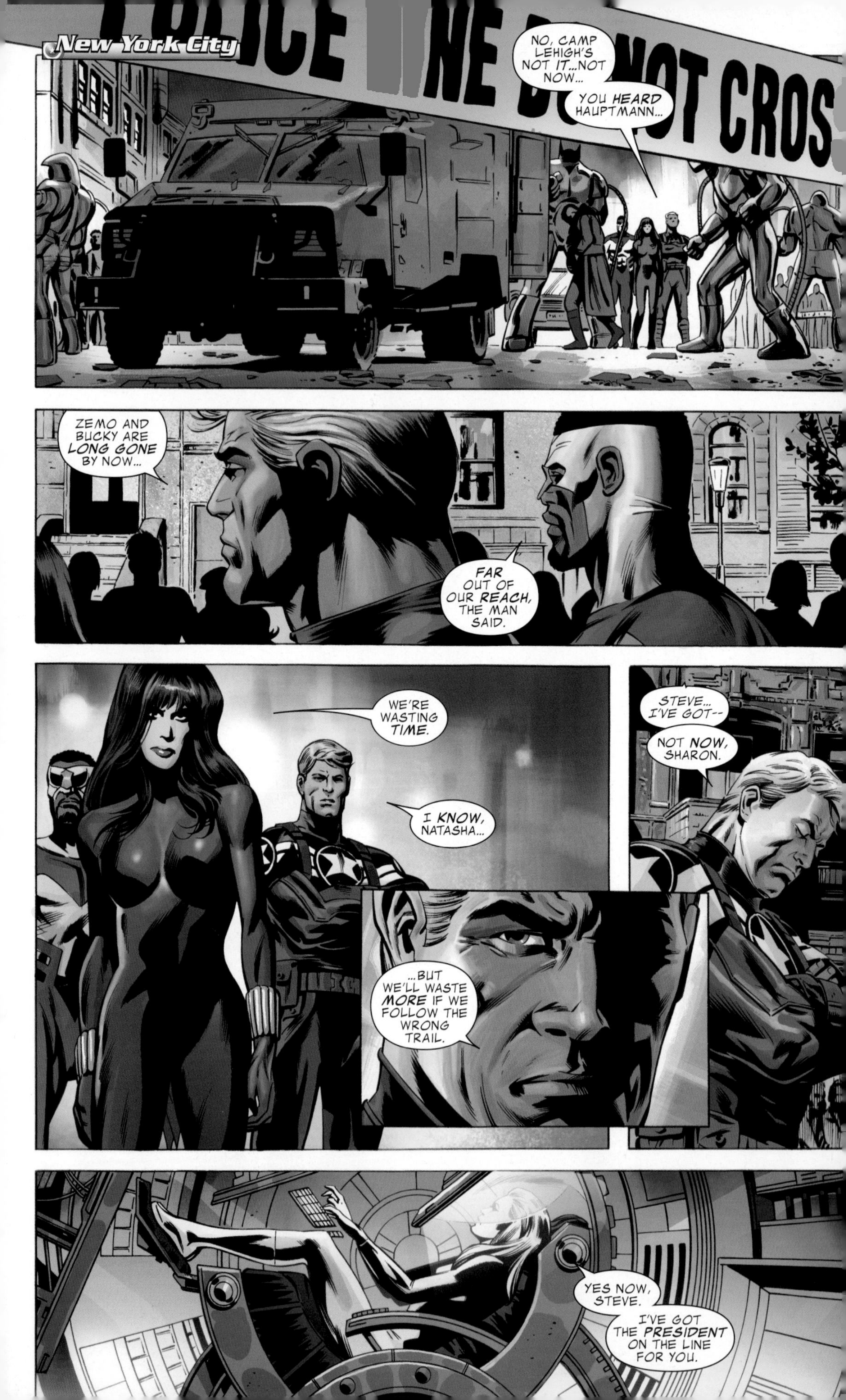
New York City
NO, CAMP LEHIGH'S NOT IT...NOT NOW...
YOU HEARD HAUPTMANN...
ZEMO AND BUCKY ARE LONG GONE BY NOW...
FAR OUT OF OUR REACH, THE MAN SAID.
WE'RE WASTING TIME.
I KNOW, NATASHA...
...BUT WE'LL WASTE MORE IF WE FOLLOW THE WRONG TRAIL.
STEVE... I'VE GOT--
NOT NOW, SHARON.
YES NOW, STEVE.
I'VE GOT THE PRESIDENT ON THE LINE FOR YOU.

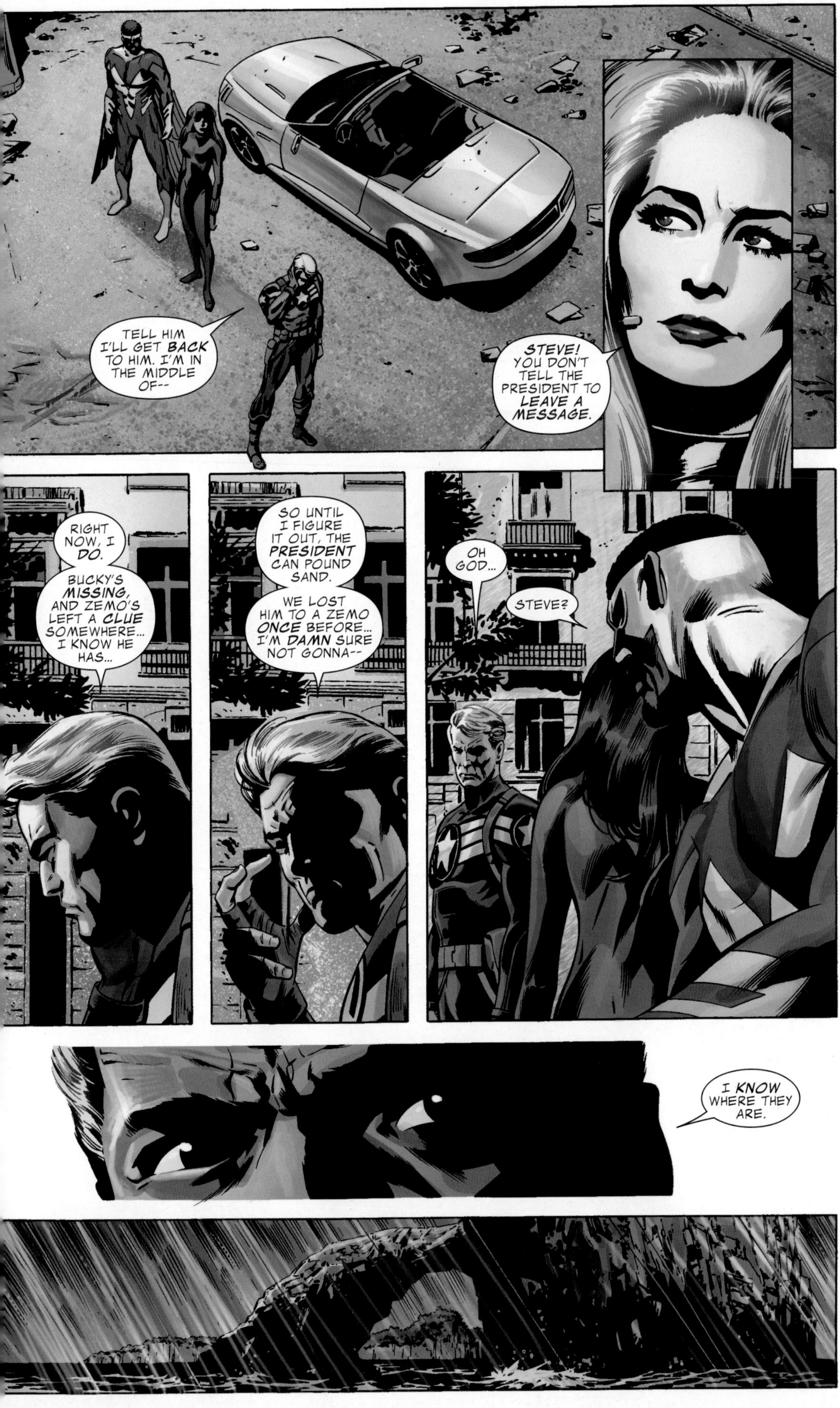

TELL HIM I'LL GET BACK TO HIM. I'M IN THE MIDDLE OF--
STEVE! YOU DON'T TELL THE PRESIDENT TO LEAVE A MESSAGE.
RIGHT NOW, I DO.
BUCKY'S MISSING, AND ZEMO'S LEFT A CLUE SOMEWHERE... I KNOW HE HAS...
SO UNTIL I FIGURE IT OUT, THE PRESIDENT CAN POUND SAND.
WE LOST HIM TO A ZEMO ONCE BEFORE... I'M DAMN SURE NOT GONNA--
OH GOD...
STEVE?
I KNOW WHERE THEY ARE.

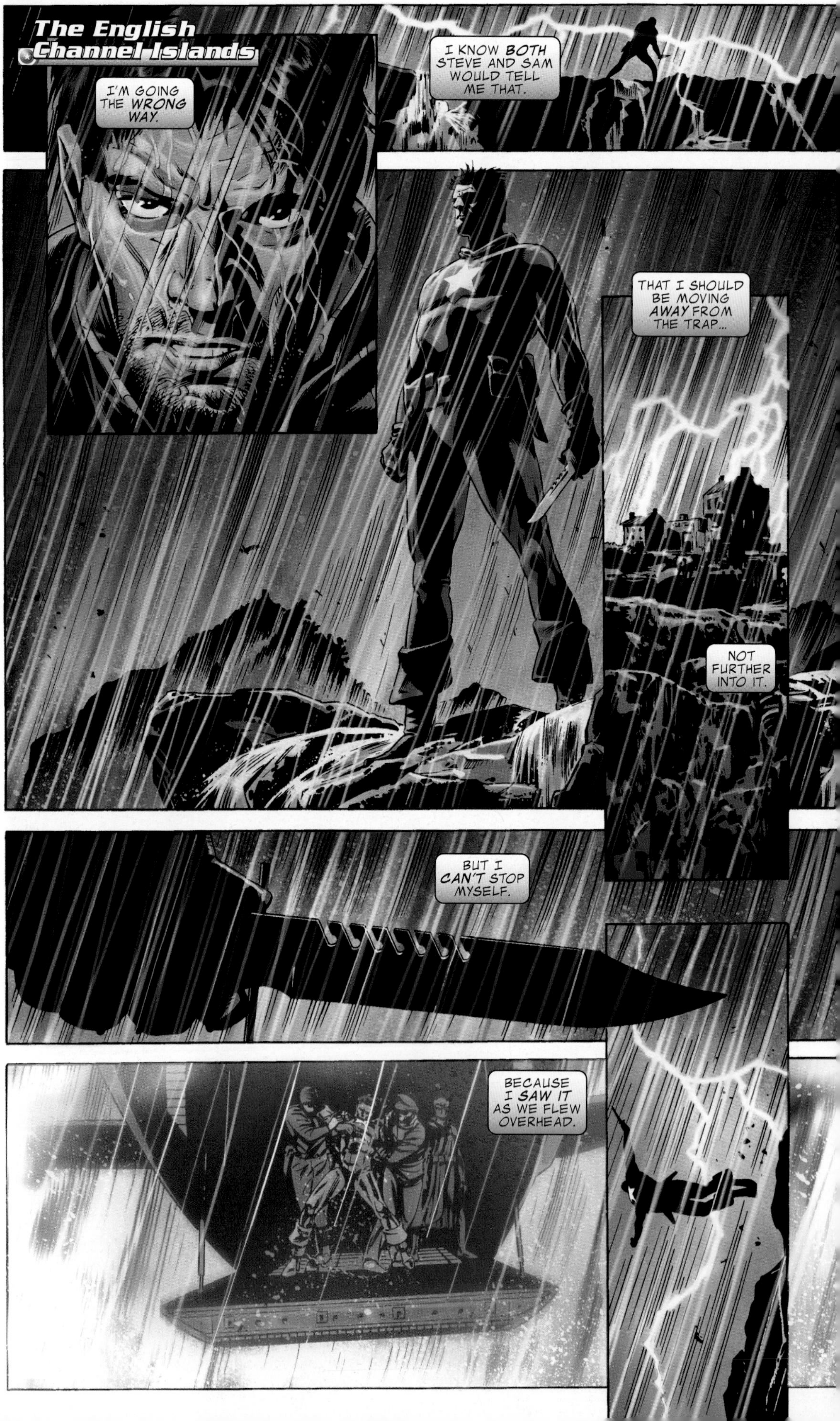
The English Channel Islands
I'M GOING THE WRONG WAY.
I KNOW BOTH STEVE AND SAM WOULD TELL ME THAT.
THAT I SHOULD BE MOVING AWAY FROM THE TRAP...
NOT FURTHER INTO IT.
BUT I CAN'T STOP MYSELF.
BECAUSE I SAW IT AS WE FLEW OVERHEAD.

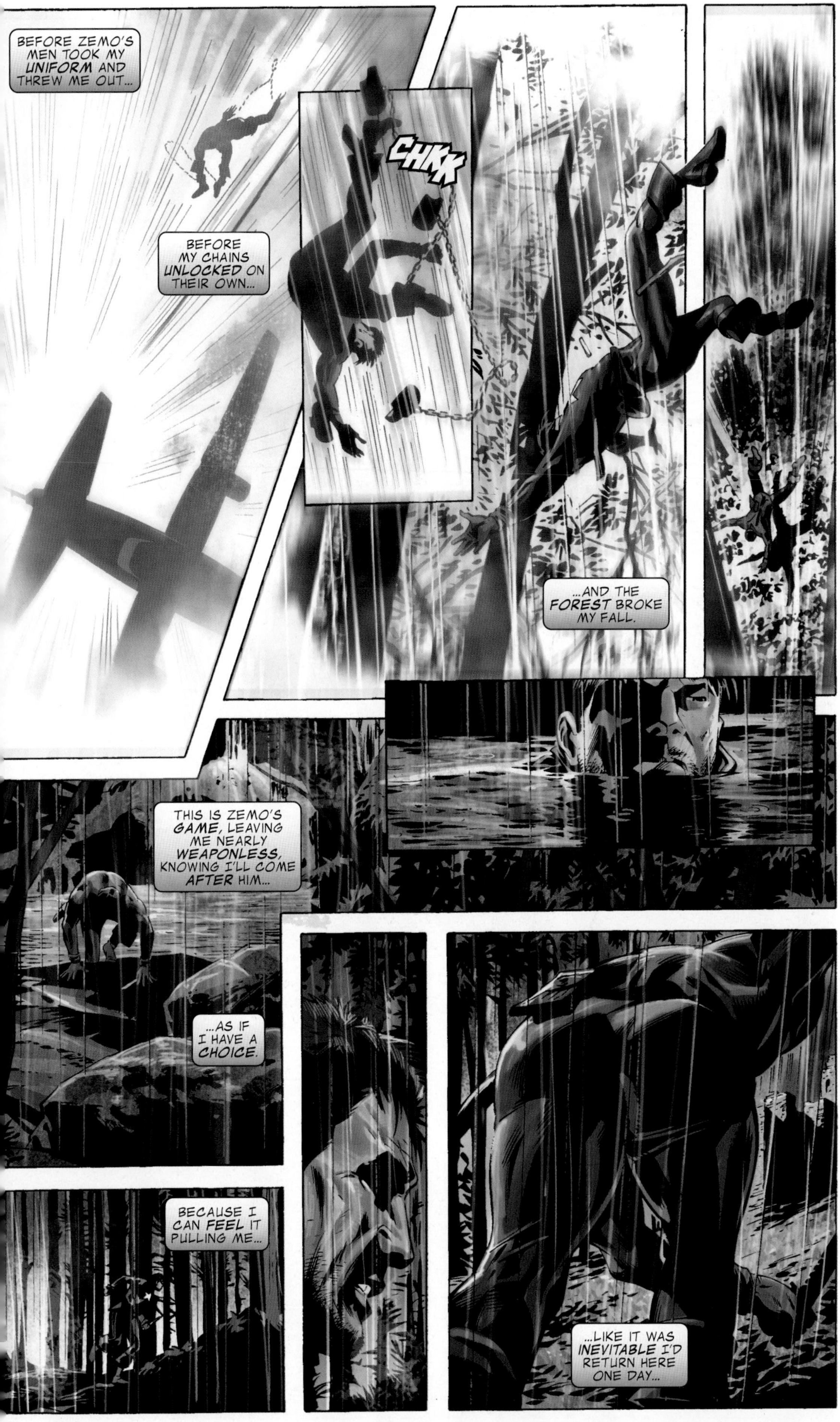
BEFORE ZEMO'S MEN TOOK MY UNIFORM AND THREW ME OUT...
BEFORE MY CHAINS UNLOCKED ON THEIR OWN...
CHKK
...AND THE FOREST BROKE MY FALL.
THIS IS ZEMO'S GAME, LEAVING ME NEARLY WEAPONLESS, KNOWING I'LL COME AFTER HIM...
...AS IF I HAVE A CHOICE.
BECAUSE I CAN FEEL IT PULLING ME...
...LIKE IT WAS INEVITABLE I'D RETURN HERE ONE DAY...

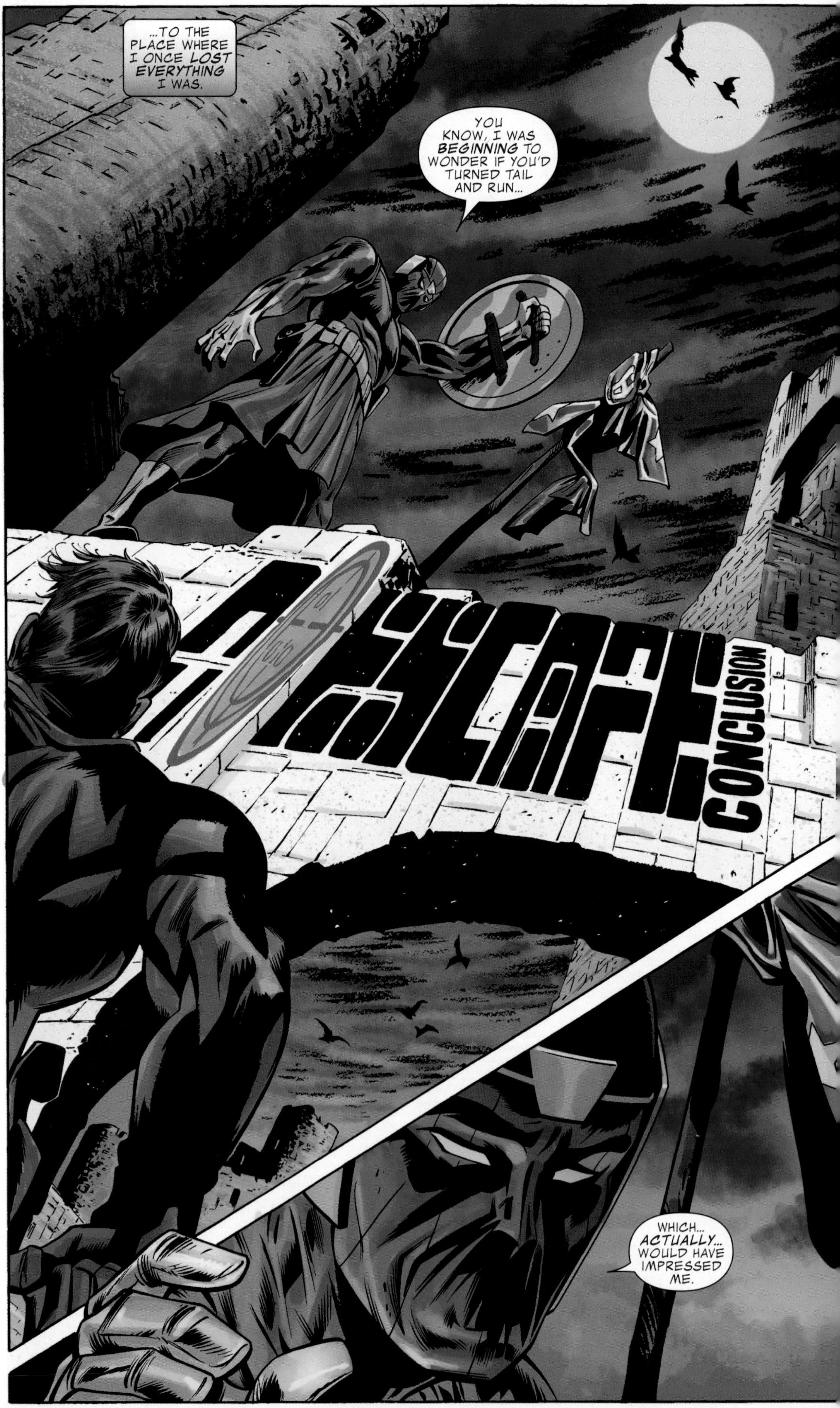
...TO THE PLACE WHERE I ONCE LOST EVERYTHING I WAS.
YOU KNOW, I WAS BEGINNING TO WONDER IF YOU'D TURNED TAIL AND RUN...
CONCLUSION
WHICH... ACTUALLY... WOULD HAVE IMPRESSED ME.

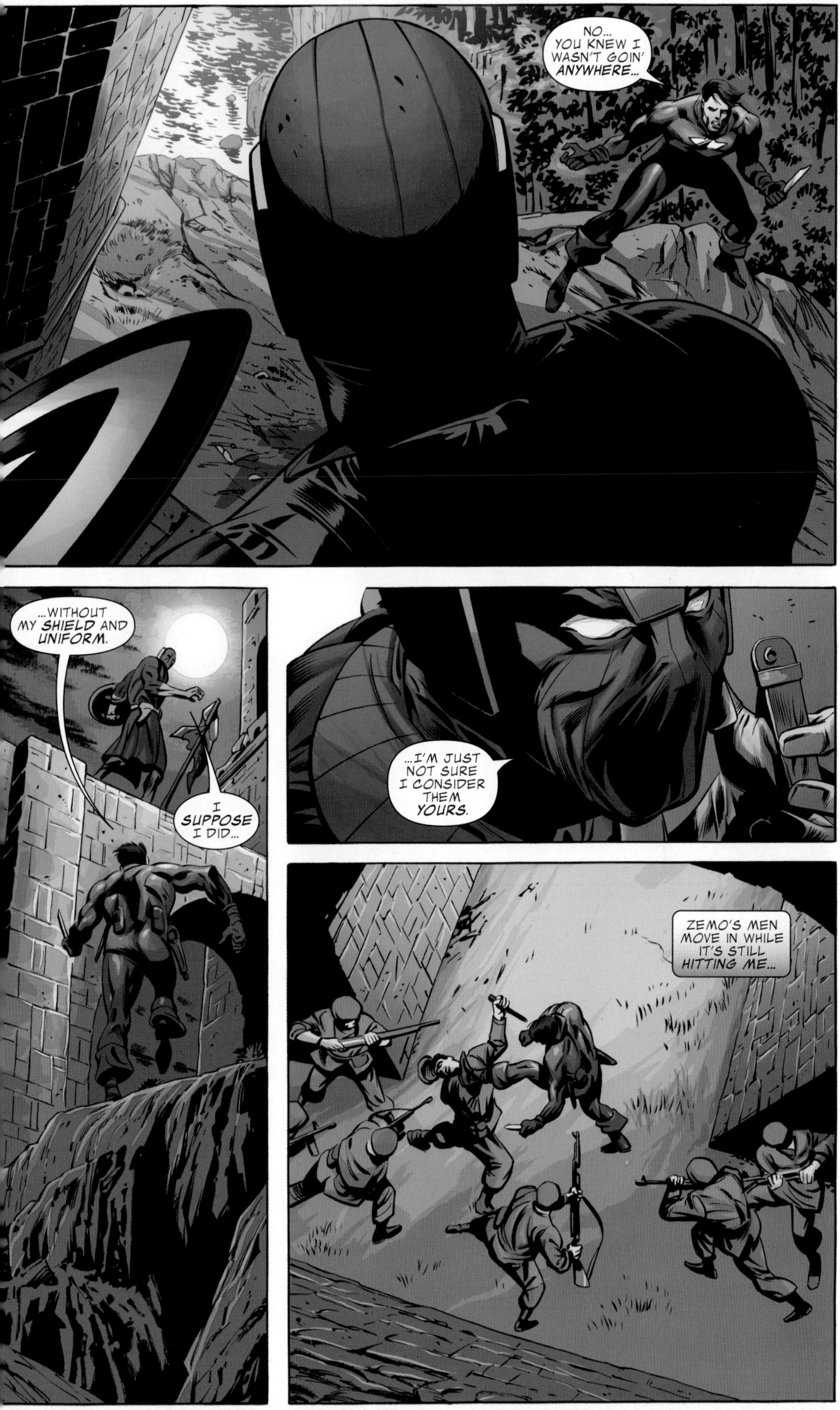
NO... YOU KNEW I WASN'T GOIN' ANYWHERE...
...WITHOUT MY SHIELD AND UNIFORM.
I SUPPOSE I DID...
...I'M JUST NOT SURE I CONSIDER THEM YOURS.
ZEMO'S MEN MOVE IN WHILE IT'S STILL HITTING ME...

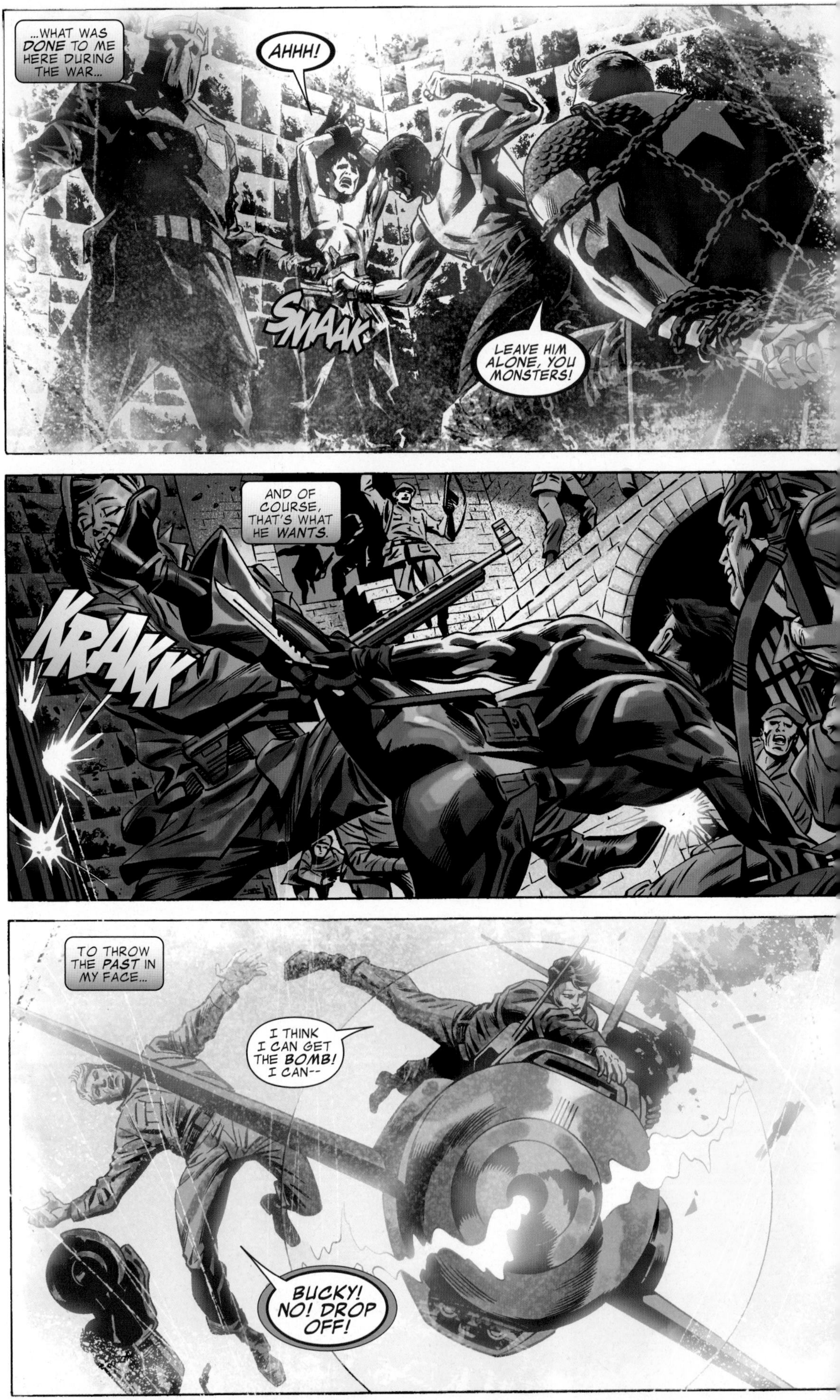
...WHAT WAS DONE TO ME HERE DURING THE WAR...
AHHH!
SMAAK
LEAVE HIM ALONE, YOU MONSTERS!
AND OF COURSE, THAT'S WHAT HE WANTS.
KRAKK
TO THROW THE PAST IN MY FACE...
I THINK I CAN GET THE BOMB! I CAN--
BUCKY! NO! DROP OFF!

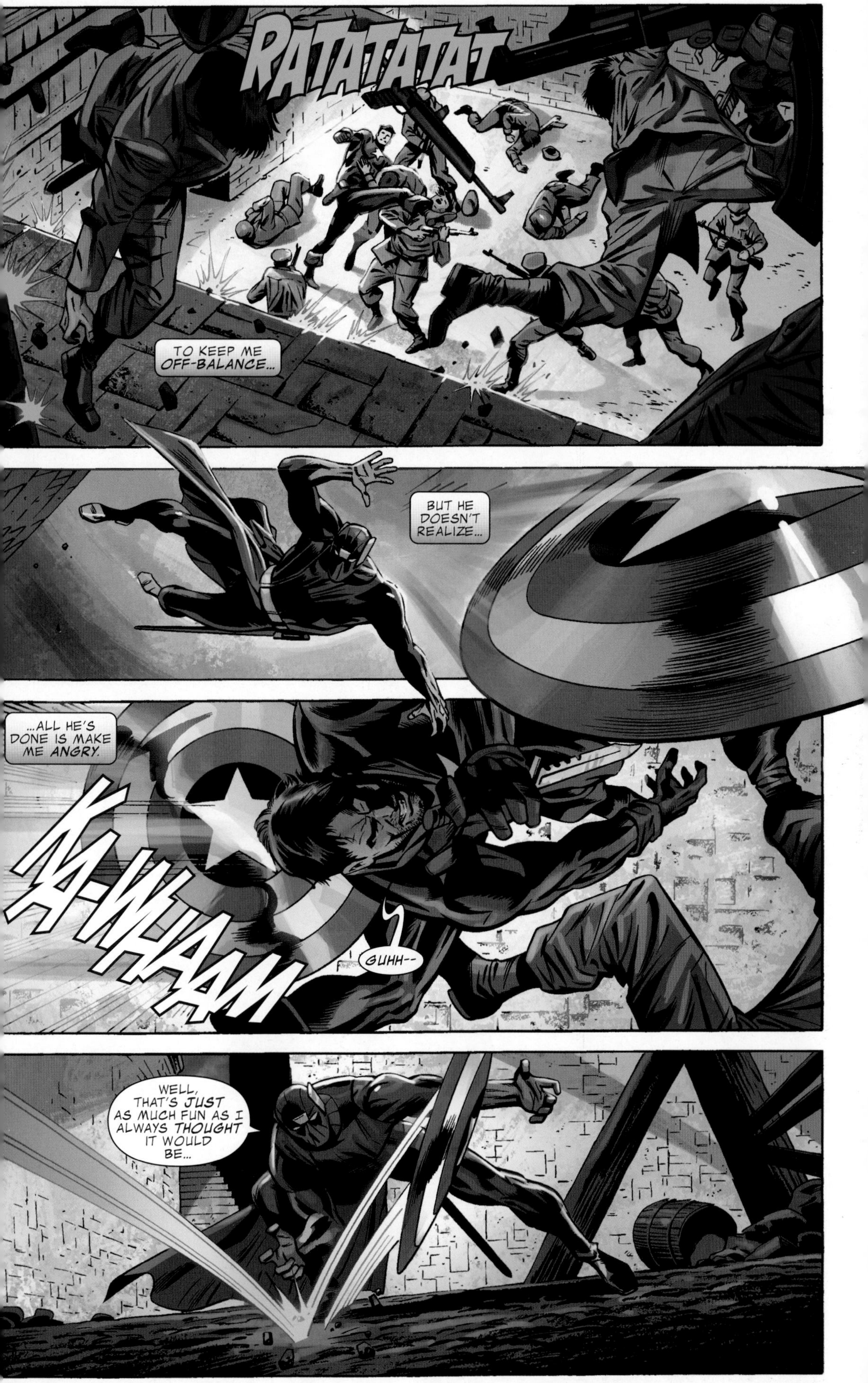
RATATATAT
TO KEEP ME OFF-BALANCE...
BUT HE DOESN'T REALIZE...
...ALL HE'S DONE IS MAKE ME ANGRY.
KA-WHAAM
GUHH--
WELL, THAT'S JUST AS MUCH FUN AS I ALWAYS THOUGHT IT WOULD BE...

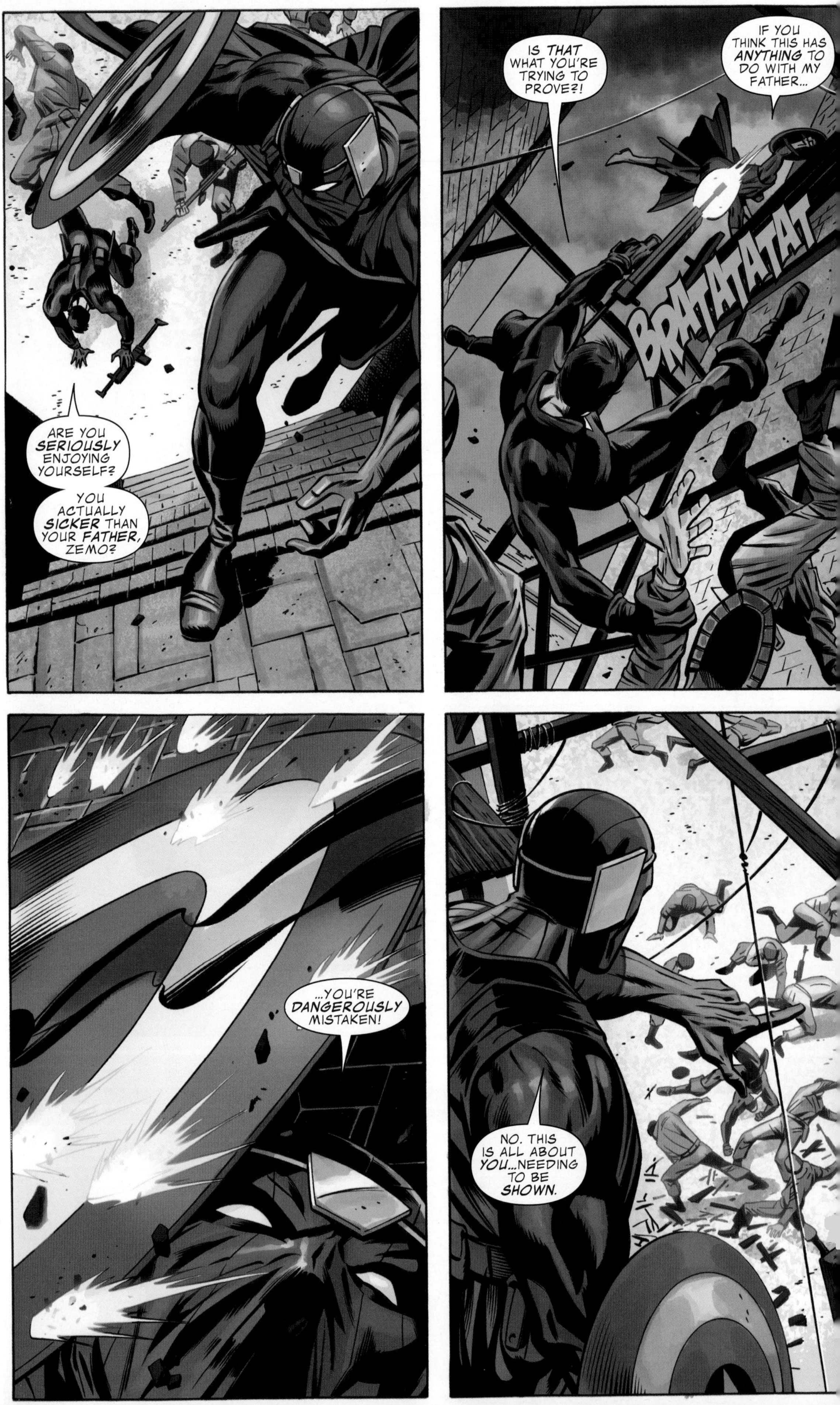
ARE YOU SERIOUSLY ENJOYING YOURSELF?
YOU ACTUALLY SICKER THAN YOUR FATHER, ZEMO?
IS THAT WHAT YOU'RE TRYING TO PROVE?!
IF YOU THINK THIS HAS ANYTHING TO DO WITH MY FATHER...
BRATATATAT
...YOU'RE DANGEROUSLY MISTAKEN!
NO. THIS IS ALL ABOUT YOU...NEEDING TO BE SHOWN.

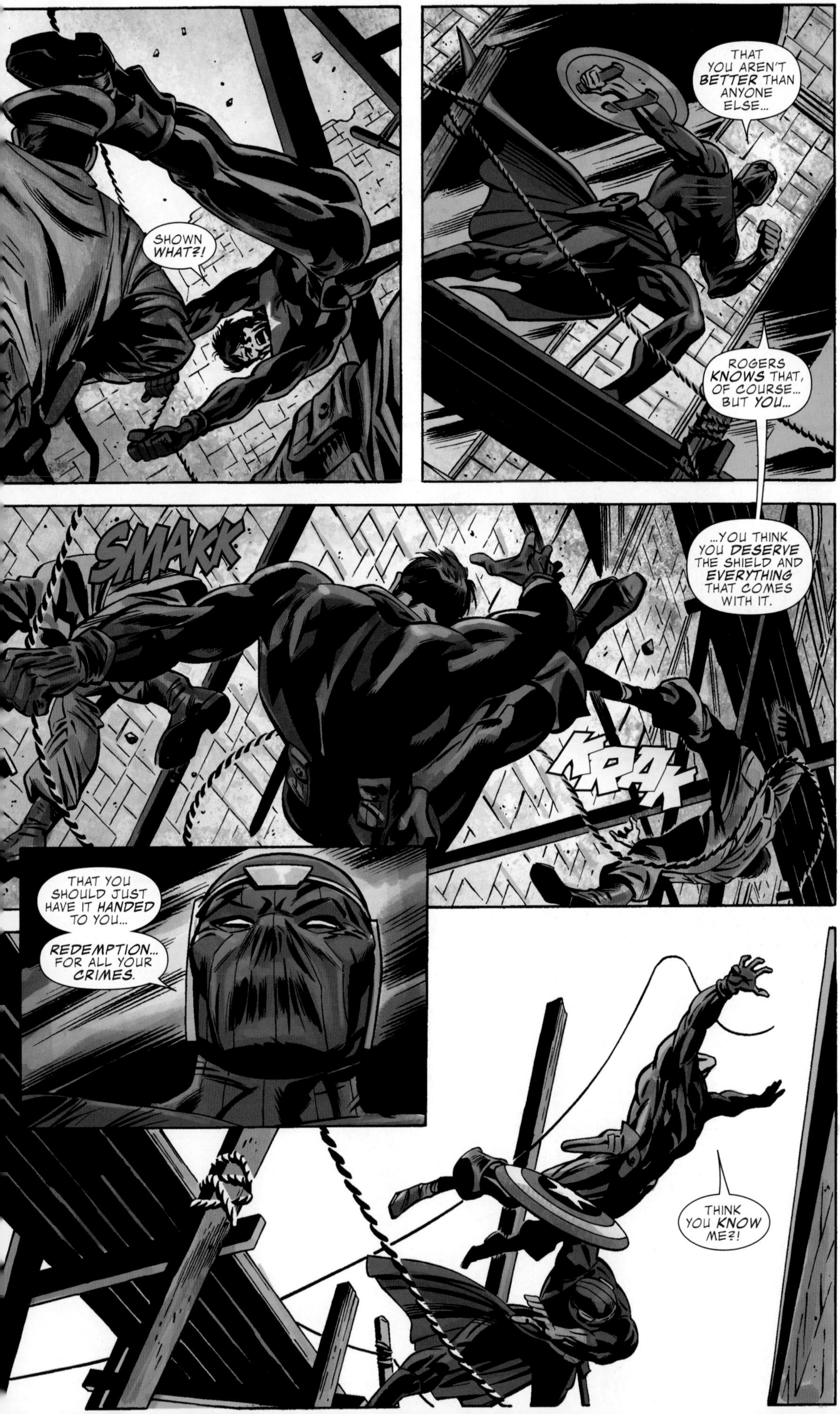
SHOWN WHAT?!
THAT YOU AREN'T BETTER THAN ANYONE ELSE...
ROGERS KNOWS THAT, OF COURSE... BUT YOU...
...YOU THINK YOU DESERVE THE SHIELD AND EVERYTHING THAT COMES WITH IT.
SMAKK
KRAK
THAT YOU SHOULD JUST HAVE IT HANDED TO YOU...
REDEMPTION... FOR ALL YOUR CRIMES.
THINK YOU KNOW ME?!

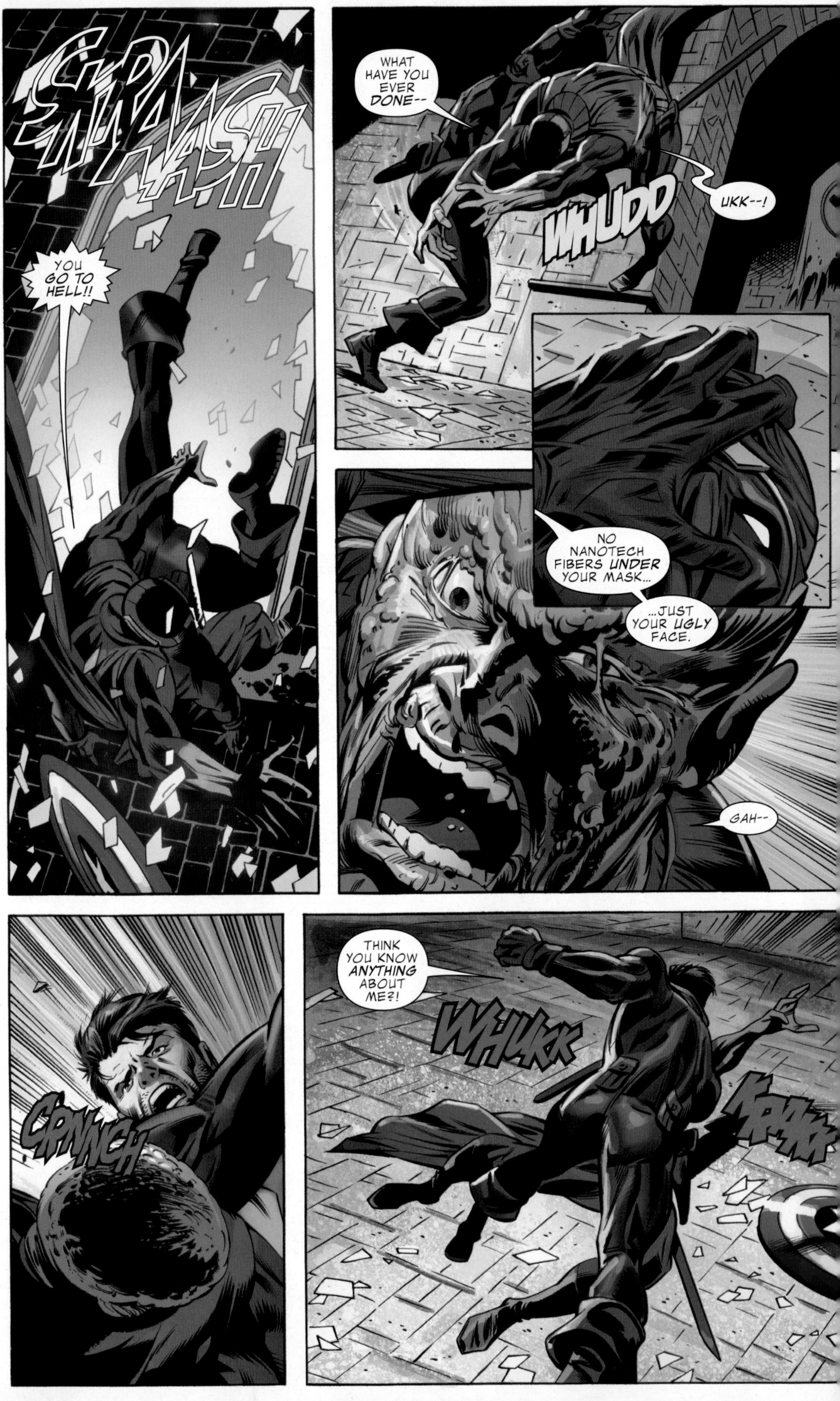
SKRAASH
YOU GO TO HELL!!
WHAT HAVE YOU EVER DONE--
WHUDD
UKK--!
NO NANOTECH FIBERS UNDER YOUR MASK...
...JUST YOUR UGLY FACE.
GAH--
CRNNCH
THINK YOU KNOW ANYTHING ABOUT ME?!
WHUKK
KRAKK

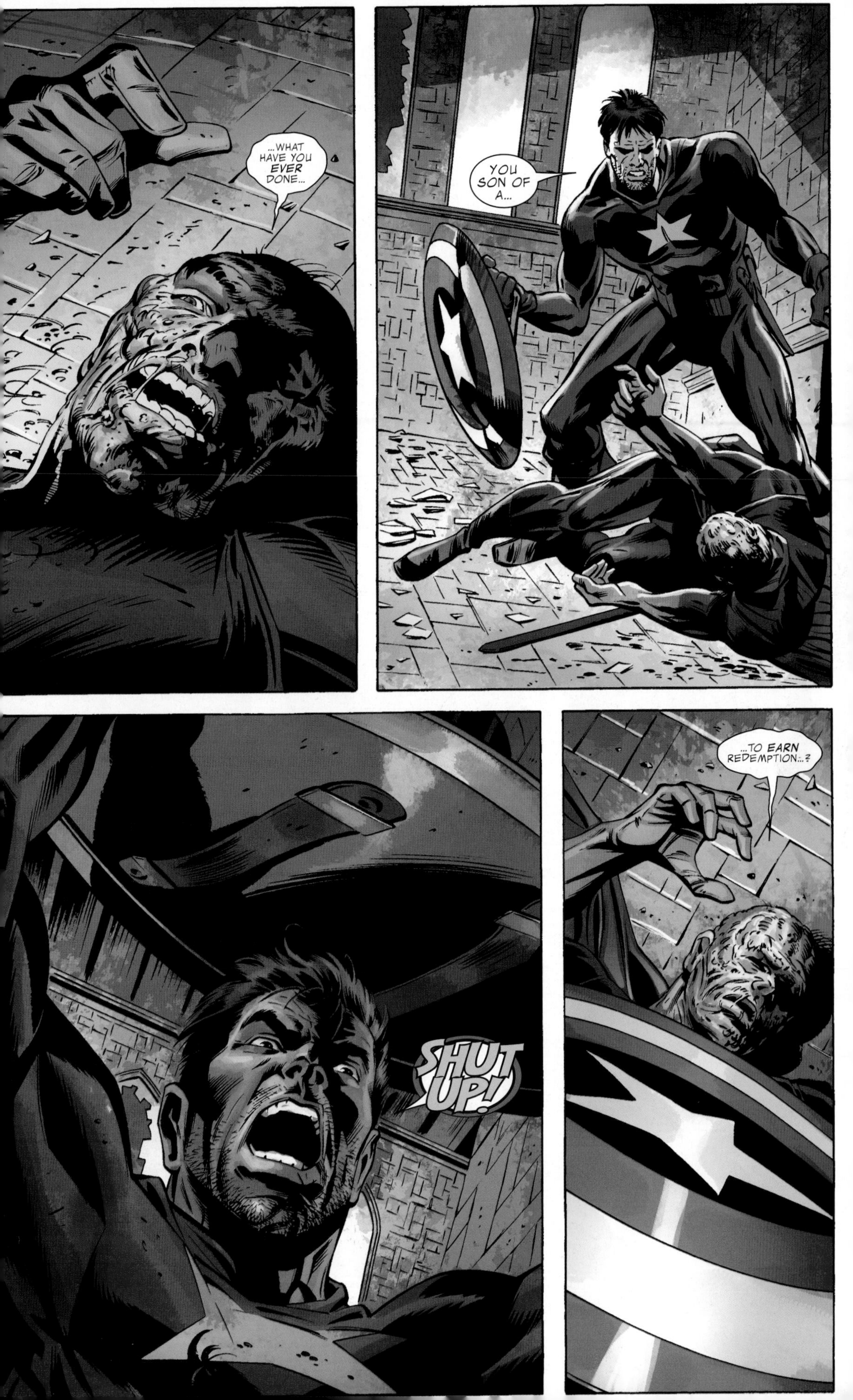
...WHAT HAVE YOU EVER DONE...
YOU SON OF A...
SHUT UP!
...TO EARN REDEMPTION...?

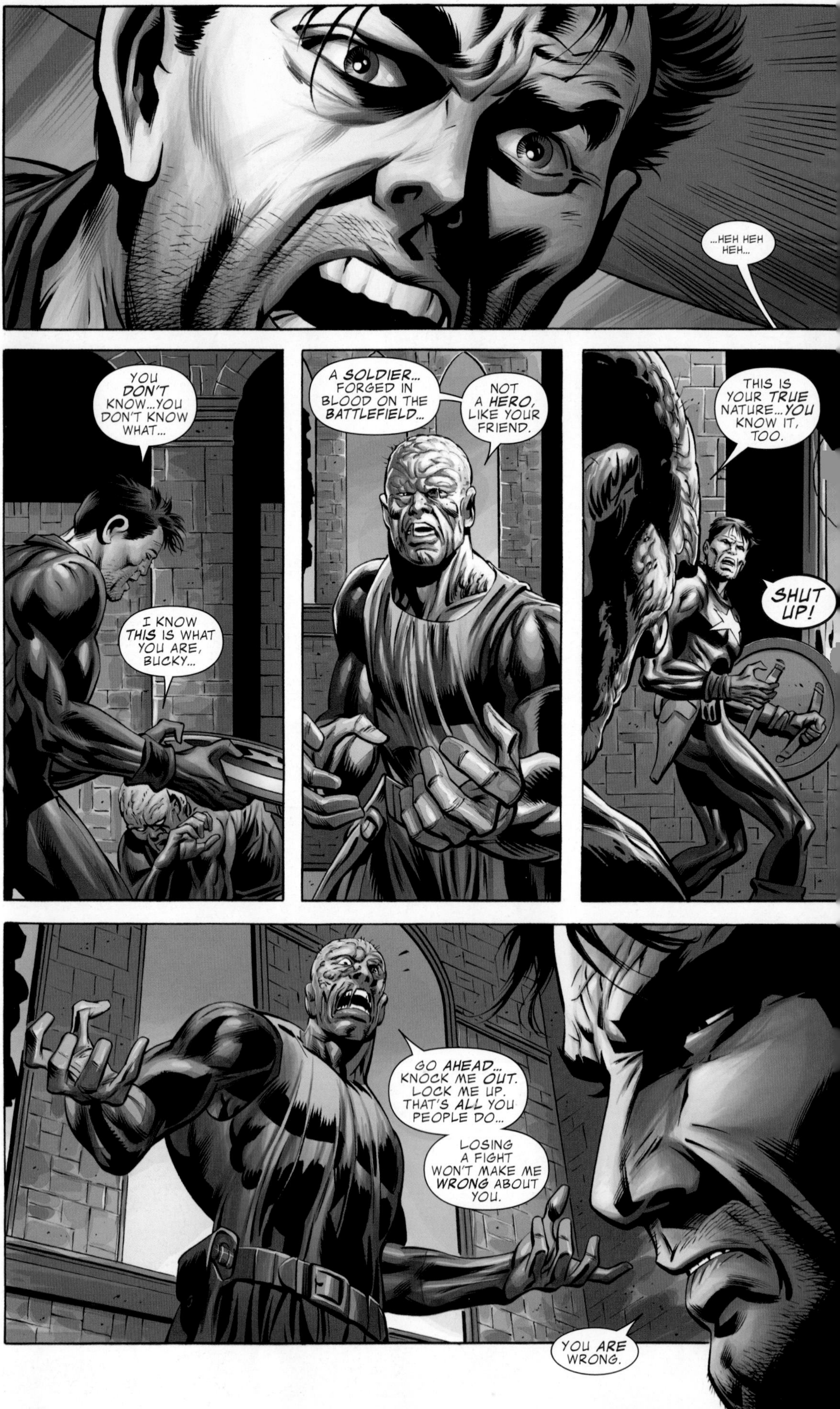
...HEH HEH HEH...
YOU DON'T KNOW...YOU DON'T KNOW WHAT...
I KNOW THIS IS WHAT YOU ARE, BUCKY...
A SOLDIER... FORGED IN BLOOD ON THE BATTLEFIELD...
NOT A HERO, LIKE YOUR FRIEND.
THIS IS YOUR TRUE NATURE...YOU KNOW IT, TOO.
SHUT UP!
GO AHEAD... KNOCK ME OUT. LOCK ME UP. THAT'S ALL YOU PEOPLE DO...
LOSING A FIGHT WON'T MAKE ME WRONG ABOUT YOU.
YOU ARE WRONG.

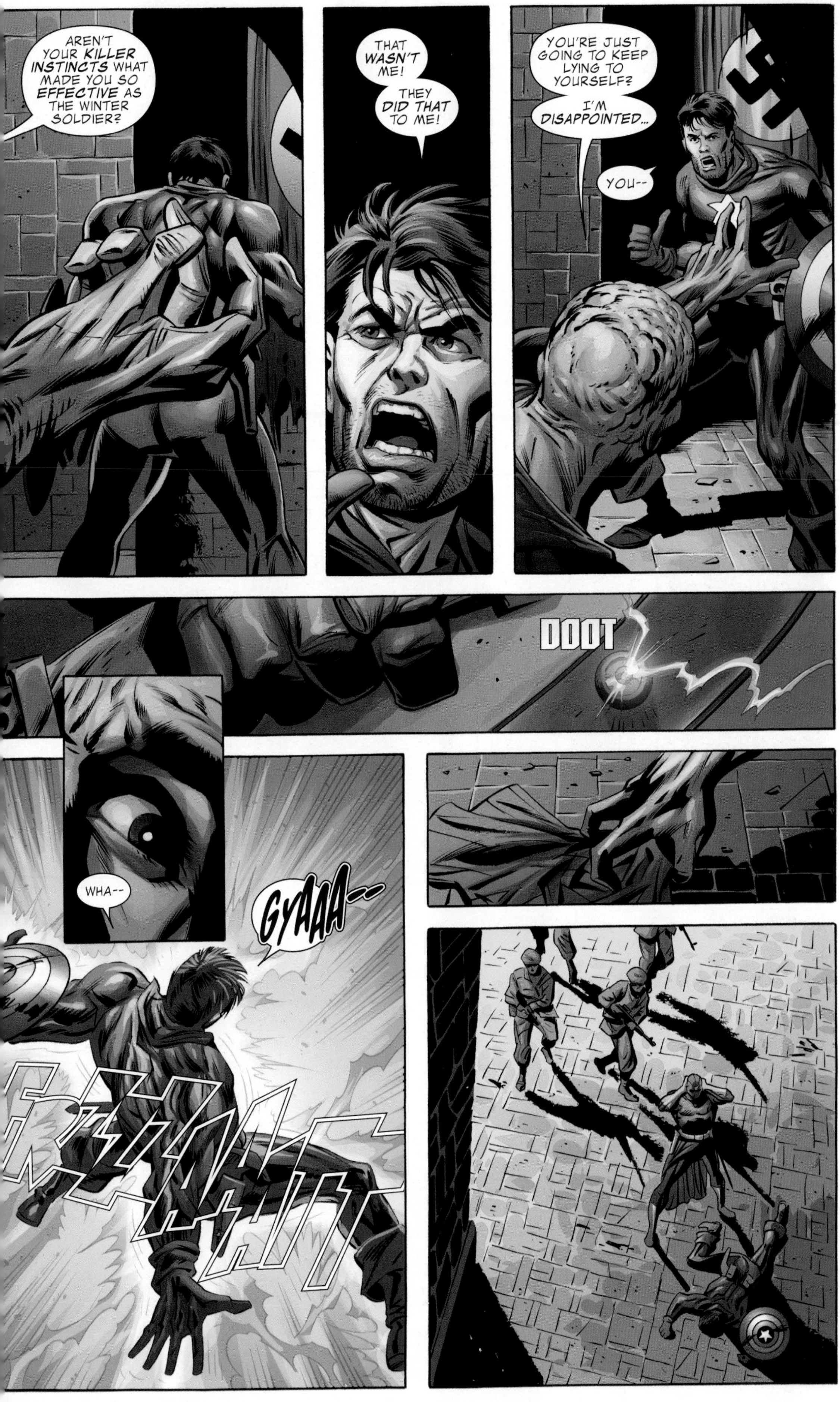

AREN'T YOUR KILLER INSTINCTS WHAT MADE YOU SO EFFECTIVE AS THE WINTER SOLDIER?
THAT WASN'T ME!
THEY DID THAT TO ME!
YOU'RE JUST GOING TO KEEP LYING TO YOURSELF?
I'M DISAPPOINTED...
YOU--
DOOT
WHA--
GYAAA--

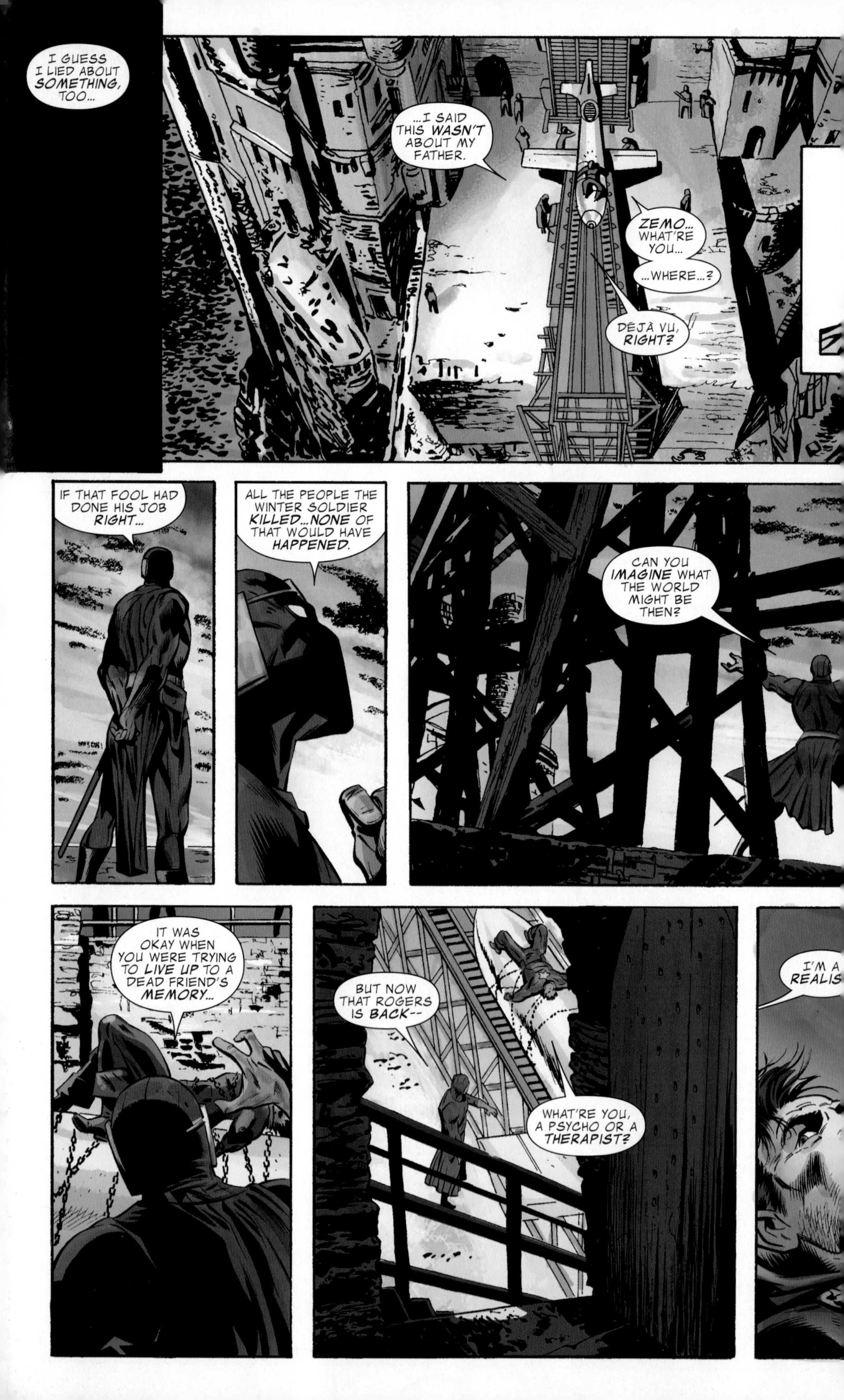
I GUESS I LIED ABOUT SOMETHING, TOO...
...I SAID THIS WASN'T ABOUT MY FATHER.
ZEMO... WHAT'RE YOU...
...WHERE...?
DÉJÀ VU, RIGHT?
IF THAT FOOL HAD DONE HIS JOB RIGHT...
ALL THE PEOPLE THE WINTER SOLDIER KILLED...NONE OF THAT WOULD HAVE HAPPENED.
CAN YOU IMAGINE WHAT THE WORLD MIGHT BE THEN?
IT WAS OKAY WHEN YOU WERE TRYING TO LIVE UP TO A DEAD FRIEND'S MEMORY...
BUT NOW THAT ROGERS IS BACK--
WHAT'RE YOU, A PSYCHO OR A THERAPIST?
I'M A REALIS

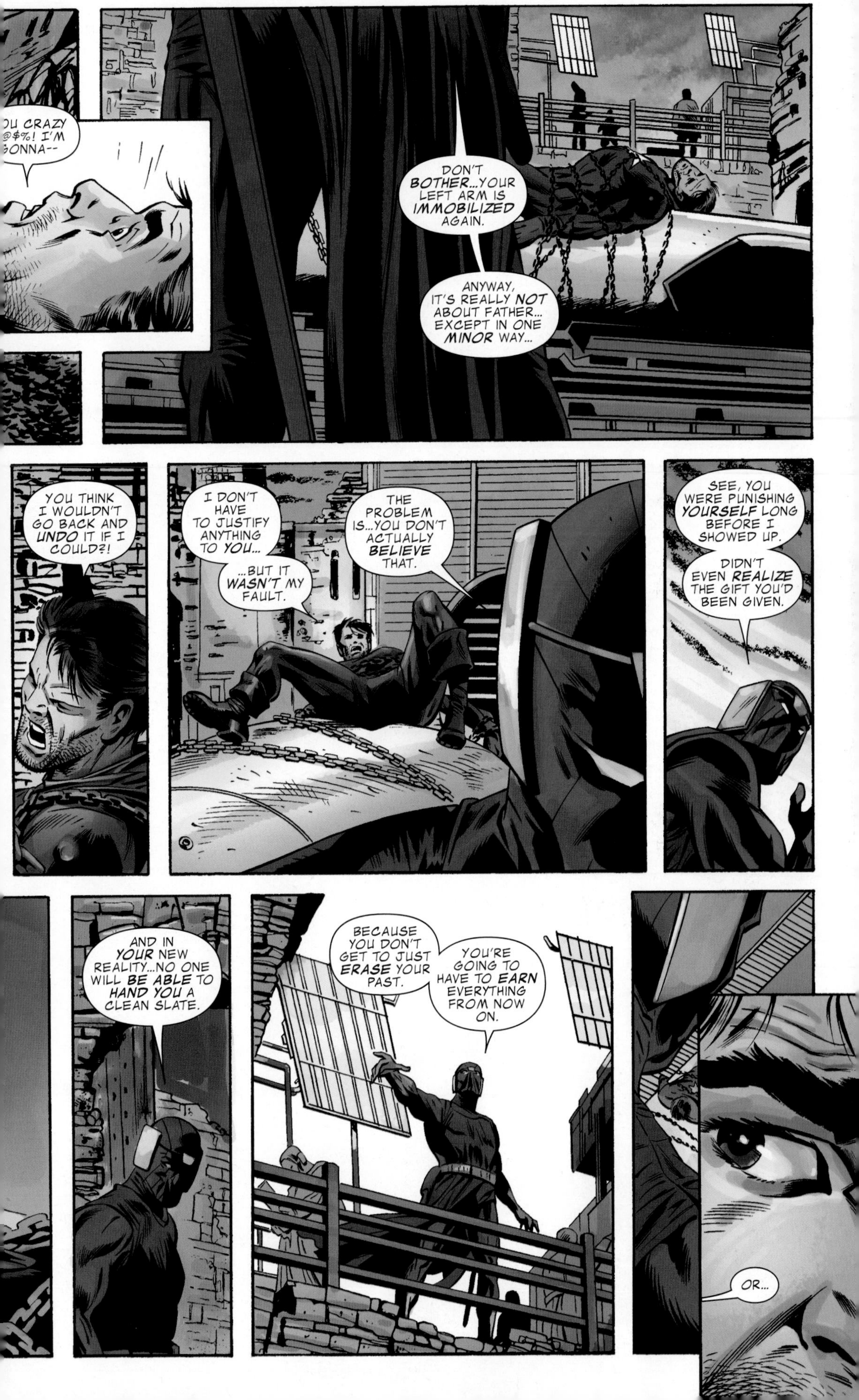

OU CRAZY @$%! I'M GONNA--
DON'T BOTHER...YOUR LEFT ARM IS IMMOBILIZED AGAIN.
ANYWAY, IT'S REALLY NOT ABOUT FATHER... EXCEPT IN ONE MINOR WAY...
YOU THINK I WOULDN'T GO BACK AND UNDO IT IF I COULD?!
I DON'T HAVE TO JUSTIFY ANYTHING TO YOU...
...BUT IT WASN'T MY FAULT.
THE PROBLEM IS...YOU DON'T ACTUALLY BELIEVE THAT.
SEE, YOU WERE PUNISHING YOURSELF LONG BEFORE I SHOWED UP.
DIDN'T EVEN REALIZE THE GIFT YOU'D BEEN GIVEN.
AND IN YOUR NEW REALITY...NO ONE WILL BE ABLE TO HAND YOU A CLEAN SLATE.
BECAUSE YOU DON'T GET TO JUST ERASE YOUR PAST.
YOU'RE GOING TO HAVE TO EARN EVERYTHING FROM NOW ON.
OR...

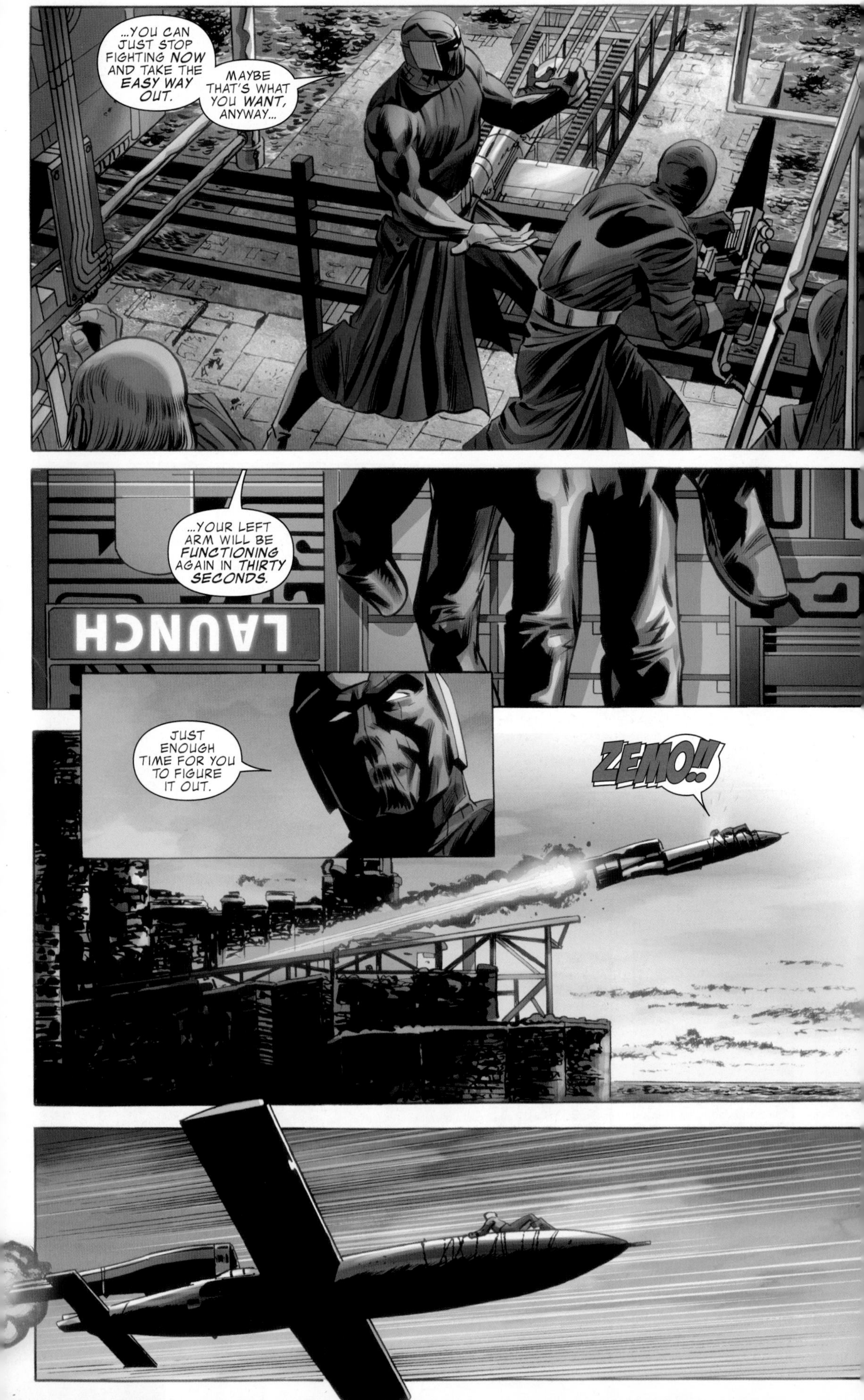

...YOU CAN JUST STOP FIGHTING NOW AND TAKE THE EASY WAY OUT.
MAYBE THAT'S WHAT YOU WANT, ANYWAY...
...YOUR LEFT ARM WILL BE FUNCTIONING AGAIN IN THIRTY SECONDS.
LAUNCH
JUST ENOUGH TIME FOR YOU TO FIGURE IT OUT.
ZEMO!!

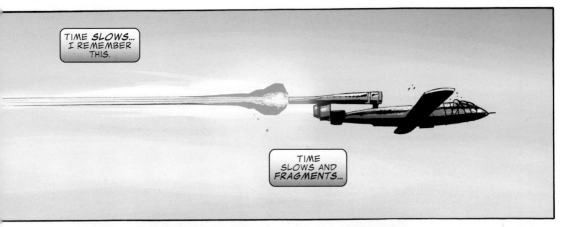

TIME *SLOWS...*
I REMEMBER
THIS.

TIME
SLOWS AND
FRAGMENTS...

OW *LONG*
UNTIL IT
LOWS UP?

ZEMO WOULD
BE SURE IT'S
THE SAME AS
LAST TIME...

...WHEN I
SHOULD
HAVE DIED.

MAYBE HE'S
RIGHT...MAYBE
THIS *IS* WHAT
I DESERVE...

TIME
FRAGMENTS
AND....I SEE IT
ALL AGAIN...

...SLIVERS OF
THE *WINTER
SOLDIER* IN
MY MIND...

...*MEMORIES...*

...OF THINGS
DONE WITH
MY HANDS.

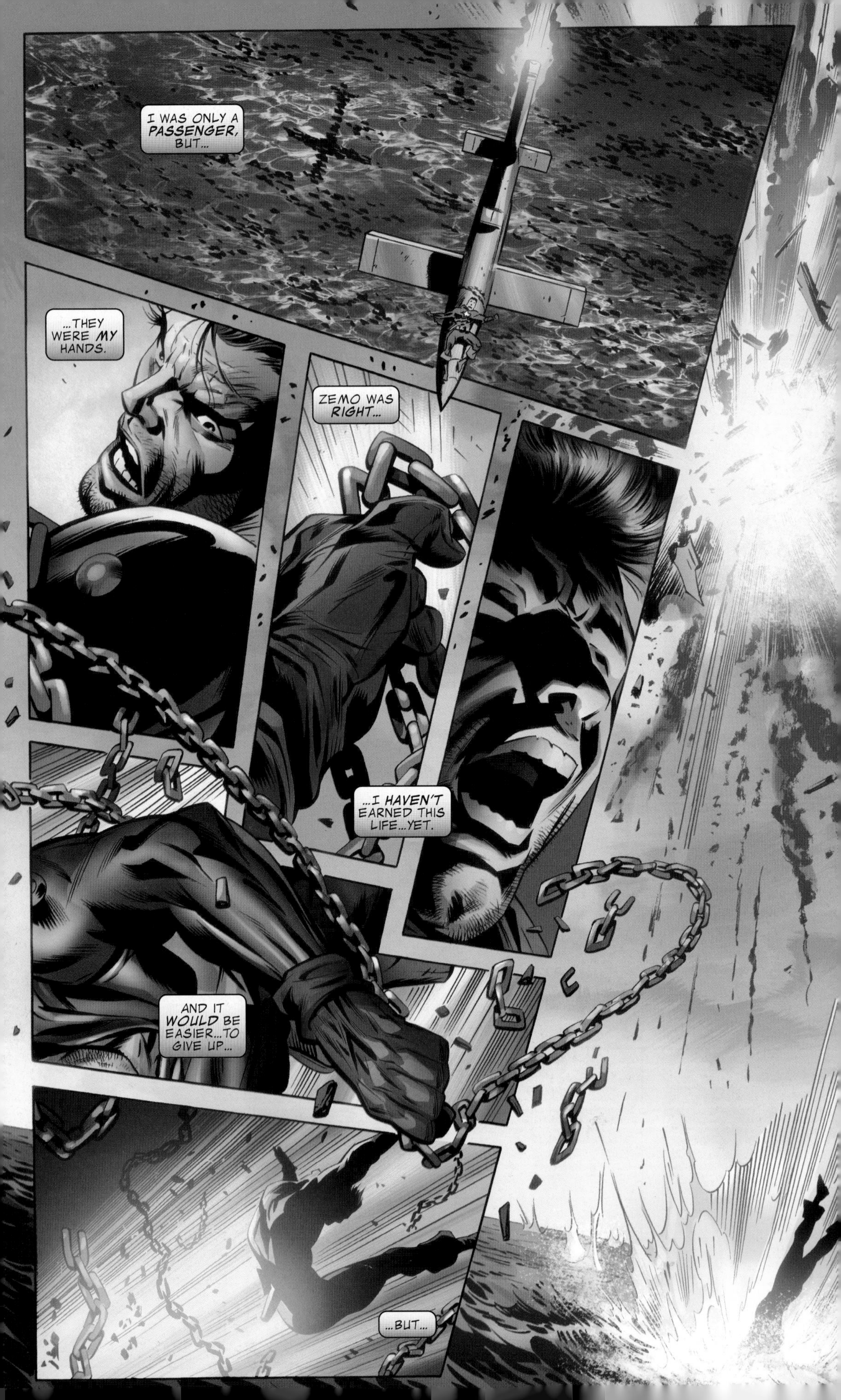
I WAS ONLY A PASSENGER, BUT...
...THEY WERE MY HANDS.
ZEMO WAS RIGHT...
...I HAVEN'T EARNED THIS LIFE...YET.
AND IT WOULD BE EASIER...TO GIVE UP...
...BUT...

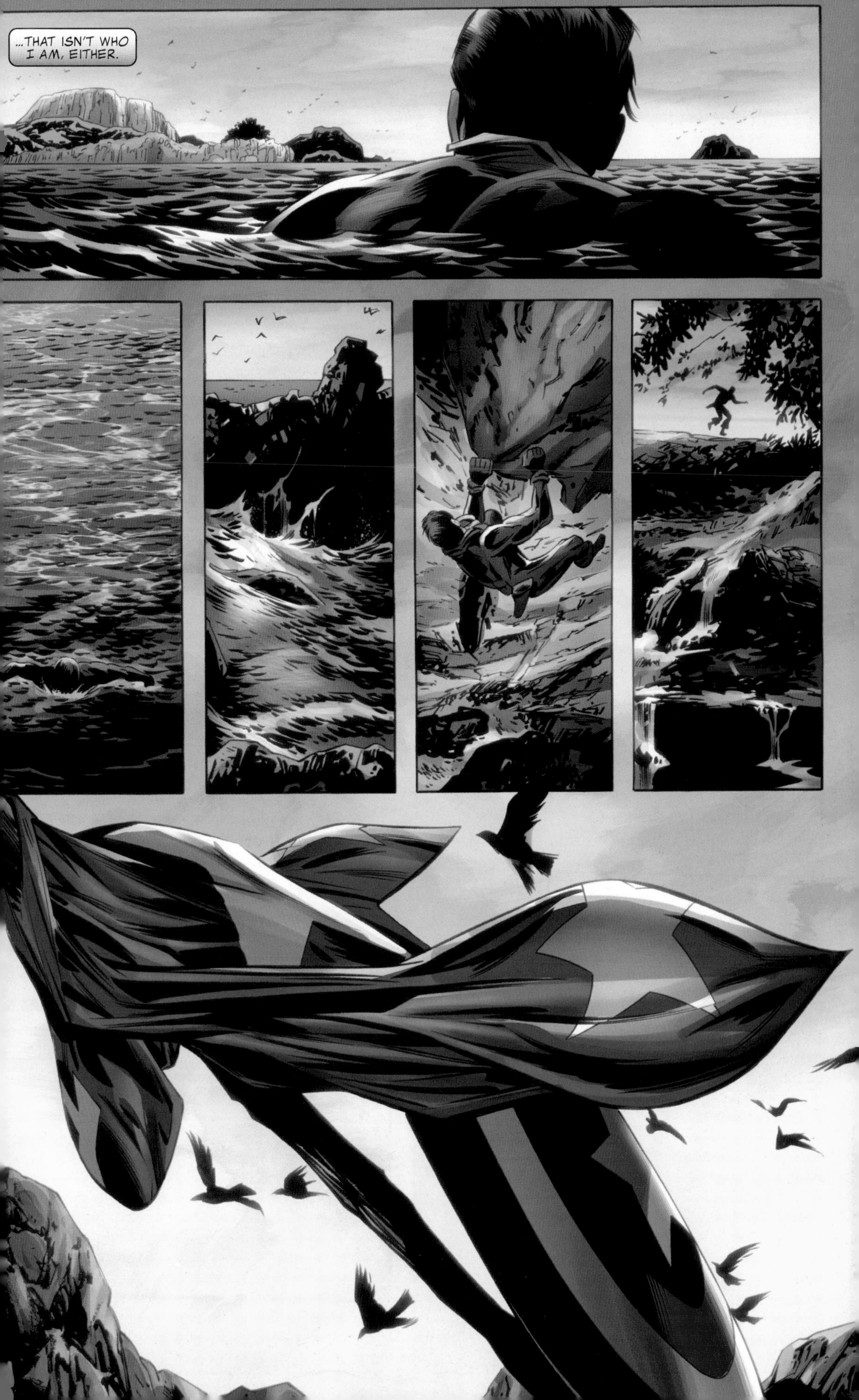
...THAT ISN'T WHO I AM, EITHER.

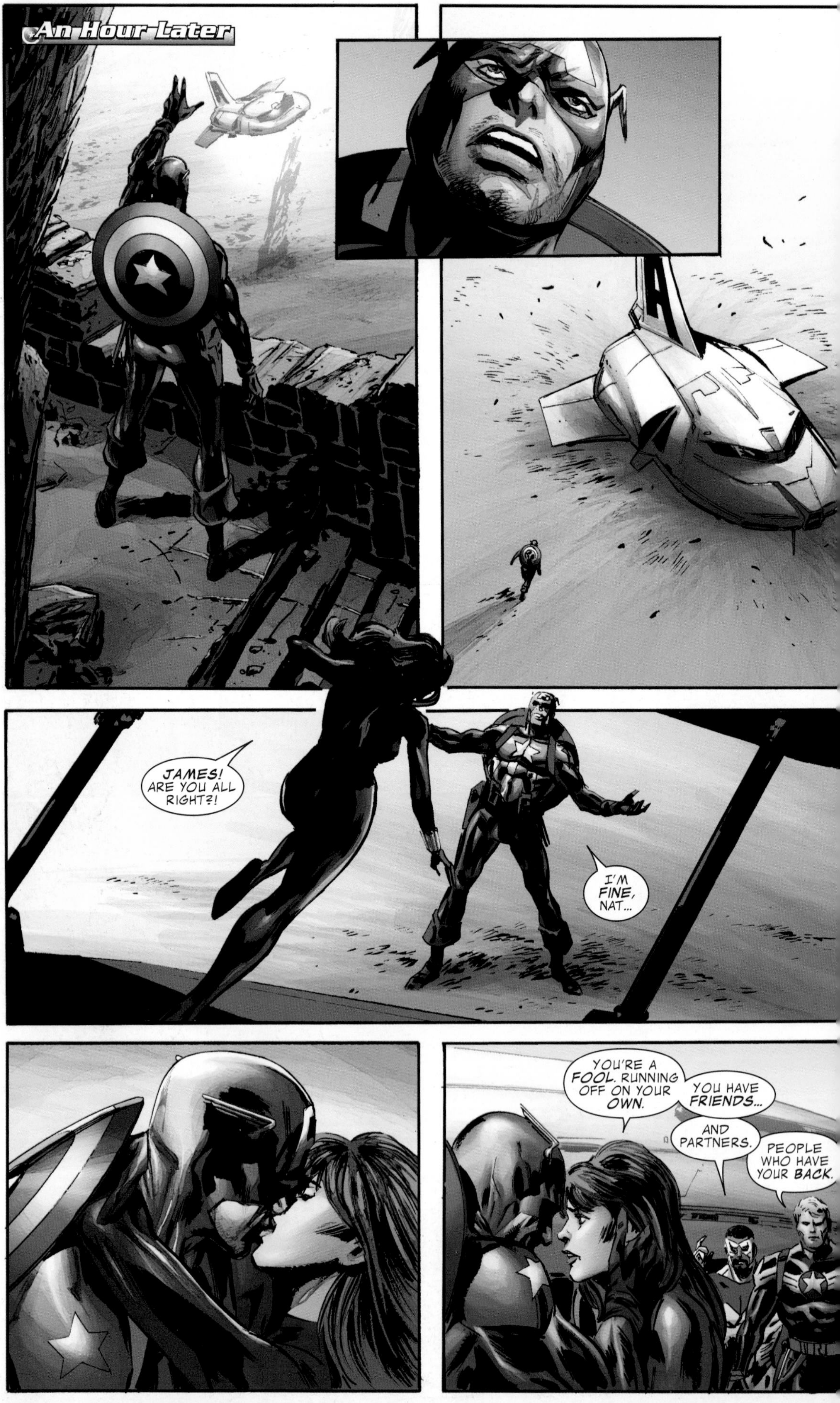
An Hour Later
JAMES! ARE YOU ALL RIGHT?!
I'M FINE, NAT...
YOU'RE A FOOL. RUNNING OFF ON YOUR OWN.
YOU HAVE FRIENDS...
AND PARTNERS.
PEOPLE WHO HAVE YOUR BACK.

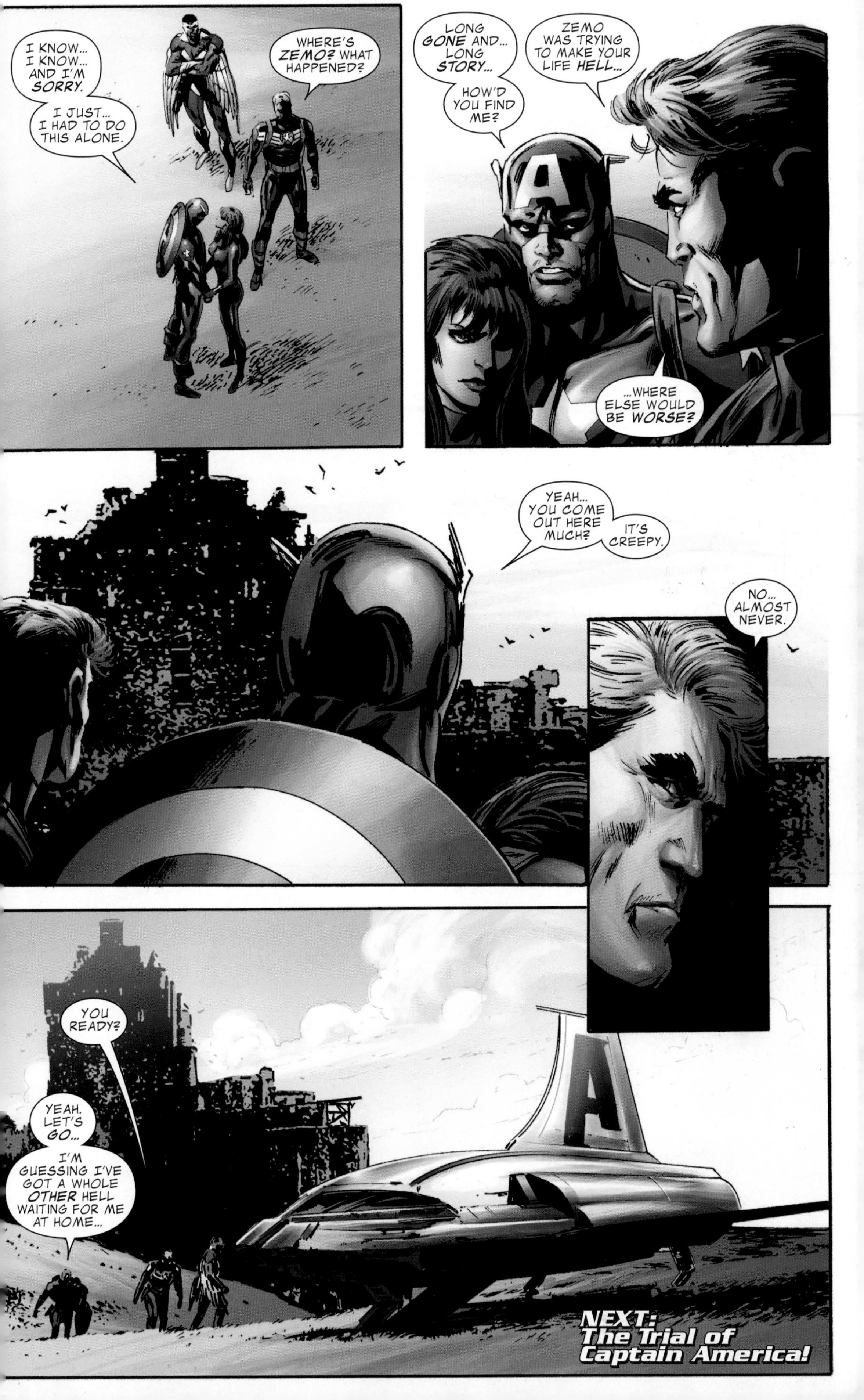
I KNOW... I KNOW... AND I'M SORRY.
I JUST... I HAD TO DO THIS ALONE.
WHERE'S ZEMO? WHAT HAPPENED?
LONG GONE AND... LONG STORY...
HOW'D YOU FIND ME?
ZEMO WAS TRYING TO MAKE YOUR LIFE HELL...
...WHERE ELSE WOULD BE WORSE?
YEAH... YOU COME OUT HERE MUCH?
IT'S CREEPY.
NO... ALMOST NEVER.
YOU READY?
YEAH. LET'S GO...
I'M GUESSING I'VE GOT A WHOLE OTHER HELL WAITING FOR ME AT HOME...
NEXT: The Trial of Captain America!

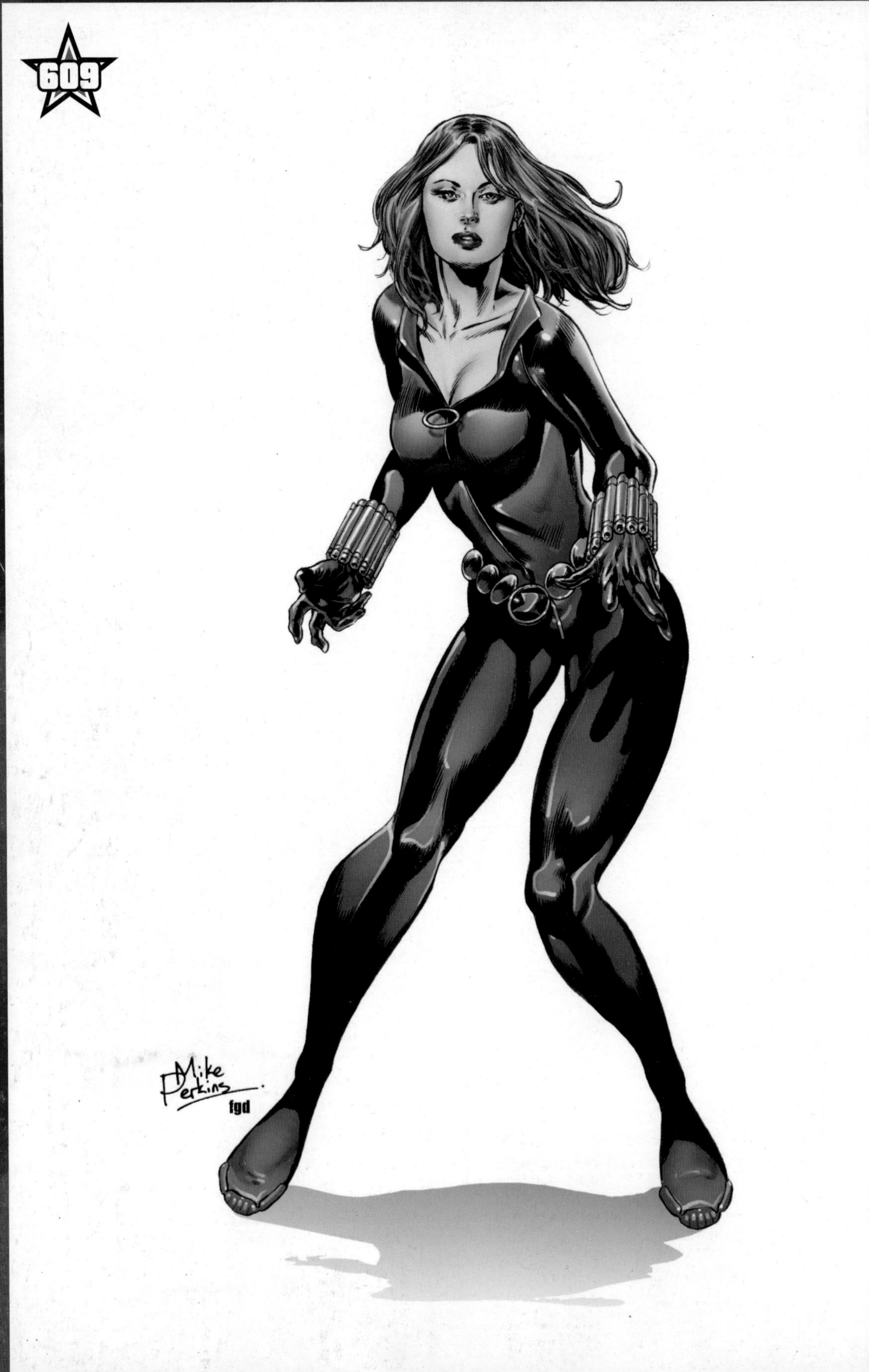
609
Mike Perkins
fgd

WOMEN OF MARVEL FRAME VARIANT BY
MIKE PERKINS & FRANK D'ARMATA